BICENTENNIAL
1807
WILEY
2007
BICENTENNIAL

THE WILEY BICENTENNIAL—KNOWLEDGE FOR GENERATIONS

*E*ach generation has its unique needs and aspirations. When Charles Wiley first opened his small printing shop in lower Manhattan in 1807, it was a generation of boundless potential searching for an identity. And we were there, helping to define a new American literary tradition. Over half a century later, in the midst of the Second Industrial Revolution, it was a generation focused on building the future. Once again, we were there, supplying the critical scientific, technical, and engineering knowledge that helped frame the world. Throughout the 20th Century, and into the new millennium, nations began to reach out beyond their own borders and a new international community was born. Wiley was there, expanding its operations around the world to enable a global exchange of ideas, opinions, and know-how.

For 200 years, Wiley has been an integral part of each generation's journey, enabling the flow of information and understanding necessary to meet their needs and fulfill their aspirations. Today, bold new technologies are changing the way we live and learn. Wiley will be there, providing you the must-have knowledge you need to imagine new worlds, new possibilities, and new opportunities.

Generations come and go, but you can always count on Wiley to provide you the knowledge you need, when and where you need it!

WILLIAM J. PESCE
PRESIDENT AND CHIEF EXECUTIVE OFFICER

PETER BOOTH WILEY
CHAIRMAN OF THE BOARD

Technology in Emergency Management

John C. Pine
Louisiana State University

BICENTENNIAL
1807
WILEY
2007
BICENTENNIAL

Credits

Publisher
Anne Smith

Development Editor
Laura Town

Marketing Manager
Jennifer Slomack

Senior Editorial Assistant
Tiara Kelly

Production Manager
Kelly Tavares

Production Assistant
Courtney Leshko

Creative Director
Harry Nolan

Cover Designer
Hope Miller

Cover Photo
Bob Sacha/Corbis Images

This book was set in Times New Roman, printed and bound by R.R. Donnelley. The cover was printed by Phoenix Color.

This book is printed on acid free paper.

To order books or for customer service please, call 1-800-CALL WILEY (225-5945).

ISBN-13 978-0-471-78973-4

ISBN-10 0-471-78973-9

Printed in the United States of America

10 9 8 7 6 5 4 3 2 1

Library of Congress Cataloging-in-Publication Data
Pine, John C., 1946–
     Technology in emergency management/John C. Pine.
        p.   cm.
     Includes bibliographical references and index.
     ISBN-13: 978-0-471-78973-4 (pbk.)
     ISBN-10: 0-471-78973-9 (pbk.)
     1. Emergency management—Technological innovations.   2. Emergency management—Data processing.   3. Information storage and retrieval systems—Emergency management.   4. Emergency communication systems   I. Title.
     HV551.2.P56 2007
     363.34028'4—dc22   2006023389

ABOUT THE AUTHOR

John C. Pine is Director, Disaster Science and Management (see http://www.dsm.lsu.edu) and Professor-Research with the Department of Environmental Studies and currently serving as Interim Chair of the Department of Geography & Anthropology at LSU. He is also currently serving as co-director of the LSU Hurricane Katrina and Rita Clearinghouse which is providing permanent storage of data associated with these hurricanes (http://www.katrina.lsu.edu). He received his Doctorate from the University of Georgia. His research involves using hazard modeling and mapping to understand the social, environmental and economic impacts of disasters with funding provided by the National Science Foundation, FEMA and the Department of Homeland Security, Department of Interior, the Environmental Protection Agency, and Sea Grant. His publications focus on hazards analysis and emergency management; his book Tort Liability Today: Claims against State and Local Governments (published by the Public Risk Management Association and the National League of Cities) is in its tenth edition. He also has numerous book chapters and articles concerning task assessment published by the Social Science Quarterly, Hazardous Materials Journal, Oceanography, Journal of Homeland Security and Emergency Management, Natural Disaster Review, American Society of Professional Emergency Planners Journal, Journal of Environmental Health. He was also the lead developer of FEMA's Higher Education Project courses on Technology and Emergency Management and Hazard Modeling and Mapping (see http://www.training.fema.gov/EMIWeb/edu/coursesunderdev.asp)

PREFACE

College classrooms bring together learners from many backgrounds with a variety of aspirations. Although the students are in the same course, they are not necessarily on the same path. This diversity, coupled with the reality that these learners often have jobs, families, and other commitments, requires a flexibility that our nation's higher education system is addressing. Distance learning, shorter course terms, new disciplines, evening courses, and certification programs are some of the approaches that colleges employ to reach as many students as possible and help them clarify and achieve their goals.

Wiley Pathways books, a new line of texts from John Wiley & Sons, Inc., are designed to help you address this diversity and the need for flexibility. These books focus on the fundamentals, identify core competencies and skills, and promote independent learning. The focus on the fundamentals helps students grasp the subject, bringing them all to the same basic understanding. These books use clear, everyday language, presented in an uncluttered format, making the reading experience more pleasurable. The core competencies and skills help students succeed in the classroom and beyond, whether in another course or in a professional setting. A variety of built-in learning resources promote independent learning and help instructors and students gauge students' understanding of the content. These resources enable students to think critically about their new knowledge, and apply their skills in any situation.

Our goal with *Wiley Pathways* books—with its brief, inviting format, clear language, and core competencies and skills focus—is to celebrate the many students in your courses, respect their needs, and help you guide them on their way.

CASE Learning System

To meet the needs of working college students, *Technology in Emergency Management* a four-step process: The CASE Learning System. Based on Bloom's Taxonomy of Learning, CASE presents key emergency management topics in easy-to-follow chapters. The text then prompts analysis, synthesis, and evaluation with a variety of learning aids and assessment tools. Students move efficiently from reviewing what they have learned, to acquiring new information and skills, to applying their new knowledge and skills to real-life scenarios. Each phase of the CASE system is signaled in-text by an icon:

▲ Content
▲ Analysis
▲ Synthesis
▲ Evaluation

Using the CASE Learning System, students not only achieve academic mastery of emergency management *theories,* but they master real-world emergency management *skills.* The CASE Learning System also helps students become independent learners, giving them a distinct advantage whether they are starting out or seek to advance in their careers.

Organization, Depth and Breadth of the Text

Technology in Emergency Management offers the following features:

▲ *Modular format.* Research on college students shows that they access information from textbooks in a non-linear way. Instructors also often wish to reorder textbook content to suit the needs of a particular class. Therefore, although *Technology in Emergency Management* proceeds logically from the basics to increasingly more challenging material, chapters are further organized into sections (4 to 6 per chapter) that are self-contained for maximum teaching and learning flexibility.

▲ *Numeric system of headings. Technology in Emergency Management* uses a numeric system for headings (for example, 2.3.4 identifies the fourth sub-section of section 3 of chapter 2). With this system, students and teachers can quickly and easily pinpoint topics in the table of contents and the text, keeping class time and study sessions focused.

▲ *Core content.* Emergency managers are given the awesome task of protecting lives and property from every conceivable hazard. To carry out their complex role effectively, they need all available tools. Technology provides tools and ways to support the entire emergency management process; from planning for potential disasters to recovering from disasters. The applications of technology will enhances the acquisition of information and resources and the use of technology in all elements of decision making by those involved in emergency management. Mobile wireless technology extends intra and inter-agency communications and offer access to a variety of resources currently only available at a very high cost and in limited situations. As a result of a greater interconnectedness of public, private, and non-profit emergency management agencies, traditional organizational boundaries have undergone significant change. Resource allocation will become more efficient and the capacity to analyze more complex issues in time of crisis will be more available to decision-makers.

This book was written with emergency management student in mind, and includes detailed examples of how technology has been applied to real-world scenarios. The application of *Technology in Emergency Management* will provide a background for understanding how technology is being applied in emergency preparedness, response, recovery and mitigation. Examples of current and emerging technology applications will be illustrated along with an explanation of critical issues that are a part of the technology application. Special issues and problems associated with the use of technology in emergency management will be examined. Strategies to overcome these issues and problems will be outlined.

This text begins with an introductory chapter entitled, "Using Technology." This chapter provides an introduction and overview of the application of technology in emergency management. It clarifies the role of technology in the support of emergency planning, response, recovery and mitigation efforts and the key elements that must be in place for technology to enhance the emergency management process.

Chapter 2 examines the use of the Internet as a tool in the emergency management process. The Internet involves a digital communications network that facilitates the communication of information between users by means of digital transmission technology. Once information is converted to digital form, it can easily be processed, searched, sorted, enhanced, converted, compressed, encrypted, replicated, and transmitted in ways that are conveniently matched to today's information processing systems. It is a global system of networked computers that allow user-to-user communication and transfer of data files from one machine to any other on the network.

Chapter 3 discusses the Internet as a network as well as other types of networks. This session provides an introduction to telecommunications and networks and their applications to emergency management. A comparison between wire-line and wireless networks will be explored.

Chapter 4 examines GIS and GPS tools and their applications are assessed. This chapter explains that Geographic Information is information which relates to specific locations. It involves the physical environment with data associated with it. Geographic Information System (GIS) is an organized collection of computer hardware and software designed to efficiently create, manipulate, analyze, and display all types of geographically or spatially referenced data. A GIS allows complex spatial operations that are very difficult to do otherwise.

Chapter 5 examines Direct and Remote Sensing which are essential for the prediction of hazards. This chapter examines the types of direct and remote sensing data available for hazards analysis and emergency response. Sources of natural hazards data including river / stream gages, weather stations, and National Weather Service forecasts will be discussed. Chemical air monitoring systems and data sources will be examined. Information gathered from direct and remote sensing is often used in conjunction with decision support systems and databases which is the topic for the sixth chapter.

Chapter 6 provides an introduction and overview of emergency management information and decision support systems. An examination of three information systems will be made including the National Emergency Management Information System and CAMEO (Computer Aided Management of Emergency Operations).

Chapter 7 is "Hazard Analysis and Modeling." This chapter provides an introduction to modeling and its application to emergency management. It will clarify the elements of hazard models and the major issues present when using hazard models. Uses of modeling programs in emergency response will be discussed. Limitations of modeling programs will be examined.

Chapter 8 is "Warning Systems". Warning systems have been a part of our emergency management system for many years. Initial efforts centered on radio broadcast warning systems. Today, warning systems include more sophisticated radio networks, cable over-ride systems, phone messaging systems, and sirens. The following materials highlight several warning systems from a national prospective (FEMA's Emergency Alert System), the National Weather Service's weather alert messages, and private sector alert systems.

Chapter 9, "Operational Problems and Technology," examines a series of operational problems that the emergency management community face on an ongoing basis including interagency collaboration and communication, data integration, systems security and compatibility, budgets, and organizational learning.

No book on technology would be complete without some predictions about the direction of technology. Chapter 10, "Emerging Technologies," examines the potential impact of new technologies on emergency management. Technology applications in emergency management are constantly changing. New developments including communications, information access, learning strategies, and Internet mapping and modeling will be highlighted during this session. Software innovations will continue along with more powerful personal computers will continue to enable emergency managers to use new technologies never before considered possible.

By working through all ten chapters, students will earn a greater understanding and appreciation of how to use technology to protect their community from any and all hazards.

Learning Aids

Each chapter of *Technology in Emergency Management* features the following learning and study aids to activate students' prior knowledge of the topics and orient them to the material.

▲ **Pre-test.** This pre-reading assessment tool in multiple-choice format not only introduces chapter material, but it also helps students anticipate the chapter's learning outcomes. By focusing students' attention on what they do not know, the self-test provides students with a benchmark against which they can measure their own progress. The pre-test is available online at www.wiley.com/college/Pine.

▲ **What You'll Learn in This Chapter and After Studying This Chapter.** These bulleted lists tell students what they will be learning in the chapter and why it is significant for their careers. They also explain why the chapter is important and how it relates to other chapters in the text. "What You'll Learn..." lists focus on the *subject matter* that will be taught (e.g. why a website outlining emergency management precautions is needed). "After Studying This Chapter..." lists emphasize *capabilities and skills* students will learn (e.g. how to determine what information should be included in an emergency management website).

▲ **Goals and Outcomes.** These lists identify specific student capabilities that will result from reading the chapter. They set students up to synthesize and evaluate the chapter material, and relate it to the real world.

▲ **Figures and tables.** Line art and photos have been carefully chosen to be truly instructional rather than filler. Tables distill and present information in a way that is easy to identify, access, and understand, enhancing the focus of the text on essential ideas.

Within-text Learning Aids

The following learning aids are designed to encourage analysis and synthesis of the material, and to support the learning process and ensure success during the evaluation phase:

▲ **Introduction.** This section orients the student by introducing the chapter and explaining its practical value and relevance to the book as a whole. Short summaries of chapter sections preview the topics to follow.

▲ **"For Example" Boxes.** Found within each section, these boxes tie section content to real-world organizations, scenarios, and applications.

▲ **Self-Check.** Related to the "What You'll Learn" bullets and found at the end of each section, this battery of short answer questions emphasizes student understanding of concepts and mastery of section content. Though the questions may either be discussed in class or studied by students outside of class, students should not go on before they can answer all questions correctly. Each *Self-Check* question set includes a link to a section of the pre-test for further review and practice.

▲ **Summary.** Each chapter concludes with a summary paragraph that reviews the major concepts in the chapter and links back to the "What you'll learn" list.

▲ **Key Terms and Glossary.** To help students develop a professional vocabulary, key terms are bolded in the introduction, summary and when they first appear in the chapter. A complete list of key terms with brief definitions appears at the end of each chapter and again in a glossary at the end of the book. Knowledge of key terms is assessed by all assessment tools (see below).

Evaluation and Assessment Tools

The evaluation phase of the CASE Learning System consists of a variety of within-chapter and end-of-chapter assessment tools that test how well students have learned the material. These tools also encourage students to extend their learning into different scenarios and higher levels of understanding and thinking. The following assessment tools appear in every chapter of *Technology in Emergency Management:*

▲ **Summary Questions** help students summarize the chapter's main points by asking a series of multiple choice and true/false questions that emphasize student understanding of concepts and mastery of chapter content. Students should be able to answer all of the Summary Questions correctly before moving on.

▲ **Review Questions** in short answer format review the major points in each chapter, prompting analysis while reinforcing and confirming student understanding of concepts, and encouraging mastery of chapter content. They are somewhat more difficult than the *Self-Check* and *Summary Questions,* and students should be able to answer most of them correctly before moving on.

▲ **Applying This Chapter Questions** drive home key ideas by asking students to synthesize and apply chapter concepts to new, real-life situations and scenarios.

▲ **You Try It Questions** are designed to extend students' thinking, and so are ideal for discussion or writing assignments. Using an open-ended format and sometimes based on Web sources, they encourage students to draw conclusions using chapter material applied to real-world situations, which fosters both mastery and independent learning.

▲ **Post-test** should be taken after students have completed the chapter. It includes all of the questions in the pre-test, so that students can see how their learning has progressed and improved.

Instructor and Student Package

Technology in Emergency Management is available with the following teaching and learning supplements. All supplements are available online at the text's Book Companion Website, located at *www.wiley.com/college/pine*.

▲ **Instructor's Resource Guide.** Provides the following aids and supplements for teaching:

- *Diagnostic Evaluation of Grammar, Mechanics, and Spelling.* A useful tool that instructors may administer to the class at the beginning of the course to determine each student's basic writing skills. The Evaluation is accompanied by an Answer Key and a Marking Key. Instructors are encouraged to use the Marking key when grading students' Evaluations, and to duplicate and distribute it to students with their graded evaluations.

- *Sample syllabus.* A convenient template that instructors may use for creating their own course syllabi.

- *Teaching suggestions.* For each chapter, these include a chapter summary, learning objectives, definitions of key terms, lecture notes, answers to select text question sets, and at least 3 suggestions for classroom activities, such as ideas for speakers to invite, videos to show, and other projects.

▲ **Test Bank.** One test per chapter, as well as a mid-term and a final. Each includes true/false, multiple choice, and open-ended questions. Answers and page references are provided for the true/false and multiple choice questions, and page references for the open-ended questions. Available in Microsoft Word and computerized formats.

▲ **PowerPoints.** Key information is summarized in 10 to 15 PowerPoints per chapter. Instructors may use these in class or choose to share them with students for class presentations or to provide additional study support.

ACKNOWLEDGMENTS

Taken together, the content, pedagogy, and assessment elements of *Technology in Emergency Management* offer the career-oriented student the most important aspects of the emergency management field as well as ways to develop the skills and capabilities that current and future employers seek in the individuals they hire and promote. Instructors will appreciate its practical focus, conciseness, and real-world emphasis. We would like to thank the following reviewers for their feedback and suggestions during the text's development. Their advice on how to shape *Technology in Emergency Management* into a solid learning tool that meets both their needs and those of their busy students is deeply appreciated.

Barbara Russo, Wayne Community College
Ed Leachman, M.S., Arkansas Tech University
Jack Rozdilsky, Ph.D.,
Eamon Doherty, Ph.D.,

I would like to acknowledge Dr. Wayne Blanchard, Emergency Management Institute, Federal Emergency Management Agency for the opportunity to develop the Technology and Emergency Management course as a part of FEMA's Higher Education Project. His guidance and suggestions provided a basis from which to prepare this book. I would also like to acknowledge the support from Ms. Laura Town for her editing, formatting, and guidance in the development of this book. Finally, I would like to acknowledge so many people who applied technology is many ways in the response and recovery to Hurricanes Katrina and Rita that impacted our state. These storms revealed the extensive application of technology in emergency response, recovery, mitigation and now in preparing for the 2006 Hurricane season. The creative use of the technology really made a difference to helping emergency managers in these storms.

BRIEF CONTENTS

CONTENTS

1

USING TECHNOLOGY
Technology as a Tool

Starting Point

Go to www.wiley.com/college/pine to assess your knowledge of using technology.
Determine where you need to concentrate your effort.

What You'll Learn in This Chapter

▲ The definitions of focusing events and windows of opportunity
▲ The types of technology used in the emergency management process
▲ How technology can assist in the emergency management process

After Studying This Chapter, You'll Be Able To

▲ Examine what technology and equipment your community needs
▲ Examine what technology tools are needed during disasters
▲ Use focusing events to attain community support for greater emergency management resources

Goals and Outcomes

▲ Select technology to improve response during a disaster
▲ Perform a technology-needs assessment
▲ Persuade the community to commit greater resources toward emergency management by using focusing events and the needs assessment

INTRODUCTION

We all live in a global village. We can receive and transmit information within seconds. We can communicate from anywhere, at anytime, and anyplace. The use of technology in emergency management provides links between local, regional, and national resources. This enhances all elements of decision making. We can only imagine the new devices that will be used in the future. Resource allocation will become more efficient. We will be able to better analyze complex issues in times of crisis.

Emergencies and disasters are extreme events that cause significant disruption. They require immediate response. They require a coordinated application of resources, facilities, and efforts beyond those regularly available to handle routine problems. They arise from both natural and man-made events. Fortunately, we now have more **technology** available than ever before to help us handle disasters. Technology is the application of scientific methods or objects to achieve a practical purpose. Technology is used throughout the emergency management process. Technology used in emergency management includes the following:

▲ Cell phones
▲ Satellite phones
▲ Satellite dishes
▲ Scanners
▲ Teleconference communication devices
▲ Desktop, laptop, and handheld personal computers
▲ Local and wide area network connections
▲ Lnternet
▲ Digital cameras
▲ Geo-positioning systems
▲ Hazard modeling software

Technology is enabling organizations to contribute to the emergency management process in ways that were only imagined in the past. We can identify the location of callers on cell phones for emergency response. We can communicate by voice and video with multiple partners to plan and respond more effectively. We can reach an unlimited audience. We can retrieve data in real time during disaster events. We can incorporate the information with existing data sets. We can place the information into a geographic information system. The use of technology is expanding and contributing to more effective plans, mitigation efforts, as well as response and recovery efforts.

Every day, technology affects emergency management in a different way. Although we cannot rely on technology to do our jobs, we must use it as a tool.

To do so, we must learn fast and have continuous training. In this chapter, we will learn how technology fits in the emergency management process, how to prioritize what technology tools are needed, and how to attain community support for the resources to purchase and use these tools.

1.1 Technology as a Management Tool

We use technology to manage our time. We use technology to manage our organization. We also use technology to manage disasters and **hazards.** Hazards are events or conditions that have the potential to create loss. Technology can be used to prepare for, respond to, recover from, and mitigate future disasters. We prepare for disasters before they happen, often without definite knowledge that they will happen. We respond to disasters when they happen. We recover from disasters after they happen. During and after recovery and preparation, we try to **mitigate** disasters. To mitigate a disaster means that we try to lessen the effects of the disaster. For example, to mitigate a levee collapse, the Army Corps of Engineers would try to strengthen it with sandbags or use barges to prevent the water from flooding an area. To mitigate the effects of a hurricane, many home and business owners board up their property to prevent damage. Throughout the entire emergency management cycle, technology is key. Technology helps us in many ways. We can be better prepared by recording weather data in remote locations. We can do this by using satellites. We can also process information in new ways. We can directly observe disaster events. In an emergency response, computer applications allow us to access detailed information, such as data about hazardous chemicals, in more assessable ways. In mitigation and recovery, we use technology to model disasters and devise an emergency response plan. Technology is especially important in conducting mitigation activities. Mitigation activities include boarding up homes before a hurricane, evacuating an area, and other actions that reduce losses.

Technology gives us the ability to receive and send information quickly. Information is critical for all involved in the emergency management process. Weather, chemical, security, and transportation information are just a few types of essential data. Quick access to information is not only important to emergency managers, but also to citizens. The quicker emergency managers can give orders to evacuate or to shelter in-place, the more lives are saved. Technology ranges from individual sensors that record information to internal and external organization networks, including the Internet, to the Emergency Broadcast System. Communication devices are ever changing, from vehicle-mounted applications to remote satellite systems and real-time video teleconferencing.

Technology needs to be easy to use for anyone in the emergency management process. It should not be viewed as an "expert system" only available to a select few. Ongoing training for officials will be critical in the effective use of technology in crisis situations.

Also, not every new technology will be applicable for every hazard. Not every new technology will be applicable to every emergency management organization. For example, you may live in California and fear an earthquake. You are therefore concerned about being able to prepare for and predict earthquakes. Another emergency manager may live in Texas and be concerned about the next hurricane. You must be careful to use technology effectively within your own region and within your own budget constraints. Figure 1-1 diagrams the role of technology in the emergency management prrocess.

Figure 1-1

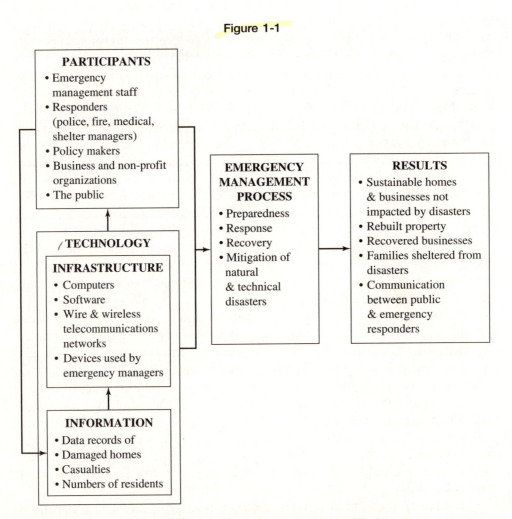

The role of technology in the emergency management process.

FOR EXAMPLE

When Technology Fails

In May 2006, a strong earthquake with a magnitude of 6.0 hit near Tonga, a group of 170 islands. The Pacific Tsunami Warning Center in Hawaii issued a tsunami alert. Tonga, however, failed to receive the warning due to power outages. Although a tsunami did not occur there, the inability to receive the warning was troubling and is forcing the Pacific Tsunami Warning Center to create additional methods for sending warnings.

SELF-CHECK

- Define **hazards.** Name two types of hazards.
- Define **mitigate.** Give one example of how a hazard can be mitigated.
- How does an emergency manager's budget affect the selection of technology?

1.2 Using Technology Effectively

Emergency management is an ever-changing process. We manage emergencies in an effort to reduce losses. Losses are defined as loss of property and loss of life. As we saw with Hurricane Katrina, natural hazards can create great losses. As we saw with the terrorist attacks of 9/11, human-caused hazards can cause substantial losses as well. Emergency managers try to reduce any and all potential losses. To do this, we have to prepare for disasters, have a good response plan when there is a disaster, and reduce our vulnerability to hazards. Emergency management is based on a systems approach, which means that every agency has a unique role in reducing losses. In addition, local, state, and federal agencies have to all work together to successfully prepare for and respond to hazards.

To reduce losses, emergency managers and agencies have to achieve a high degree of performance. Any misstep could cost lives. Technology not only enhances performance in times of crisis, but also helps predict when there will be a time of crisis. Technology has also had major effects on all organizations, allowing emergency managers to do the following:

1. **Predict hazards more quickly.** Whether the hazard is a natural disaster or a terrorist attack, technology helps us understand it. Satellites help us

detect and track storms with accuracy. Chemical sensors help us detect harmful chemicals. After the devastating tsunami of 2005, the Pacific Rim has now installed a tsunami warning system.

2. **Respond more effectively.** There are several software programs that help model what would happen if an area were hit by a disaster. For example, before Hurricane Katrina, emergency managers simulated what a Category 5 storm would do to New Orleans. The software-modeling program showed emergency managers that the city of New Orleans would flood. These modeling programs help responders know what outcome of different hazards could be, and therefore, know what planning should address. Also, with GPS software, emergency managers can track supplies and get them to their target destination very quickly. They can pinpoint where to direct emergency personnel for rescue operations or post-disaster cleanup of chemical containers, boats, or building debris.

3. **Communicate quickly.** With cell phones, the Internet, e-mail, and satellite phones, we can now communicate in any type of disaster, regardless of the damage to the area's infrastructure. We can also quickly send large amounts of information instantaneously through e-mail. Plus, we can quickly warn people to evacuate through the use of information on Web sites and e-mails in addition to the traditional media of television, radio, and newsprint.

4. **Develop a better understanding of hazards.** With our advanced equipment, we can better understand how hazards occur. For example, with the tsunami sensor system in place in the Pacific Rim, we can gain a better understanding of tsunamis and increase our ability to predict and warn residents of a tsunami.

5. **Improve response.** With the enhanced ability to communicate quickly, we also know when response activities are not going well. For example, during Hurricane Katrina we all saw that there were problems getting supplies to New Orleans. Based on that information, public and nonprofit agencies were able to adapt their efforts to get supplies to the hurricane victims.

6. **Increase coordination.** With increased communication and an increased ability to predict hazards, it is easier for emergency managers to work with first responders in their own community. It is also easier for emergency managers to work with state emergency management agencies and FEMA.

7. **Improve efficiency.** Computers and other forms of technology have made all organizations more efficient, which has led to a reduction in the amount of people needed in each organization.

8. **Improve training and risk communication programs.** With software programs, it is very easy to scan the results of surveys on training and risk communication programs and evaluate the results. This evaluation process leads to improvements in the programs.

FOR EXAMPLE

Training

For the use of technology to be effective, staff members must be trained. Research has indicated that many tools that are available to emergency managers and staff, such as software modeling programs, are not used because the staff is not properly trained on how to use it. FEMA and state emergency management agencies offer different types of training. Not only should staff members be trained initially on the technology, but refresher courses should also be held periodically.

SELF-CHECK

- Give three examples of how technology can be used to understand hazards.
- How can technology be used in training programs?
- How can software programs be used in emergency management?

1.3 Completing a Needs Assessment

Participants in the emergency management system from public agencies, non and profit, business organizations, and the general public all make use of technology. Each has their own perspective, role, needs, and capabilities, which enables the emergency management system to function. Understanding the players in the system is critical to effective use of technology. Not every emergency management organization has a budget for all the software and computers that they would like to have. Nonetheless, there are certain items that every organization should have:

▲ **Satellite phones.** During Hurricane Katrina, the New Orleans infrastructure was badly damaged. Mayor Ray Nagin was cut off from all communications and could not contact anyone at the state and federal level to update them on the situation. Mayor Nagin's staff ended up breaking into an office supply store and taking satellite phones so they could communicate their needs. This is just one example of why every emergency manager needs satellite phones.

▲ **Web sites.** Web sites are a great way to warn people of hazards, provide information on hazards, and outline mitigation strategies. For large jurisdictions, you can give specific neighborhood information. For example, some neighborhoods may be in the hazard's direct path and will be more affected than those neighborhoods outside the hazard's path. Web-based resources are being used today by public agencies, are citizens, businesses, and nonprofit agencies in gathering information about disasters. The National Hurricane Center provides ongoing information about hurricanes for state and local emergency management agencies, businesses, and the general public to support decision making. The number of people who rely on Web sites for information is growing every day. At the very least, many people will use the Web as one of their sources for information.

▲ **Digital cameras.** You may need to take photos of hazard damage and transmit them quickly over the Internet to state or federal authorities. Digital cameras were an essential resource in documenting property damage following Hurricanes Katrina and Rita.

▲ **Access to HAZUS-MH.** HAZUS-MH stands for the software program Hazards US-Multi Hazard. You can use this program to estimate losses from earthquakes, floods, and hurricane winds. The program analyzes the impact of a disaster. The program also displays estimates of damages and losses. You can request this program through the FEMA Web site (www.fema.gov).

You may be the emergency manager of a small community. If so, you may need only the basic equipment. Or you may be the emergency manager of a large jurisdiction and need every advantage new technology offers. Before you can submit a budget request for new technology, you must determine what you truly need.

To Complete a Needs Assessment

Step 1: Inventory your use of technology today. How are you using technology and contributing to the emergency management system? What do you need to know to identify other means of utilizing technology?

Step 2: Determine your community's vulnerability. For example, if you have several industrial facilities that work with hazmat, then you may need chemical sensors installed. If you live in a community that is on the transportation route for dangerous nuclear waste, you may need cameras installed along the route within your community in an effort to prevent a terrorist hijacking. If you have completed a Hazard Vulnerability Assessment (HVA), this will go a long way in determining what type of technology you need.

Step 3: Determine how to educate the community on mitigation strategies. For example, you may determine that one way to educate the public is to provide a comprehensive Web site. You may decide that you need to send e-mail messages to residents. Or you could decide to hold several news conferences. Your strategy will most likely consist of reaching people through several different media.

Step 4: Determine how the emergency management community can better coordinate efforts between agencies (including first responders). For example, you may need satellite phones, GPS devices, or a Web portal to streamline communication and provide assistance more efficiently.

Step 5: Determine how you could be more effective in predicting hazards. For example, you may need modeling software to determine what parts of the jurisdiction would be affected by a hurricane.

Step 6: Determine how you could be more effective in responding to hazards. For example, if all traditional lines of communication are knocked out, you may need satellite phones or some other means of communication.

Step 7: Assess the threat and your needs. What is the most likely threat? What hazard would cause the most damage? What equipment and software would help you the most?

Once you determine your needs, you need to prioritize them based on the greatest need. You will want to submit budget requests for new equipment and software that can be useful for all hazards. You will also want to submit budget requests for equipment that will have a direct impact should you get hit with the hazard that your community is most vulnerable to. Public organizations have been facing critical financial limitation. Expenditures for technology must be viewed as cost effective, especially in serving the community in non-emergency operations.

Outside the normal budget cycle, a good time to submit a request for new equipment is when there is a **focusing event.** A focusing event is a national disaster resulting in large losses that receives extensive media coverage. Hurricane Katrina is a focusing event. The tsunami in the Pacific Rim is a focusing event. These events give you a **window of opportunity** to advocate for better and newer equipment. A window of opportunity is the chance to argue that a focusing event could occur locally if certain precautions are not taken. During this window of opportunity, you will need to make the argument that such a disaster "could happen here." Because this window of opportunity will not be open for long, you must take advantage of it as soon as you can. Once decision makers are over the shock of the magnitude of the disaster, they will turn their attention to the annual necessities for the community. For example, the decision makers know they have to fund the school bus system, as this is a definite need. Your job is to convince decision makers to prepare for a disaster that may or may not happen.

Technology innovations have resulted in more than just new devices; they have also resulted in changes in human interactions. The changes, especially those in communications, provide more information for decision making. This would be a positive impact if it were not for the possibility of inaccurate, incomplete, or misdirected information. So often our developments in technology suggest that there is a quick fix for whatever our problems are (Quarantelli 1997). A focus on gadgetry leads us in the wrong direction; we need to view technology as simply a tool with strengths and limitations. Technology brings us unprecedented amounts of information that can clarify problems or confuse us (Michael 1985). For example, a geographic information system on a personal computer can provide us with extensive information about a jurisdiction; however, the emergency manager may need simple directions from one location to another as provided by many Internet sites, such as MapQuest or GoogleEarth. The key is to find the fit between technology and our emergency management needs.

The Internet provides a great resource to the emergency management community by allowing agencies to communicate in a timely manner and ensure that activities are coordinated. This Internet-based system provides federal, state, local, and nonprofit agencies an integrated system for making resource requests and task tracking. Because it is digital, it maintains a historical memory (data files) for evaluating agency response and coordination.

The photo in Figure 1-2, from New Orleans after Hurricane Katrina, illustrates several applications of technology and emergency management. First, the Red Cross, local government damage assessment teams, and insurance adjusters link photos of residents, businesses, and critical infrastructure to datasets documenting property damage from disasters. Second, the high water marks on the house were used by a survey team to document high water elevations in the city; the high water levels were used by digital surveying equipment. Finally, digital images such as this photo of a home are used by the media, public officials, and many other organizations to document in printed and online documents and presentations the social, economic, and environmental impacts of disasters.

FOR EXAMPLE

Focusing Event: 9/11

One of the many tragedies of 9/11 was the fact that so many firefighters had faulty communications equipment, and they did not hear the directive to vacate the World Trade Center. If they had heard these instructions, there is no doubt that more lives would have been saved. The 9/11 Commission issued their report months later and urged all municipalities to ensure their communications equipment is maintained and always works properly.

Figure 1-2

This photo from Hurricane Katrina illustrates applications of technology in emergency management.

SELF-CHECK

- Define **focusing event** and **window of opportunity.**
- What is the relationship between a focusing event and a window of opportunity?
- What is a needs assessment and when should it be conducted?
- Name three types of technology that are used in emergency management.

SUMMARY

In this lesson, you have defined focusing events and windows of opportunity. You have assessed different ways that technology can help you be more effective. You have evaluated how to perform a needs assessment and how to ask your community for more resources. Technology provides tools to link local, regional, and national resources. A technology needs assessment is critical because agencies in the emergency management system have different technology needs and financial resources. Once you know your needs, you can ask for the tools that will help you mitigate and respond to hazards more effectively.

KEY TERMS

Focusing event	A national disaster resulting in losses that receives extensive media coverage.
Hazard	An event or physical condition that has the potential to create loss (economic, social, or environmental).
Mitigate	To take Action and enact strategies taken that reduce vulnerability to hazards.
Technology	The application of scientific methods or objects to achieve a practical purpose.
Window of opportunity	A chance to compare the local area to areas that have garnered media coverage due to disasters. This chance allows emergency management officials to argue that the "same thing could happen here" in an effort to attain greater resources and funds for emergency management.

ASSESS YOUR UNDERSTANDING

Go to www.wiley.com/college/pine to evaluate your knowledge of using technology. *Measure your learning by comparing pre-test and post-test results.*

Summary Questions

1. Which of the following best illustrates the role of technology as a management tool?
   (a) allows us greater access to information for decision making.
   (b) provides an opportunity to get the newest phone or radio.
   (c) keeps emergency management as a priority in an agency.
   (d) forces agencies to use the latest device or system.
2. Technology allows emergency managers to do all of the following except
   (a) predict hazards more quickly.
   (b) respond more effectively.
   (c) communicate more quickly.
   (d) eliminate the need for training.
3. Hurricane Katrina is an example of a
   (a) focusing event.
   (b) window of opportunity.
   (c) technological disaster.
   (d) disaster where no technology was used.
4. Technology can be used in
   (a) mitigating disasters.
   (b) responding to disasters.
   (c) recovering from disasters.
   (d) all phases of emergency management.
5. HAZUS-MH is a software modeling program. True or False?

Review Questions

1. What technology tools would you use during hurricane season?
2. Name two technology tools that every emergency management organization should have.
3. What steps do you need to take to perform a technology needs assessment?
4. Is training important even when you have all the technology tools you need? Why?
5. Name two ways technology provides quick access to information.

Applying This Chapter

1. You work as an emergency manager for a small town that just created the position. As the local emergency management agency did not previously exist you are in charge of a new agency. What technology should you recommend for purchase and why?

2. Coordination is a critical role in emergency preparedness, response, recovery, and mitigation. What technology would be extremely helpful in enhancing your capabilities in your efforts to coordinate between local public agencies, businesses, and not-for-profit agencies?

3. Your organization has been given a donation by a local nonprofit group that wants to help the community be better prepared for disasters. You have a choice between a digital camera or a digital video camera, both of equal quality, value, and support if you had a question on their use. Which would you select? How would you determine which one you would select?

4. You are the emergency manager for New Orleans, Louisiana. You need to create a Web site that addresses issues and concerns that often come up during hurricane season. What information do you post and why?

Submitting a Budget Request

You are the emergency manager of a small town in Florida. You, unfortunately, do not have the equipment you would like to have in case of a hurricane. Before you submit your budget request, how do you make sure that you are asking for the right equipment? How can you be sure that what you are asking for is really what you need?

Choosing Technology

You are the emergency manager of a small town in Florida. Because the town is in Florida and close to the coast, it is vulnerable to hurricanes. Write a paper listing all the technology that is on your wish list and why. Also list technology items that you would not need and/or use along with the reasons why.

Needs Assessment

The first step in conducting a needs assessment is taking stock of what you have and how you are using technology in present operations. Select a local emergency response agency and interview the emergency manager. Then determine what technology is currently in use and what is needed. Write a paper outlining your suggestions.

2

EMERGENCY MANAGEMENT AND THE INTERNET
The Information Superhighway

Starting Point

Go to www.wiley.com/college/pine to assess your knowledge of the basics of emergency management and the Internet.
Determine where you need to concentrate your effort.

What You'll Learn in This Chapter

- ▲ Ways in which the Internet was used during Hurricane Katrina
- ▲ The evolution of the Internet
- ▲ The difference between closed and open systems
- ▲ The strengths and limitations of the Internet as an emergency management tool
- ▲ Helpful emergency management Web sites

After Studying This Chapter, You'll Be Able To

- ▲ Examine ways to use the Internet in disasters
- ▲ Describe the history of the Internet
- ▲ Compare and contrast closed and open systems
- ▲ Assess the limitations of the Internet and capitalize on the strengths of the Internet as an emergency management tool
- ▲ Examine helpful emergency management Web sites

Goals and Outcomes

- ▲ Evaluate the lessons of Internet use during Hurricane Katrina and applies them to other disasters
- ▲ Examine the history of the Internet
- ▲ Evaluate the differences between open and closed systems
- ▲ Evaluate the strengths and limitations of the Internet as an emergency management tool
- ▲ Assess how the Internet can be used in hazard-mitigation activities
- ▲ Assess how the Internet can be used in response activities
- ▲ Compare emergency management Web sites

INTRODUCTION

The **Internet** is a digital transmission technology that allows users to search, sort, convert, and transfer information over a network. The Internet has changed the world. You can quickly communicate through the Internet without picking up a phone or sending a fax. You can work closely with others halfway across the world. The **Web** is a distributed information system. Through the Web, you can provide hazard information, issue evacuation instructions, and apply for disaster relief. In this chapter, you will go back to the beginning of the Internet and see how it has evolved as a system. You will compare and contrast open and closed systems. You will assess the strengths and limitations of the Internet. You will also review helpful emergency management Web sites. And finally, you will see how you can use the Internet in managing emergencies. First, however, we begin with a real-world case study how the Internet was used during Hurricane Katrina.

2.1 Case Study: Hurricane Katrina and the Internet

The Internet has changed society in many different ways. It has also changed emergency management. Consider Hurricane Katrina. Residents who chose to evacuate New Orleans looked up evacuation information on the Internet. Many read about the devastation of the hurricane on the Internet. Responders used the Web to find the location of addresses in New Orleans to direct rescue operations. Operations support staff used e-mail, teleconferencing, and Web-based response information systems to record and track response operations. After the hurricane, people used the Web to post pictures of their loved ones. Throughout the hurricane, the public and the emergency management community made extensive use of e-mail. The Red Cross established a database on the Internet of people staying in shelters in an effort to reunite families. Even pictures of pets were posted on the Internet in an effort to reunite them with their owners. Those who were affected by the hurricane applied for financial aid on the FEMA Web site. Many of the sites provide access to public and private groups that provide services to the community.

One of the advantages of the Web is the research capability it offers. You can easily search the entire Web for sites that offer services to disaster victims. For example, immediately after Hurricane Katrina, Web sites were thrown together by churches, nonprofits, and concerned citizens who offered to help the victims. By examining the sites obtained from searches, you can identify resources for information, products, or services. The sites also provide a basis for communicating to a group of organizations that want to help in response and recovery. These groups increase your network of contacts. For example, citizens formed a Web site that offered housing to people who had lost their homes. This Web site was launched on September 1, 2005, by a group of computer programmers who wanted to help the victims of Katrina. They immediately received financial support and free services from several nonprofit groups.

As we can see, there are many applications for the Internet. Federal, state, and local governments use the Internet. Nonprofit agencies use the Internet. Information and resources on emergency preparedness, response, recovery, and mitigation activities can be found on the Internet. FEMA allows businesses and citizens to apply for financial resources using the Internet (Figure 2-1). FEMA also has its complete Web site in Spanish. This is a great way to reach those who are not native English speakers. State agencies and local governments make information available to citizens. Hazard warnings are on the Internet. Recommendations on evacuation routes or when reentry may be made in a community impacted by a disaster are on the Internet. These sites are constantly changing, so visit your state, local, FEMA, or Red Cross Web site and explore what is available today.

The FEMA Web site (www.fema.gov) provides examples of how technology is used in emergency management. For example, this site offers the following:

▲ **Information access.** The site provides access to information on programs and activities of FEMA offices at the national or regional level. There is also information on training and exercises, weather information, or flood insurance information. FEMA also posts the results of several research projects online. This research could help you develop solutions for problems in your own jurisdiction.

Figure 2-1

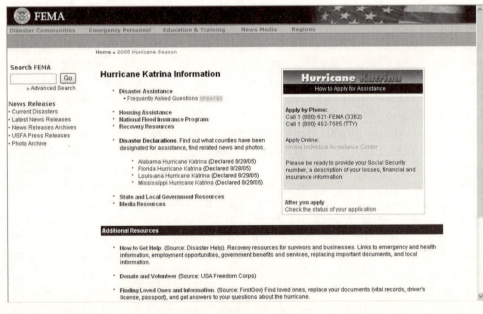

FEMA Web page providing information about Hurricane Katrina.

> ## FOR EXAMPLE
>
> ### Links
>
> With Web sites, you have an unlimited amount of space to display information. For example, you can get all kinds of statistics, and reports from the Department of Homeland Security Web site (www.dhs.gov). You can also link with other sites on a Web site. For example, the FEMA Web site can provide links to victims of natural disasters, such as links to the Red Cross or the Salvation Army, to enable people to get the help they need.

▲ **Communication links.** The site provides information on how to contact the FEMA staff, including e-mail addresses that can be used.

▲ **Information on aid or making donations.** Disaster victims can apply for aid through the Web site and check on the status of their application. Those wanting to help can donate by using the Web.

▲ **Grant applications.** FEMA provides grant and funding applications for local and state emergency management associations online.

▲ **Employment opportunities.** Emergency management and first-responder vacancies are posted on the FEMA site.

▲ **Directory.** A directory of FEMA directory is posted online.

SELF-CHECK

- Define **Internet**.
- Give two examples of how the Internet was used during Hurricane Katrina.
- What services does the FEMA Web site provide?
- What information can be posted on the Internet to help people who are trying to evacuate before a natural disaster?

2.2 The Beginning of the Internet

The Internet is a digital communications network that makes it easy to communicate to others. Not only can you send short e-mails, for example, through the Internet to friends, but you can also have a Web site that contains hundreds of pages of information. The Internet uses digital transmission technology. Information is first converted to digital form. It can then be easily processed, searched, sorted, enhanced, converted, compressed, encrypted, replicated, and transmitted. All this happens in ways that are conveniently matched to today's information processing systems.

The foundation of the Internet is a network that is a communication system that connects users around the world by means of links and switches as well as control software. The Internet provides a general communication infrastructure. It is targeted to a wide range of computer-based services, such as electronic mail (e-mail), information retrieval, and teleconferencing. Its roots lie in the research community. Its original funding came from the Department of Defense. It is now widely used commercially. For example, we have all done some Internet shopping or auction bidding.

The Internet originated with **ARPANET,** which was the first packet switching network. ARPANET was sponsored by the Advanced Research Projects Agency (ARPA). The first node of ARPANET was installed at the University of California at Los Angeles in 1969. The Internet was first used within the computer science community. Use of the Internet later expanded into research libraries and higher education. The Internet is now being used everywhere, including public libraries and elementary schools. The spread of Internet use is a result of federal funding decisions that were both farsighted and, at the time, risk-taking. The government's high-risk, high-payoff approach was essential to the acceleration of successful networking.

The National Science Foundation (NSF) expanded the Internet in 1986. This was the beginning of a grand experiment as part of the National Research and Education Network (NREN) program. At this time, the computer science community had become enthusiastic users of the early Internet. However, the larger science research community had only limited exposure to the technology. It was far from clear that the Internet would be critical to research. The NSF, with the support of other federal agencies and the Office of Science and Technology Policy (OSTP), discussed how the Internet could be used. These agencies concluded that the way to support science research was to build and operate a network to encompass the nation's vast research community. The result was greater, broader, and faster communication, collaboration, and sharing of new data. The results also included innovations in the organization, presentation, and retrieval of information. That experiment has been a resounding success. It has demonstrated the power of networking to transform a community. It has changed how that community operates. And it has built a base of enthusiastic and committed users.

During this same time, individuals and groups within education began to benefit from access to the Internet. Now, schools and universities across the country network. Today, the demand for access to and capacity on the Internet is great. All types of people at every level of society now use the Internet for a variety of professional and personal reasons.

FOR EXAMPLE

Growth of Internet Use

The growth of Internet use in American homes has been phenomenal. According to the 1997 Census, 36.6% of all Americans had a computer and 18% had Internet access. In 2000, 51% of all Americans had a computer and 41.5% had Internet access. This translates to more than 2 in 5 households having Internet access. Ninety-four million people use the Internet at home. Many adults reported that even their three-year-old uses the Internet (U.S. Census Bureau, "Home Computers and Internet Use in the United States: August 2000" issued September 2001).

In a short amount of time, we have experienced the following phenomenon with the Internet:

▲ We now have a diverse user population; people at all levels of society use the Internet.
▲ The number of people who use the Internet continues to grow.
▲ There has been an increase in private investors who invest in Internet technologies.
▲ There are several different Internet service providers.
▲ There is a wide range of services offered on the Internet, from shopping to investing to research.
▲ There has been an enormous growth of infrastructure applications and services.

SELF-CHECK

- Define **ARPANET**.
- How did the Internet evolve from ARPANET?
- How many Americans use the Internet, and how has the usage rate changed over the years?

2.3 The Internet as a System

A **system** is composed of three elements: input, transformation, and output(see Figure 2-2). The Internet is a system and has these three elements as well. Here are some general examples of each element:

▲ **Inputs:** Web sites, users, organizations, technical support staff, computers, networks, computer programs, or financial resources

▲ **Transformation:** Web services, teleconferencing, or communication processing

▲ **Outputs:** Communication links, messages delivered, documents printed, data obtained and made available, or reports prepared

Figure 2-2

Systems Concepts		
Inputs	**Transformation**	**Outputs**
Computers, networks, Internet E-Mail, Web broadcasts, Web courses, Web map utilities, Web pages, & Web search engines.	File communication, E-Mail communication, Web broadcast communication, Web page searches, Web maps, Students using Web courses	Information used from E-Mail, Web broadcast, or Web courses; use of Web maps, use of data from shared Internet files, individual learning from Web courses or broadcasts

The Internet is a system.

To illustrate, let's look at a specific example.

▲ **Input:** You sit down at your computer and connect to the Internet. You then type in "www.fema.gov".

▲ **Transformation:** The FEMA Web site address is converted to an IP address, and the information from the Web site is being retrieved.

▲ **Output:** The FEMA Web site comes up, and you can download all the information you need.

We've all had an experience when using the Internet wasn't quite that easy! Let's look at what can go wrong.

Problems with Inputs:

▲ Breakdowns in network or cable/line connections
▲ Busy signal on the connection
▲ Lack of technical support in formatting the computer links to the Internet
▲ Phone connection to an Internet service provider is not a local call

Problems with Transformation:

▲ The Internet interface is confusing
▲ Internet system malfunctions
▲ The system takes too long to process a user request

Problems with Outputs:

▲ The message may be in a format that the user cannot process

▲ The information is confusing or too much information is provided

▲ Outputs may be in a format that is not compatible with the user's system

2.3.1 Open and Closed Internet Systems

There are two basic types of systems, closed and open.

▲ **Closed system:** A system that is not open to any inputs and does not interact with its environment.

▲ **Open system:** A group of interacting parts that interacts on an ongoing basis with its environment to achieve a specific end.

Closed systems are not influenced by and do not interact with their environment. Machines, for example, are closed systems. Machines are not affected by their environment. Machines do not interact with their environment. Traditional management theories were based on interacting with closed systems that do not change. The organization was considered to be sufficiently independent so that its problems could be analyzed in terms of internal structure, tasks, and formal relationships, without reference to the external environment.

We can view the Internet as an open system. An open system involves the dynamic interaction of the system with its environment. Systems theory maintains that everything is related to everything else. Biological and social systems fall within the open system classification. These systems are in a dynamic relationship with their environment. These systems receive various inputs, transform these inputs in some way, and export outputs. These systems are open not only in relation to their environment, but also in relation to themselves. The interactions between components affect the system as a whole. The open system adapts to its environment by changing the structure and processes of the internal components.

We often work in environments in which there are several desktop computers linked to the Internet. A computer that is linked to a local, area network or to the Internet is part of a system. If the computer has access to the Internet, then the system is characterized as open. If the computer is not linked to other computers (local or area network) or a local Internet provider, that computer is operating in a closed system. Operating in a closed computer system limits communication and contacts. The manager is then forced to depend on other communication systems.

An open system means that users or organizations are not self-contained. They interrelate to others. No organization can survive for long if it ignores government regulations, the courts, outside interest groups, private service providers, or elected officials. An organization should be judged on its ability to acquire inputs, process these inputs, channel the outputs, and maintain stability and balance.

FOR EXAMPLE

Lost Connection

Residents of Pensacola, Florida, wanted the reentry schedule for coastal communities impacted by hurricanes in the summer of 2004. Local officials, recognized that if a hurricane hit Pensacola, the Web site would not be available as the power to the servers and phone lines would be down so they arranged a duplicate Web site for Mobile, Alabama. Evacuees could log onto the Pensacola Web site despite the fact that it was run from Mobile. Emergency management officials in Pensacola provided up-to-date information about road closures and damage status from their Web site operating from Mobile. Planning and effective coordination by Florida emergency management officials allowed useful information to be communicated by way of the Web.

Outputs are the ends, and acquisition of inputs and processing efficiencies are the means. If an organization is to survive over the long term, it must remain adaptive.

The open system interacts with its environment and requires some means of maintaining continuity in a changing world. The survival of the system, in effect, would not be possible without continuous inflow, transformation, and outflow. The system is thus in a continuous recycling process. The system must receive sufficient input of resources to maintain its operations. It also must export the transformed resources to the environment in sufficient quantity to continue the cycle.

SELF-CHECK

- Define **closed system** and **open system.**
- What are the three elements in a system?
- What makes the Internet an open system?
- What is an example of an input in terms of the Internet?

2.4 Internet, the Web, and the Emergency Management Community

The Internet can help you provide information about emergencies and disasters. The Internet also makes it easier to work with others due to the ability to communicate quickly and the ability to share resources. One could argue that the Internet is even more important for small or rural communities (Pan American Health Organization), 1996. Reasons supporting the argument include the following:

▲ The Internet promotes working with other similar communities in a disaster.

▲ The Internet provides a low-cost approach for exchanging expert information on specialized topics of importance during disasters.

▲ The Internet allows researchers and practitioners in small or rural communities access to information that is not available in the emergency manager's local community.

The Internet provides a unique means of communication and information access to the emergency management community. This technology can be used in an emergency response in the following ways:

▲ **Messaging:** The Internet can be used to send or receive notification of an incident.

▲ **Information access:** The Internet can provide access to information that is stored and maintained on another computer system. An example of this can be drawn from an emergency notification system for a flood. A local emergency management agency receives a call of a storm that is likely to cause major flooding in area creeks and bayous. Businesses and residents in a specific area must be notified of rising water. The emergency operations center needs access to real-time flood levels. The U.S. Geological Survey has developed a flood-monitoring system using the Internet. A local community could maintain real-time access to the data through the Internet.

The Internet provides you with a forum of unlimited potential. Not only can you post instructions, warnings, and evacuation orders on the Internet, but you can also add video and streaming audio files. You can also experiment with creative ways to communicate. Florida, for example, has an outstanding emergency management Web site (www.floridadisaster.org). Florida is vulnerable to hurricanes. Emergency managers there are always looking for ways to prevent losses. On their Web site, they have the basic information on hurricanes, and they have put this information in different formats to encourage people to protect themselves. For example, in Figure 2-3, we have a screenshot of one of the Web pages on evacuation. The question of "Should I evacuate?" is turned into a board game that resembles Monopoly. This approach will reach some citizens that black-and-white text on a page wouldn't. Because the information is presented in an interesting way, people are immediately drawn in. People will be more likely to read about the different steps they should take when evacuating.

Figure 2-3

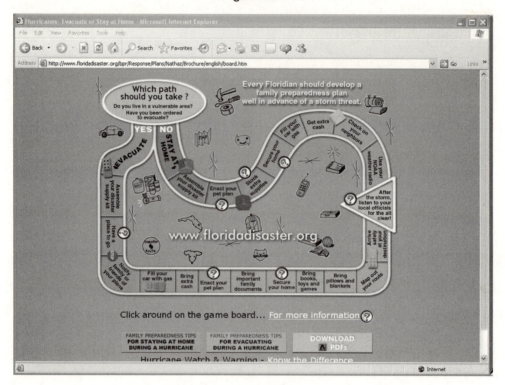

Information on evacuation on the Florida Emergency Management Web site (www.floridadisaster.org).

2.4.1 The World Wide Web

The Web began as a project designed to distribute scientific information across computer networks. A Web is a distributed information system that can be constructed on any local area or wide area network or as in the more common usage, a "World Wide Web." Information was first distributed in a system known as hypertext. The idea was to allow collaborative researchers to present their research, complete with text, graphics, and illustrations. It evolved to allow sound and video (Ecember, Randall, Tatters, 1995.)

The Web is not the same as the Internet. The Web provides the technology to interface with Internet resources. The Web is a concept. It is not just a program or system or even a specific protocol. The World Wide Web is a means of presenting and linking information dispersed across the Internet in an easily accessible way (Ecember, John, Neil Randall, Wes Tatters, Discover the World Wide Web, U.S. Robotics, Sams.net Publishing: Indianapolis, IN, 1995.)

The Internet requires a tool (browser) to allow the user to navigate the Internet without having to know, remember, or write down the lengthy and clumsy addresses and filenames that the Web needs to operate. The Web provides the system of navigation to links on the sites but also provides links to contextually related documents or specific parts of documents.

The World Wide Web today allows emergency management staff to be connected to improve communications (e-mail), economy (shared use of computer programs, printers, scanners, and storage devices), and productivity (easy access to data and communication of reports and other work products to other staff). What steps can you take to ensure that Web technology contributes to the work environment rather than inhibit work processes? The Web gives you tools to:

▲ **Train your staff:** Training or coaching on critical Web sites and their use in emergency management.

▲ **Support your staff:** Provide technical support to staff in solving common problems.

▲ **Involve your staff:** Involvement by staff in Web site design.

▲ **Communicate to your staff and staffs of other emergency management organizations:** Examine the advantages of Web communications by phone, Webcast, or electronic mail.

2.4.2 Limitations of the Internet

The Internet provides agencies with an excellent communication device to both the general public and other agencies associated with emergency management. However, the Internet does have its limitations:

▲ **Security:** The communication goes two ways. You provide information using the Internet, and those who have access to you could pose security threats. Agencies spend extensive resources to protect the information. However, we have all heard of cases in which people's credit card numbers or social security numbers were stolen by someone who was able to hack through the security. Identity theft is one of the fastest-growing crimes today and will continue to increase. Security is the number one limitation of the Internet. For example, imagine what someone could do with the information FEMA receives from applicants. The identity thief could apply for credit cards, open accounts, and ruin someone's credit.

▲ **Dependability or reliability:** When the power goes out, what do we do for backup? When your server is down, do you have a plan for an alternative Internet site to provide essential information to the public? Communication was a problem during Hurricane Katrina. All the phone lines and DSL lines were down in New Orleans. The mayor of New Orleans could only communicate by satellite phone.

▲ **Training of users:** The Internet has been with us for many years, and we expect users to know how to navigate our Internet site. However, many sites are cumbersome, and users find it difficult to find information they need. Ensuring that a site is "user friendly" is essential to making this resource an asset to a community.

▲ **Quality of the information obtained:** The design of an Internet site is a key in ensuring that it accomplishes its mission. For a Web site to be useful, it must be continually updated with new information. In addition, the information must be correct and accurate. Dissemination of sensitive data is a growing issue today. Free access to government information may conflict with agency perceptions of what may be shared with the public. An agency policy and procedure for determining what may be shared on a Web site is essential.

▲ **Information accessibility:** Information accessibility is a major concern for emergency managers. There will always be those who have access to technology and those who do not. Even among those who have access to technology, there will be those who are proficient with it and those who are not. Included in the larger group are vulnerable populations such as persons with learning disabilities or persons who do not speak English (Email and Kasperson, 1996). This is why you must not rely on the Internet as your sole means of getting out information. The Internet is a tool that can complement mitigation and response strategies, but it cannot replace those strategies.

It is essential that our communities and organizations prepare in such a way as to overcome these limitations of the Internet.

2.4.3 Helpful Web Sites for Emergency Managers

The following are descriptions of helpful Web sites for emergency managers.

▲ *The University of Colorado, Natural Hazards Research and Applications Information Center* (www.colorado.edu/hazards/resources/sites.html). The

FOR EXAMPLE

Making Web Sites Accessible

Web site forms must be accessible to everyone to be effective. Two weeks after Hurricane Katrina, Jim Rapoza wrote an article in *eweek* about the FEMA Web site applications. Initially, the FEMA applications could only be viewed by those using Internet Explorer 6.0 or higher. People trying to fill out the applications using Linux or an older version of Explorer could not access them (Repeza, 2005). When designing Web site forms, you must make them accessible to as many people as possible.

Center has developed a list of selected sites that will be useful to emergency managers and has made the list available from the its Web site. The University of Colorado site is the oldest one used by the emergency management community. On this site you will find great examples of newsletters, research reports, and conference notes. This site also provides more useful links.

▲ *The Weather Channel* (www.weather.com). This site is always on in operations centers when disaster strikes.

▲ *Online newspapers.* Many newspapers are now online, including local, regional, and national paper. Emergency managers use these links to track how disasters are covered locally, regionally, and nationally.

▲ *National Weather Service* (www.nws.noaa.gov). The National Oceanic and Atmospheric Administration has several satellites that allow emergency managers to track hurricanes and large storms.

▲ *Relief and Rehabilitation Network* (RRN; www.civilsoc.org/usnisorg/educultr/relief.htm). This Web site is a neutral forum for the exchange of information among professionals from over 150 donor, government, UN, Red Cross, non governmental organizations, and research and media organizations in the field of humanitarian assistance from more that 60 countries worldwide. The site contains the following:

  ▲ The online RRN Newsletter featuring articles and news on current developments in the field of humanitarian assistance; key policy issues; a regional focus section; and details of recent and forthcoming conferences, training courses, and publications.

  ▲ A list of RRN publications and abstracts.

  ▲ The Red Pages offering a comprehensive directory of links to non-governmental, UN, and donor organizations, news, background information and research resources relating to humanitarian assistance in both complex emergencies and natural disasters.

  ▲ A list of current members from over 150 donor, government, UN, Red Cross, NGO, and research organizations in the field of humanitarian assistance in more than 60 countries worldwide.

  ▲ Information on how to join the RRN or order RRN publications.

2.4.4 Forums and Webcasting

Two other ways the Internet is useful to you is through forums and Webcasting. A **forum** is an online chat hosted by an organization that allows you to ask questions. The EIIP Virtual Forum (www.emforum.org) is a unique resource. This Web site is designed specifically for emergency managers. Each week, the Forum provides you an opportunity to "talk" with experts in the field by way of the Web. Check out the site and tune in for a chance to talk with leaders in the emergency management field. This site also keeps transcripts of all the chats, so you don't have to be online at a specific time for the discussion to still be valuable to you. For example, one of EIIP's recent guests was Michael Domaratz, member of the National Geospatial Programs Office of the U.S. Geological Survey.

Webcasting is streaming audio and video through the Web. Webcasting is becoming a popular way to teach courses online, for example. There are also ways you can use Webcasts in emergency management. You can use a Webcast to brief other emergency managers on conditions in your state, for instance. Louisiana State University, for example, hosted a Webcast to link over 40 sites to a conference on rebuilding New Orleans. The conference was sponsored by Acorn, a national community advocacy group located in New Orleans. This is a great example of how you can use the Web to share lessons learned during a disaster and to discuss hazard mitigation. For more information on the Webcast previously mentioned, go to www.acorn.com.

SELF-CHECK

- Define **forum** and **Webcasting**.
- List and define two limitations of the Internet.
- List and explain two ways the Internet can be used in emergency management.
- Identify some examples of Web sites that have recently been useful in understanding hazards.

SUMMARY

The Internet has changed the way we communicate, the way we conduct research, the way we train others, and other daily tasks of emergency management. In this chapter, you reviewed the history of the Internet and described how it has evolved over the years. You have also defined the Internet as a system and have compared it to closed systems. You have assessed the strengths and limitations of the Internet. From there, you have evaluated ways in which the Internet can assist in all phases of emergency management.

KEY TERMS

ARPANET	The first packet switching network.
Closed system	A system that is not open to any inputs and does not interact with its environment.
Forum	An online chat hosted by an organization that allows you to ask questions.
Internet	A digital transmission technology that allows users to search, sort, convert, and transfer information over a network.
Open system	A group of interacting parts that interacts on an ongoing basis with its environment to achieve a specific end.
System	A group of interacting parts that function on a regular basis to achieve a specific end.
Web	A distributed information system that can be constructed on a local or wide area basis or an unlimited basis as with the World Wide Web.
Webcasting	Streaming audio and video through the Web.

ASSESS YOUR UNDERSTANDING

Go to www.wiley.com/college/pine to evaluate your knowledge of the basics of emergency management and the Internet.
Measure your learning by comparing pre-test and post-test results.

Summary Questions

1. FEMA's Web page can be considered an open system that is influenced by outside users and input. True or False?

2. One limitation of the Internet is
   (a) it is expensive to use.   .
   (b) it is difficult to understand.
   (c) it is not available in many homes.
   (d) it is not always secure.

3. The Internet provides an unlimited communication resource to emergency managers. True or False?

4. The Internet and the Web do not provide emergency managers with any useful tools in responding during a disaster. True or False?

5. The Internet and the Web are the same thing. True or False?

6. The Internet is
   (a) an open system.
   (b) a closed system.
   (c) a Web.
   (d) a forum.

7. One strength of the Internet is
   (a) it is easy to do research on.
   (b) all the sites are accessible to everyone, including non-English speakers.
   (c) the information online is always accurate.
   (d) the connection is always secure and available.

8. The first packet switching network was
   (a) the Internet.
   (b) the World Wide Web.
   (c) ARPANET.
   (d) Telnet.

9. Streaming audio and video through the Web is called
   (a) forums.
   (b) real-time.

    (c) Webcasting.

    (d) Weblinking.

10. The following organizations use the Internet to disseminate hazard-related information (Select all that apply):

    (a) The Red Cross

    (b) FEMA

    (c) The Weather Channel

    (d) Florida Emergency Management Agency

Review Questions

1. What are two ways that emergency managers can use the Web during a disaster?
2. What is the distinction between the Web and the Internet?
3. What are the limitations of the Internet?
4. What training needs to occur with emergency management staff with regard to the Internet?
5. In what ways can you use the Internet in emergency preparedness, response, recovery, and mitigation?
6. How did the Internet help emergency management in Hurricane Katrina?
7. How does the Internet improve emergency management?
8. Name two Web sites that offer valuable emergency management information.
9. How has the Internet evolved over the years?
10. Have you ever been frustrated with your use of the Internet? If so, why?
11. How can the Internet be used to educate others about hazards?

Applying This Chapter

1. You are the emergency manager for a small coastal community that has grown rapidly over the years. Due to the rapid changes, you have a staff that does not have much training experience. How can you use the Internet to train and involve your staff?
2. You are the emergency manager for Louisiana. You are working on revamping the state emergency management agency Web site. What types of information do you put on the Web site and why? What links to other Web sites do you include?

3. You are in a shelter working with hurricane victims who lost their homes and do not know where some of their family members are. What types of Internet resources could they use?

4. Visit your local community's emergency management Web site, if there is one. What would you change about it?

5. You are the emergency manager for a retirement community on the coast. You know a hurricane is scheduled to land. Do you use the Internet as your prime channel of communication? Why or why not?

6. You are the emergency manager for a town in Arizona that is being engulfed in wildfires. What type of information do you post on the Internet and why?

7. You are the head of FEMA. What types of services and information do you want to post on the FEMA Web site? Why?

8. You have been the victim of a hurricane and have lost everything you own. What type of help and information should you expect to be able to find on the Web?

9. You need to train emergency responders across the United States on a new mitigation technique. How can the Internet help you do this?

Disaster Information

You are the emergency manager for a coastal community that is in the path of a hurricane. According to weather forecasters, the hurricane is scheduled to hit your town in five days. What types of information do you put on your Web site and why? What external links do you include? Where do you advertise the site and why? Write three to four paragraphs answering these questions.

Searching

Perform an Internet search using the term *Hurricane Katrina* or *Hurricane Wilma* and see how many hits you receive. How many of these links are helpful to you as an emergency manager? How many would be helpful to hurricane victims? How many are not helpful? Make a two-column list and list some of the helpful and unhelpful Web sites.

Asking for Money

You are the emergency manager and you must prepare a proposal to the city, county, or agency chief executive officer justifying the preparation of an emergency management Web site. Determine the approximate costs associated with a Web design program, equipment, development fees, price options, and other direct or indirect expenditures. Assume that the emergency management unit has a computer. Prepare a one-page memo justifying this proposal. Be sure to explain how a Web page will help the community and the emergency management agency.

3

NETWORKS AND COMMUNICATIONS SYSTEMS
Working Together

Starting Point

Go to www.wiley.com/college/pine to assess your knowledge of networks and communications systems.
Determine where you need to concentrate your effort.

What You'll Learn in This Chapter

▲ What components make a network
▲ Categories of networks
▲ Types of communication networks
▲ How communication networks affect the emergency management process
▲ Trends in technology affecting networks

After Studying This Chapter, You'll Be Able To

▲ Compare and contrast wireless and wireline networks
▲ Categorize the types of communication systems that may be used in emergency management
▲ Distinguish the steps through which information is relayed
▲ Examine how the application of technology in communications or information management enhances the synergy of emergency operations
▲ Examine how networks can help save lives in a disaster
▲ Analyze how trends in technology affect networks

Goals and Outcomes

▲ Evaluate the role networks play in the emergency management process
▲ Compare and contrast LANs and WANs
▲ Evaluate solutions to challenges in implementing technology in emergency management
▲ Assess and evaluate trends in technology that will affect networks
▲ Select networks and technology that can facilitate emergency management

INTRODUCTION

As an emergency manager, you will find that communication is vitally important. The ability to communicate to the public, to first responders, and to other emergency management officials is crucial in the fight to protect lives and property. In this chapter, you will define networks and their role in communication. You will evaluate different types of networks. You will compare and contrast different categories of communication networks and their role in the emergency management process. Finally, you will assess trends in technology and how these trends will affect your daily duties.

3.1 What Is a Network?

We use networks every day. Whether we use the Internet, the telephone, or a radio, we are using a network. A **network** is a collection of parts that provide voice and data information. Networks provide a basis for communication between members of the emergency management community. They are a critical part of the infrastructure and are crucial in achieving program goals. Although we take networks for granted if they work, when they break down, there are disastrous consequences.

Many of us think of a network as a system of computers, terminals, and databases connected by communications lines (see Figure 3-1).

When we access files at work or school that other people have access to from their computer, we are using a network. Networks make sharing information easy. Networks enable people who work and live in different parts of the country to share information easily. A network connects users by links and switches and control software. A digital network communicates information between users in fractions of a second using digital transmission technology. Networks help emergency managers in many ways:

▲ **Greater efficiency:** Networking increases productivity. Staff members have instant access to volumes of information and computer applications through the network. They also have an easier time communicating internally.

▲ **Enhanced internal communication:** Networking enhances interoffice communication between staff and provides the ability to communicate with external members of the emergency management community through a wide area network.

▲ **Enhanced external communication:** Networking provides a basis for communicating with the public. For example, we use television and radio programming as well as the cable TV industry. The providers of

Figure 3-1

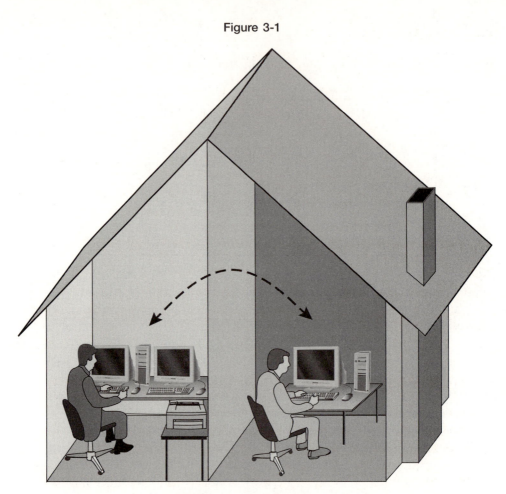

A simple home network.

both telephone and cable TV networks have changed their technology and range of services. They now offer even more uses to the emergency management community.

▲ **Access to crucial information:** Networking provides management with a means of monitoring databases and critical information.

The components of a network vary, depending on the type and size of the network. In general, networks include switches, transmission equipment, operations systems, and databases. Access is the ability to connect to networks and to receive services from networks. When a user wants to be served, he or she indicates this desire to a network and receives an indication that this service can be provided. Access occurs over an access transmission line or "local loop." If the local loop is a wire of any type (copper or fiber), the network access is wireline. If a local loop consists of radio transmission equipment, the local loop is wireless.

Today we use fiber-optic technology. A single strand of optical fiber can carry 8,000 telephone conversations, and a single fiber-optic cable has many strands of fibers. Most long-distance data is carried by fiber-optic cable, which replaced copper wire as the method for voice and data transmission. Fiber-optic cable is 20 times lighter than copper wire, it is difficult to tap into, and loses a little data during transmission. It does have some disadvantages—mainly that it is too expensive for low-volume applications because it is difficult to splice. The technology allows for a greater number of connections in a more efficient manner. In addition, we use very fast digital switches. These allow for the transmission of large databases across our networks. We now have more connections transmitting more information than ever before. Access to all of this information improves the efficiency of emergency management agencies.

FEMA uses networks to provide you with access to a variety of different databases. For example, FEMA has a risk assessment database that you can access. The data would help you reduce losses force a flood, during conventional bomb attacks or during chemical, biological, and radiological attacks. The database can import and display digital photos, emergency plans, and digital floor plans. FEMA has other databases as well.

FOR EXAMPLE

FEMA Database

One FEMA database focuses on flood mitigation. An estimated 30 million Americans are at high risk from flooding, and almost every American is at some degree of flood risk. Flood Map Modernization (Map Mod) is FEMA's approach to updating the nation's flood hazard maps. Map Mod will transform flood maps into a more reliable, easier-to-use, and readily available product. Updated, digital flood maps will become the platform for identifying multiple hazards—not just floods. Map Mod is a collaborative process and a new way of doing business for government officials, cutting across all layers of government. Officials and other stakeholders will be active in the mapping process (e.g., collecting, updating, and adopting data). Local engineering companies are contracted to do the mapping and determine where the high, medium, and low flood risk zones are located. The maps are reviewed and adopted by the local government and FEMA. Leveraging partnerships will allow states and communities to choose their level of involvement.

SELF-CHECK

- Define **network**.
- How does FEMA use networks and how can their use benefit you?
- What are the key components and equipment in networks?
- What are the advantages of creating networks to access data?

3.2 Types of Networks

A network could be local or wide area. It can be satellite, landline, or undersea, fiber, copper, or wireless. Regardless, it provides connectivity among users and host computers. Today emergency management is using several important networks.

3.2.1 Wireline Networks

Wireline networks serve users through a series of network elements and lines interconnecting them. A user is connected to a network via a hard wire over which all necessary communications between the user and the network take place. An example of a wireline network is the traditional phone system. The cell phone system, in contrast, is a wireless network. The number of wireline services and their complexity grew over time. This required networks to adapt to these new services through technological innovations. Services such as call forwarding and call waiting require sophisticated switches to support the user's needs. With the computerization of switches and digitization of transmission switches, switches became faster and smarter. Computers now control the sophisticated services such as call forwarding. A limitation of this type of process is that it is very expensive to design new switches for services and to program the switches. Wireline networks have the following characteristics:

- ▲ They provide an initial connection of two or more sites directly by way of land lines.
- ▲ They have limited interference with electromagnet waves traveling over wires.
- ▲ There are high costs of labor for installation and maintenance.
- ▲ They are inflexible (not movable).

3.2.2 Wireless Networks

Wireless networks are Communication network that connect users by radio or wireless means. The wireless environment is based on transmission techniques that adapt to unstable or broken links in the networks. It provides a stable and flexible means to communicate. Wireless technology has the following characteristics:

> ## FOR EXAMPLE
>
> ### The Internet Is a Network
>
> The Internet is a newer and different kind of network. The purpose of the Internet is to provide a very general communication infrastructure. The Internet is not targeted to one application, such as telephone or delivery of TV; rather, it is targeted to a wide range of computer-based services, such as electronic mail (e-mail), information retrieval, and teleconferencing. See Chapter 2 for a full discussion of the Internet and for examples of how you can use the Internet during disasters.

▲ Radio technology is used to establish a contact between the caller and a network.

▲ Supports mobile users.

▲ Quicker connection.

▲ Simpler installation and maintenance.

As you will see in the sidebar below, there are many applications for wireless Technology in emergency management.

DISASTER DRILL TESTS NEW WIRELESS TECHNOLOGIES DEVELOPED AT UCSD AND CALIT2

MAY 18, 2004

The disaster began with the explosion of a simulated "dirty" bomb inside a Carlsbad office building. With that, one of the largest ever emergency response drills in San Diego County—dubbed Operation Moonlight—got underway May 12, to test preparedness among first responders and emergency-relief agencies. Within 90 minutes of the detonation, police and firefighters from around the county began arriving, including some that became victims requiring treatment as paramedics and hazardous materials crews arrived on the scene. Then, a second mock explosion went off in the parking lot—this one a radiological bomb. At least 18 federal, state and local agencies participated, in addition to hospitals, Red Cross and county health and emergency systems, not to mention more than two dozen faculty, students and researchers from the UCSD Jacobs School of Engineering and California Institute for Telecommunications and Information Technology (Calit2).

The full-scale disaster drill was organized by San Diego's Metropolitan Medical Strike Team (MMST), and the contingent of researchers from UCSD and Calit2 were on hand to learn how new technologies they are developing would operate in a real emergency-response situation.

"We are working with the MMST to enhance their capabilities using wireless technology," said Leslie Lenert, a professor in the UCSD School of Medicine. "We are deeply indebted to the first-responder community for allowing us to take advantage of the drill to integrate ourselves with their activities and to learn more about how wireless systems work in this situation."

Lenert is the principal investigator on a $4 million project called Wireless Internet Information System for Medical Response in Disasters (WIISARD). Its goal: to develop and speed deployment of sophisticated wireless technology to coordinate and enhance care of mass casualties in a terrorist attack or natural disaster. The disaster drill coincided with a three-day site visit by WIISARD's funding agency, the National Library of Medicine, part of the National Institutes of Health.

Most of the new technologies tested during the drill came out of UCSD engineering labs and Calit2, where WIISARD co-PI Ramesh Rao is the division director at UCSD. "This is a real-life drill, with real paramedics and first responders reacting to a simulated attack on the building," said Rao, who is also a professor of electrical and computer engineering at the Jacobs School. "We deployed a series of ad hoc systems and networks, and we got to see if those technologies are robust enough to work in such an environment. And they were."

Both Rao and Calit2 director Larry Smarr were on hand for the disaster drill that involved more than 250 people from across the county. MMST officials, including physician-director Theodore Chan (who is also an associate clinical professor of medicine at UCSD), pulled in a broad cross-section of first responders for the drill, including paramedics, Red Cross, fire, sheriff's deputies, police, SWAT teams and hazardous-materials crews from throughout San Diego County. At the same time, UCSD engineering faculty, researchers and students showcased several technologies developed for or adapted for use by WIISARD—underscoring the speed at which Calit2 and the Jacobs School are pushing safety technologies out of the lab and into the field.

The day started with a tour of the CyberShuttle, which was used as a mobile command center. Developed by Calit2 researchers, the CyberShuttle is a regular campus commuter bus outfitted with an 802.11b (Wi-Fi) local area network connected to a wide-area, third-generation (3G) cellular network recently launched by Verizon Wireless and based on QUALCOMM's 1xEVDO technology. The bus, which now displays computing and display capabilities, became the hub for wireless data transmission at the site, including victim tracking and vital-signs monitoring.

Researchers, and potential new industry partners, also set up an ad hoc, multi-hop "mesh" video transmission network. Each camera was equipped with wireless, and each video feed was transmitted over the Wi-Fi network to the command center, and from there, to the Internet. The video gave emergency officials the ability to "see" the disaster site remotely, prior to dispatching hazmat and other crews to the scene. The video component is also under development by Ericsson engineer Rajesh Mishra as part of Rao's Always Best Connected project—and was not originally part of WIISARD—but "we didn't want to miss out on an opportunity to test this new idea," said Rao.

The hazmat team also tested a helmet-mounted camera on the system. "There is a hazmat person wearing a wireless camera and he's transmitting to our command center in the UCSD CyberShuttle," noted Lenert. "From there, paramedics can be in contact with the hazmat team, so they can be debriefed about the situation inside."

After SWAT and hazmat teams entered the building, they found more than a dozen "victims"—most of them students in the Jacobs School's ECE 191 class working on a project supervised by Calit2 principal development engineer Douglas Palmer. The class projects are designed to give engineering students hands-on experience in real-world electrical engineering. The students had good reason to volunteer for the disaster drill, because it would give them a close-up look at how the first responders used wireless technology that allowed the mobile command center to monitor continuously the vital signs of anyone "hurt" in the presumed attack.

The class started with a pulse oximeter built into a Pocket PC by Dolphin Medical. Pulse oximeters measure a patient's pulse as well as the level of oxygen in the blood via a clamp on the tip of a finger. For their part, Palmer's students incorporated Wi-Fi access into each of the devices. "The class is working on the signal processing, the wireless backhaul, and the processing subsystem required to get all this data back and collated," said Palmer. "Blood oxygen is one of the best indicators and predictors of patient health."

"What I told them is, 'You're a senior engineering student, and to experience what an engineer goes through, you have to be in the field to meet with the customer,'" added Palmer. "And in this case, the customer is the first responder community."

The pulse oximeters as well as communications between first responders and the command center required high-speed Wi-Fi connectivity, which was provided by Entrée Wireless. The briefcase-sized devices each created a 1,000-ft. radius mobile "bubble" of Wi-Fi access over the emergency area and channeled all the data to the Web over Verizon's 3G network (eliminating the need for each responder to carry a separate 3G device). Each bubble can support hundreds of victims and thirty or forty first responders. They also allow those responders communicating through one bubble to communicate with each other at about 5 megabits per second, with each bubble contributing 300K to 500K to an Internet connection depending on cellular coverage.

The test marked the first commercial deployment of Entrée's devices, as well as the first commercial product based on public-domain research done at Calit2.

"The original concept came from the CyberShuttle that they have on campus to allow students to have Wi-Fi access on the road to make some of their downtime more productive," said Entrée Wireless president David Ahlgren. "It allows you in a very economical way to bring communications to first responders."

The mobile Wi-Fi devices were also used for location-based tracking of patients—similar to the ActiveCampus Explorer technology developed by Jacobs School computer science and engineering professor Bill Griswold. Griswold directed research by WIISARD staffers Steve Brown and Ricky Huang to develop complex software systems for the ad hoc networks at the disaster scene. "Our team worked on the software to deliver the vital-signs and location tracking data to a server at UCSD and back out to command center software," said Griswold. "It allows first responders to keep track of how victims are doing and where they are located in targeted areas such as triage, decontamination, walking wounded, and the like."

"We have also tagged four first responders with GPS-enabled cell phones from Verizon and QUALCOMM," added Lenert. "We are testing the ability of that technology to monitor the positions of the first responders."

After a series of debriefings that began immediately following the drill, WIISARD researchers will work on improvements to the new technologies. They will also start work on the next phase of the project: a first-responder computer system. "We are going to try to give these guys situational awareness on a handheld device," said Lenert. "It would allow them to see the field, where the plumes are, where the victims are, and help them to organize better their own responsive care."

—By Doug Ramsey (This article reprinted courtesy of Calit2)

SELF-CHECK

- Define **wireline networks** and **wireless networks**.
- What characteristics do wireless networks have?
- How can wireless networks be effectively used to support emergency management activities?
- What are the limitations and potential risks of relying solely on cellular phone wireless networks for communication during disasters?

3.3 Communication Networks

A **communication network** is a set of devices linked to transfer information. Each device is called a *node*. Figure 3-2 shows you the basics of how a network operates. The basic steps of how information is relayed is are follows:

Figure 3-2

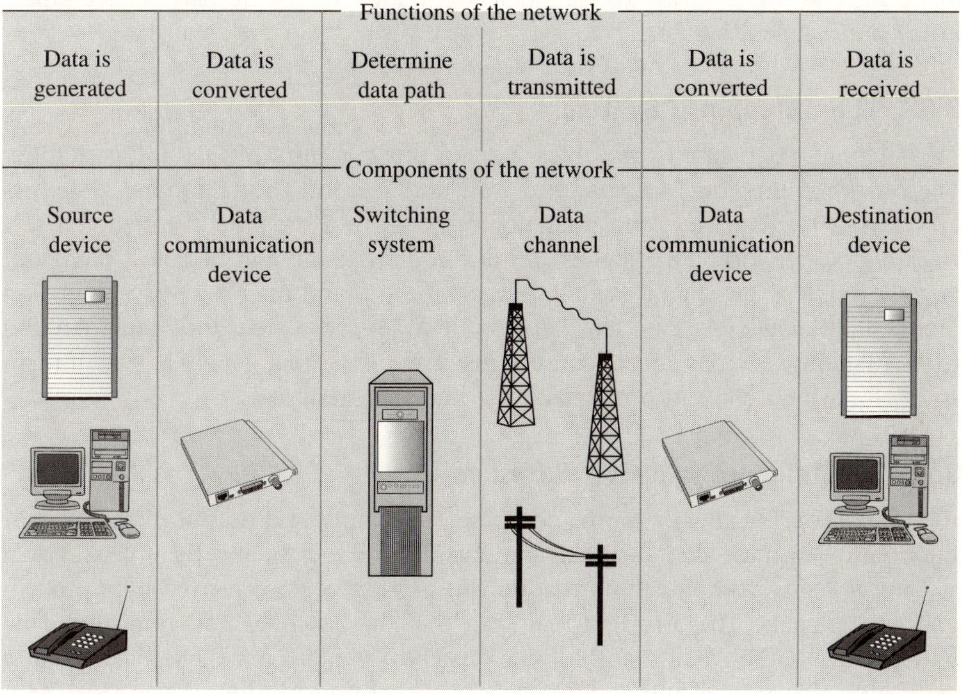

Functions of the network					
Data is generated	Data is converted	Determine data path	Data is transmitted	Data is converted	Data is received
Components of the network					
Source device	Data communication device	Switching system	Data channel	Data communication device	Destination device

How networks operate.

1. **Data is generated.** For example, a telephone caller creates data by speaking. The words in an e-mail are data as well.
2. **Data is converted.** Data must be converted from its original form into a form for transmission. This is called *encoding*. In a conversation on the telephone, the mouthpiece encodes sounds into electrical impulses.
3. **Determine the data path.** The path for the data must be determined. This process is called *switching*. Telephone systems, for example, require switching so the information goes from the source to the correct destination.
4. **Data is transmitted.** The data is sent along wireline or wireless systems. In a landline telephone conversation, the data is sent along telephone lines.
5. **Data is converted.** The data must be converted to be understood. In a telephone conversation, the handset decodes the conversation into audible, clear sounds.
6. **Data is received.** The data has been converted to its original form and is being accessed and understood by the receiver.

Communication systems used in emergency management include teleconferencing, e-mail, and fax. These systems help by linking the many parts of the emergency management system.

3.3.1 The Telephone System

The telephone network is the oldest part of our communications infrastructure. The service it provides is stable and well understood. The telephone system is evolving. It is changing from an analog network to a broadband integrated services digital network. This makes simultaneous transmission of voice, data, and video possible. New digital switching machines, digital microwave systems, and digital light wave systems can all handle digitized voice and data. **Analog transmission services** are a continuous wave or signal (such as the human voice) for which conventional telephone lines are designed.

3.3.2 Digital Transmission Services

As you're probably already aware, computers use input and output digital signals. Information in these digital signals is transmitted using 1s and 0s and is known as *binary*. Before computer information can be sent, it is converted by a modem to analog signals. The analog signals can then be accepted and transmitted by phone lines. Rather than using a binary system (digital), analog signals are in a wave form that normal phone lines are capable of transmitting. When these analog signals are received, another modem converts them to digital signals that can be used by computers. These information transmission systems are constantly converting digital signals to analog signals and then back again.

3.3.3 Microwave Radio Services

Microwave radio has been the backbone transmission system of the long-distance telephone network in the United States and Canada for the past 35 years. Until the mid-1970s, nearly all radio systems were analog. The radio systems transmitted analog multiplexed signals originating from analog telephone systems. They provide good voice telephone service. However, they are currently less than satisfactory for data transmission at high speed and low error rates. Digital transmission systems detect and reshape the transmitted pulses. As we discussed before, fiber-optic cable has incredible bandwidth. Microwave systems are now trying to expand to match the bandwidth of land-based optical fiber systems. Figure 3-3 shows you how microwaves, satellites, and cellular telephones transmit signals.

3.3.4 Satellite Communications

Geostationary satellites orbit at an altitude of 36,000 kilometers (km) above the equator. This is called geostationary earth orbit (GEO). The satellite maintains an orbit that allows the satellite to maintain a fixed position in relation to the

Figure 3-3

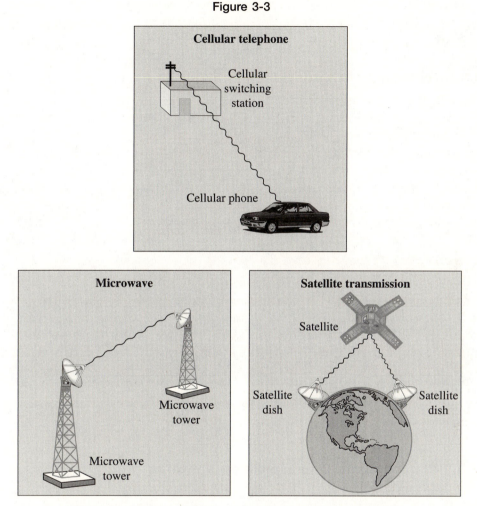

How microwaves, satellites, and cell phones transmit signals.

Earth. At this height, communications through a GEO travel at the speed of light and entail a round-trip transmission latency of about one-half second. This means that GEO can never provide fiberlike continuous services. This delay is noticeable in many intercontinental phone calls, impeding understanding and distorting the personal nuances of speech.

Networks on the ground have evolved from centralized systems built around a single mainframe computer to **distributed networks** of interconnected systems. Space-based satellite networks are evolving from centralized networks relying on a single geostationary satellite to distributed networks of interconnected low Earth orbit satellites. In geostationary systems, any single satellite loss or failure is catastrophic to the system.

Figure 3-4

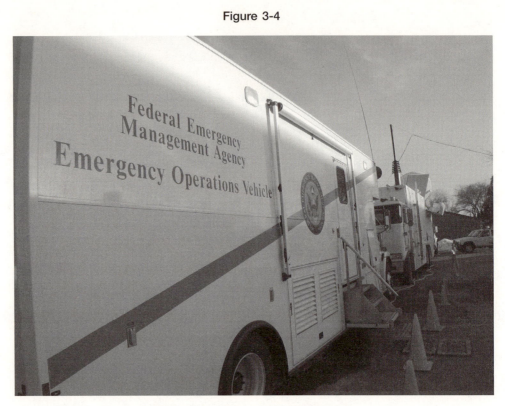

FEMA mobile communications center.

3.3.5 Disruptions in Communication Networks

Disasters may cause a major disruption in communications. During Hurricane Katrina, the mayor of New Orleans could not communicate to anyone. He could not communicate through e-mail, landline phone, or cell phone. His staff had to break into an office supply store and take satellite phones so they could talk to emergency management officials.

FEMA can solve this problem. They help people communicate during a disaster and can deploy a mobile communications center. They deployed such centers in Louisiana after Hurricane Katrina. The communications provided by this unit include the following:

▲ Restored telephone service
▲ Video teleconferencing
▲ Full broadcast video
▲ High-frequency, long-distance radio

Figure 3-5

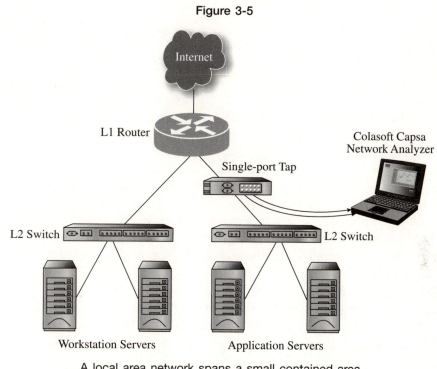

A local area network spans a small contained area.

▲ Local radio
▲ Integrated radio and wire communication

In addition to this support, the unit provides generators, heating and air-conditioning units, water-purification units, and tractor-trailer support units (see Figure 3-4). The Red Cross also has similar mobile communications centers that they use once they are sent to an area.

3.3.6 Local Area Network (LAN)

A **local area network (LAN)** is a communication network. It is usually owned and operated by the business customer (see Figure 3-5). A LAN enables many independent peripheral devices, such as terminals, to be linked to a network through which they can share expensive central processing units. These devices communicate over distances up to 2 km. For example, these devices can communicate within an office building.

Local networks can be categorized according to their transmission bandwidth. They are either baseband or broadband. In baseband LANs, the entire bandwidth is used to transmit a single digital signal. In broadband networks, the capacity of the cable is divided into many channels, which can transmit higher-speed signals. In the past, broadband networks have typically operated over coaxial cables.

One of the most popular LANs in use today is Ethernet. Developed by Xerox, it operates at 10 Mb/s over **coaxial cable**. Coaxial cable is a copper data transmission wire that has an outer insulator and electrically grounded shielding. *Twisted pair wiring* is another name for copper telephone wiring. Copper telephone wiring consists of a pair of copper wires that are twisted to help minimize distortion of the signal by the other telephone lines bundled in the same cable. Unshielded twisted pair wiring allows an unlimited number of devices to be connected (in reality up to 200).

You may want to connect a computer to an office network. Fiber-optic cables will initially cost more than coaxial cable; however, the fiber-optic cable allows for faster communication and in the long run may be more cost effective.

The local area network gives you many advantages. By connecting to a city, county, regional, or agency network, you have greater access to agency data sets. You can share resources such as printers, plotters, scanners, and storage devices. You will have enhanced security for data sharing and communication.

3.3.7 Wide Area Network (WAN)

Wide area networks (WANs) are communication networks that span a large geographical region. WANs, for example, could span the entire length of the United States. WANs are used for different purposes. Police officers around the country can link into a wireless WAN that provides instant access to several law enforcement databases. Figure 3-6 shows a wide area network.

FOR EXAMPLE

Networks in Disaster Recovery

After Katrina devastated Louisiana, Mississippi, and Alabama, the Red Cross was quick to arrive on the scene. The Red Cross collected names, addresses, and other information about victims and inputted the information into wireless laptops. The information was then transmitted wirelessly over portable servers to a central database. The records could then be accessed at any time by any Red Cross worker from anywhere in the network. Using this database allowed for more timely, efficient, and accurate distribution of emergency funds to the victims.

WANs are often in the form of a virtual private network (VPN). A virtual private network is a private network configured within a public network. For example, many Americans work at home during the week or weekend for their company. Although they are not in the office, they need access to company files and databases. A company can set up a VPN, a private network, and access to company files can be gained by going through the Internet, a public network.

As technology changes and improves, so will networks. For example, value added networks (VANs) are public networks that transmit data and provide access to commercial databases and software. VANs have largely been replaced by the Internet due to the lower cost and higher efficiency of the Internet.

SELF-CHECK

- Define **analog transmission services.**
- Define **local area network (LAN)** and **wide area network (WAN).**
- How could local agencies such as the Red Cross, health care providers, school systems, or public utilities be connected in times of disaster to support emergency response activities?
- When a **communication network** fails, how are communications maintained?
- What are the steps in how information is relayed?

3.4 Trends in Technology Affecting Networks

There are many trends in technology that will not only affect networks, but will also affect your job. We will examine each of these trends.

3.4.1 Remote Access to Information

Critical information is now more available as a result of our expanding networks. As an illustration, the U.S. Geological Survey worked with the National Weather Service. They installed a system of stream monitoring gauges to provide timely information on water levels in streams and rivers and weather sensors. The information from the sensors is available to the emergency manager. Because the information can be sent over networks, it can be sent to any emergency manager regardless of location. More widespread use of sensors can generate valuable information to be used in a crisis. This information can be sent over the Internet.

Figure 3-6

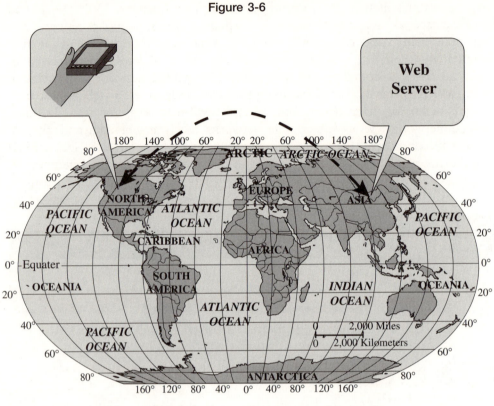

A wide area network spans a large geographical region.

Another example is tsunami detection. Gauges that detect earthquake activity, a precursor to a tsunami, can be viewed remotely over networks. Once a tsunami is detected, evacuation warnings can be issued and lives can be saved.

3.4.2 Information Overload

With so much information streaming over networks at the same time, the system can get overloaded. If a communication system is highly centralized, even a limited emergency can result in communication bottlenecks. For example, we have all experienced times when we tried to make a call and the call didn't go through because "all circuits were busy." This could have been when you tried to call a loved one on 9/11. It also could have been when you tried to call your mother on Mother's Day. When your call can't go through, it's because the telephone network is overloaded. Imagine how difficult it would be to reach a loved one after a major terrorist attack. Subnetworks may need to be created to divert communication from the operations center. A planned distributed computing

> **FOR EXAMPLE**
>
> **Satellite Images**
>
> FEMA also established a joint data resource with Louisiana State University. They obtain and make available high-resolution images of the areas impacted by Katrina. Commercial satellite images were procured by FEMA. These images are available to federal, state, and local emergency responders and to the research community. The data is accessible through the Internet. It is used for many tasks. The high-resolution images are provided for emergency rescue to calculate the time it would take to pump New Orleans of the floodwaters. The public may download many of these images from http://atlas. lsu.edu. The Internet gives you a way to view critical data sources at a high speed. You can use the data for critical response and recovery purposes.

capability can be designed by examining elements of the emergency management system. To design a communication network, you need to know who needs to communicate directly and frequently with other officials and co-workers.

3.4.3 Data Integration

Many organizations have been struggling to cope with increasing demands for timely and accurate data to support ongoing decision making. Many organizations have data in different databases, documents, and paper files. The challenge here is to sort through all the data, choose the relevant data, and integrate it into one central database. Once this is done, the decision makers will have access to the essential data that helps them form a decision. Hurricane Katrina illustrated the need for making data available to emergency responders. For example, the EPA needed access to property ownership records (local assessor databases) to determine whose property may have been impacted by a chemical spill. Finding the appropriate data and gaining access to it in a timely manner was critical to an effective response. Data must be linked so that users know of the data and can use it. In the future, data will include more databases (relational), as well as digital libraries and multimedia databases. Documentation on the source of data and data types will be critical to ensure that information is used for its intended purpose.

3.4.4 Real-Time Response Data

In a disaster, complex computing may not be possible but emergency managers still need real-time data. As in other disaster management situations, a rear support team can be organized to carry out high-performance modeling and analysis.

Figure 3-7

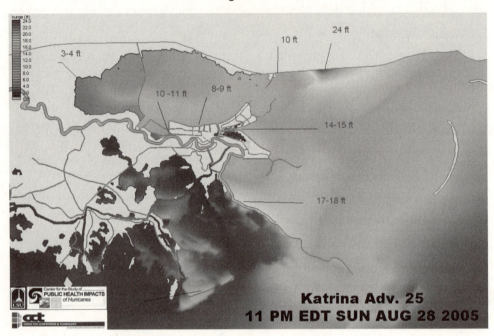

Digital animation map of Hurricane Katrina.

Dependable networks should be designed to allow for detailed analysis to occur even during stressful events. The lines of communication between support staff and operations units must be maintained. Communication also must be in a secure environment. For example, a hazmat team responding to a biological attack needs to be able to communicate to the first responders. The hazmat team can let the EMTs know what agents were likely used. The first responders can then alert the medical teams at the hospital and more effectively treat or evacuate the victims. The storm surge modeling for Hurricane Katrina and Rita were completed at Louisiana State University (LSU) based on data from severe weather warnings provided by the National Hurricane Center (NHC). Digital animation maps (See Figure 3-7) representing the storm surge water depths were posted on the Web for use by FEMA, as well as by state and local emergency management officials in both Louisiana and Texas. The Internet provided officials with information (from the surge model) to help support evacuation warnings, routing of vehicles, and road closures (see http://hurricane.lsu.edu/floodprediction/).

3.4.5 Capability and Compatibility Issues in Networks and Communications

You may face many issues in utilizing networks and communication systems. These include:

System Capacity

Responders rely heavily on technology for support in decision making and operations. This leads to the networks becoming overloaded. Procedures for managing a system and establishing priorities must be created. These cannot interfere with ongoing operations of the system. Response organizations should participate in exercises that overextend their communication capacity. This will force the system to adjust.

Interoperable Systems

Most industry efforts are targeted to the commercial market. The focus is on providing a static communications infrastructure (placement of routers and sites as hosts). Current systems are designed to carry anticipated loads and provide security. Backup options must be developed and mobile options considered. Communication patterns in times of crisis may be unpredictable. It may be impossible to establish and maintain a static routing structure because the host and units are inherently unstable. A "self-organizing" system may need to be designed.

Security

Many emergency management officials are concerned with the security of their system. They want to safeguard personal or business information that may be contained in data files. Emergency responders communicating individual health care information by radio should be sensitive to laws and regulations limiting access to information.

Lack of Current Relevant Information on Technology

Many databases are not updated on a regular basis. Users often assume they are and often believe they are examining the most recent, accurate, and relevant information when they are looking at old or inaccurate data.

Financial and Training Constraints

Powerful computers are expensive. They are often beyond the reach of local governments. In addition, emergency management works with many other local agencies. Employees of these agencies may not have a strong technology background.

Collaboration with Other Agencies

In times of crisis, agencies benefit from help from other groups. The interdependence of organizations must be recognized. It is important that their offices are linked on a secure network. This ensures that they work together in a disaster.

3.4.6 Using Technology to Create Synergy

The combined and coordinated actions of a parts of a system achieve more than all of the parts acting independently. The systems approach also suggests that if the performance of an enterprise is a product of interaction rather than the sum of its parts, it is entirely possible for the action of two or more parts to achieve an effect of which either is individually incapable. The notion of the whole being greater than the sum of its parts is called **synergy**.

For the emergency management system to function effectively, all of its parts must work together. The application of the synergy concept helps us to explain why the performance of a system as a whole depends more on how its parts relate than on how well each part operates. Indeed, the interdependence of utilities, local education, health care, public safety, and private and nonprofit partners shows that even if each part independently performs as efficiently as possible, the system as a whole may not. They must work together. Synergy is an important concept for managers. It emphasizes the need for individuals, as well as departments, to work together in a cooperative fashion.

During the early response efforts in Hurricane Katrina, the Louisiana State Office of Emergency Preparedness and Homeland Security asked Louisiana State University to provide GIS support in the state operations center. A team composed of faculty, research associates, and graduate students from LSU volunteered. They set up and provided GIS support throughout the response to Hurricanes Katrina and Rita. The group was composed of eight different academic units and research labs on the campus. Each had special data sets that would prove extremely useful during the response. The blend of experienced GIS users showed that each person contributed from their knowledge and experience in working with hazards data. Further, each member of the team worked with many state and local agency GIS staff members in the state operations center. When a request came from someone in the state operations center, this group found the appropriate data and quickly prepared map products for the responders. Truly, this team was more than just an assembly of individuals. Their merged knowledge, experience, and contacts offered much more than any one member could It was truly a synergistic effort.

A second example of synergy is illustrated in efforts to respond to the 911 calls in Orleans Parish. Beginning on the morning of August 29 when Katrina made landfall, the 911 Orleans Communication Center began receiving calls for help from people trapped by the flood waters. A database of the calls, including the time of the call, address, and nature of the emergency, was passed along to GIS staff from the USGS operating from the LSU campus in Baton Rouge. This group passed the file on to an experienced group in Maryland that geocoded the addresses into a geospatial map layer. This map layer was sent back to the USGS staff in Baton Rouge and placed on high-resolution images of New Orleans. Each call was noted on the map along with the address of the caller. The digital maps prepared by the USGS staff were then passed along to the Louisiana Geologic Survey (LAGS) staff at LSU for printing. The maps were broken down into 16 map grids. Responders used these the next morning in carrying out the rescue. The LAGS team along with the USGS team printed 16 copies of each of the large and small maps and delivered their maps to the Louisiana State Police each morning. The state police then took the printed maps to New Orleans for use by the assembled rescue teams. The rescue teams composed of U.S. Coast Guard boats and helicopters, U.S. Army and National Guard helicopters, fire and police boat teams, and Louisiana Fish and Wildlife agents. This was not just a team effort. No one group could have done this alone. By working together, they were able to do much more than just the sum of their individual efforts. Many have seen the pictures of people being rescued from the New Orleans area after Hurricane Katrina. The combined efforts of so many people made this rescue effort possible.

SELF-CHECK

* Define **synergy**.
* Many network capability and compatibility issues face the emergency manager today. Which of these issues must be confronted to ensure effective recovery in a disaster?
* Considering the continued expansion of networks and the integration of large amounts of information, how would you effectively guard against information overload?
* In the future, networks will play an increasing role in local emergency management agencies. How will they be used?
* How would you use networks to increase the collaboration between agencies during disasters?

SUMMARY

We use networks every day. For an emergency manager, networks are essential means of sharing information. In this chapter you have defined *networks* and *communication systems*. Networks facilitate information sharing in all phases of emergency management. Emergency management utilizes many forms of networks, including wireline and wireless communication technologies. Networks use land- and satellite-based technologies to support voice, video, and data communication systems. Networks may serve local or wide area systems and include secure access for users.

In this chapter, you have also identified several trends in technology that will affect networks. These trends include real-time response data, data integration, remote access to data, and information overload. The technologies used in networks will be ever changing, but we must manage the system to minimize information overload, and ensure data integration, and provide information in real time. In the future, network communication systems will change but must continue to address issues involving flexibility, interoperability, security, and financial constraints.

KEY TERMS

Analog transmission services
A continuous wave or signal (such as the human voice) for which conventional telephone lines are designed.

Coaxial cable
A copper data transmission wire that has an outer insulator and electrically grounded shielding.

Communication network
A set of linked devices that transfer information between users.

Distributed network
A collection of interconnected related network systems that facilitate information sharing.

Local area network (LAN)
A collection of users within an enterprise (business or public agency) that facilitates information sharing.

Network
A collection of parts that provide information to users.

Synergy
The notion that the whole is greater than the sum of its parts.

Wide area network (WAN)
A collection of selected users that may span a large geographical region and include multiple enterprises or agencies.

Wireless network
A communication network that connects users by radio or wireless means.

Wireline network
A series of network elements and the hard-wire lines interconnecting them.

ASSESS YOUR UNDERSTANDING

Go to www.wiley.com/college/pine to evaluate your knowledge of networks and communications systems.

Measure your learning by comparing pre-test and post-test results.

Summary Questions

1. A network is only used to enhance internal communications. True or False?

2. A wireless network would include only radio technology. True or False?

3. A wide area network could include users throughout the United States. True or False?

4. Communication bottlenecks can occur in most wire or wireless networks because
   (a) demand has exceeded the capacity of the network.
   (b) rules have been established that are mandated.
   (c) the system capacity was intentionally limited.
   (d) subnetworks must be controlled.

5. A network
   (a) is a system of computers.
   (b) provides voice information.
   (c) provides data information.
   (d) is a collection of parts that provide voice and data information.

6. A wireline network
   (a) has low costs of labor and installation.
   (b) is movable.
   (c) provides limited interference with electromagnet waves traveling over wires.
   (d) does not use land lines.

7. Most databases are kept up-to-date. True or False?

8. Disasters can make complex computing difficult. True or False?

9. Synergy is
   (a) energy.
   (b) when technology works.
   (c) when the sum of the parts is greater than the whole.
   (d) when the whole is greater than the sum of its parts.

Review Questions

1. What is a local area network (LAN)?
2. Name two trends affecting technology.
3. What advantages do wireless communication networks have over wireline networks?
4. Is it important to keep databases up-to-date? If so, why?
5. Give an example of how an emergency manager can use technology to create synergy.
6. Disasters can disrupt communications. What are two things you as an emergency manager can do to ensure you still have communications ability during a disaster?

Applying This Chapter

1. You are the local emergency manager for a large city that is implementing a new network system, and you have to decide what types of networks to implement. What do you consider to be the strengths and weaknesses of the wireless network system? What do you consider to be the strengths and weaknesses of the wireline system?
2. You are the local emergency manager for a town that is directly in the path of a hurricane. You have 24 hours before the hurricane is scheduled to make landfall. How can you use networks to save lives?
3. You are the director of FEMA. How do you use networks to help the state emergency management agencies? How does the ability to have remote access to information affect your job?
4. You are the local emergency manager for a city that was attacked by terrorists. All of the networks were disrupted due to the attack. What steps do you take so you can continue to communicate during the initial response?
5. Assuming that you want to develop a collaborative environment with other emergency management agencies during disasters, what types of information would you share and what types of technology would you use to share it?

YOU TRY IT

Enhancing Communication

Make a drawing of local agencies and organizations (public, private, and nonprofit) that could work together in an emergency or disaster. Make circles to represent each organization that contributes to the emergency response or recovery. Make the circles larger for those organizations that have a greater role in disaster response or recovery. Use lines to connect the agencies on a network. Where agencies have a greater interconnectedness, make the lines thicker. This drawing will demonstrate the importance of communications between agencies. By what means do these agencies currently communicate in a disaster? How could their communication be enhanced by the use of networks and emerging communication technology?

Networking in the Office

What advantages does networking give to emergency management offices? How does networking enable emergency management personnel to complete their daily duties?

Technology Constraints

You are a local emergency manager, and you work in a small town. You want to install a wide area network to link with neighboring emergency management offices in other nearby towns. Write a one-page paper on what obstacles you will face.

4

GIS AND GPS TOOLS
Maps and Geographic Systems

Starting Point

Go to www.wiley.com/college/pine to assess your knowledge of GIS and GPS tools.
Determine where you need to concentrate your effort.

What You'll Learn in This Chapter

▲ Benefits and challenges of using GIS, including the investment needed in computer hardware and software, geographic data, procedures, and training staff and technical support
▲ Benefits and challenges of using GPS to aid in location, navigation, tracking, mapping, and timing
▲ How to interpret different types of data
▲ Advantages image maps have over feature-based layer maps
▲ The uses of geocoding in emergency management
▲ Types of data available to emergency managers

After Studying This Chapter, You'll Be Able To

▲ Define GIS as a system and describe what investment is needed to implement a GIS system
▲ Use GIS to identify populations and areas at risk for certain hazards
▲ Assess how GPS can be used to create accurate maps
▲ Interpret vector and raster data
▲ Select appropriate data types for your goals
▲ Evaluate geocoding and its uses in emergency management activities

Goals and Outcomes

▲ Assess GIS capabilities and the best way to use them in emergency planning and response
▲ Evaluate the role of GPS in emergency management
▲ Choose data that pinpoints special facilities during disasters
▲ Use flood zone maps for hazard mitigation
▲ Compare and contrast feature-based maps and image-based maps
▲ Evaluate TIGER files and how they can be used in planning and recovery
▲ Evaluate map resources on the Internet

INTRODUCTION

When Hurricane Katrina flooded New Orleans, the Coast Guard went in to rescue people from the roofs of their flooded homes. Calls from stranded people came in nonstop. The members of the Coast Guard were not familiar with the area. The street signs were down. Street addresses were not useful. The Coast Guard, with support from United States Geological Survey (USGS), solved the problem by **geocoding** the addresses from 911 calls. Geocoding is the graphic representation, usually in the form of a point on a map of information in a database that includes street addresses or other location information. The street addresses were converted to longitude and latitude coordinates that allowed the Coast Guard to locate those who were stranded. This is just one of the ways an emergency manager can use technology to save lives.

In this chapter, you will learn other ways geographic and information technology tools can save lives. You will assess the investment needed to implement a GIS system. You will assess how to develop a GIS system. You will compare and contrast different map data types and how the data can help you in all phases of emergency management. All of these tools, like the geocoding, can help you in preparedness, mitigation, response, and recovery.

4.1 Geographic Information System: A Review of the Technology

Organizing information so it can be accessed by pointing to a region or a specific location on a map is used in a variety of applications. A system that supports this task is called a **geographic information system (GIS).** The information available is data that relates to specific locations. For example, it could be a map of your neighborhood that shows the precise locations of where all the violent crimes occurred in the past year. The data includes the physical identifier location along with the information associated with it. This information is geographic in that it is related and referenced by a system of coordinates. Objects, the data associated with them, and their locations are the building blocks of a GIS. A GIS is an organized collection of computer hardware and software designed to create, manipulate, analyze, and display all types of geographic data. A GIS allows complex spatial operations that are difficult to do otherwise. A GIS can assist in emergency rescue operations by identifying where help is needed and helping to direct resources in an efficient manner. GIS is also referred to as a "smart map" tool. It allows users to search, analyze, and edit data. For example, the New York City Office of Emergency Management uses a language map created by their GIS team. This map shows the breakdown of languages spoken in the neighborhoods of Brooklyn. The map also highlights areas where English is not understood. This information would be used during an evacuation. Emergency managers would issue evacuation orders in languages the residents would understand (see Fig. 4.1).

A GIS is one of the most important tools that you have. You can use GIS's and their programs, data, maps, charts, and tables to make valuable decisions. From planning decisions on the locations of shelters to response decisions concerning the best evacuation route to the examination floodplains, GIS is a tool that provides needed information for decision making.

A GIS is an information system, but one in which the data is geographically referenced. A GIS, for example, could create and edit lists of schools, hospitals, nursing homes, or shelters, but also the capability to display the records in the tables in a graphic or map format.

Map data comes in three forms, including **lines, points,** and **polygons,** that are used in a vector format (a coordinate-based map). A second type of format is image oriented (raster data). The image may be a high-resolution photo from an aircraft or U.S. Geological Survey (USGS) digital elevation data that has quantitative attributes referring to cells in a rectangular grid that reflect elevation. We will discuss these in-depth later in this chapter.

A GIS is a system. A GIS system includes data, graphics, and a program to manipulate both the data and the graphics. A GIS stores, retrieves, manipulates, analyzes, and displays these data according to user-defined specifications. Ideally the GIS is used as a decision support system involving the integration of spatial data in a problem-solving environment. As a system, GIS includes the basic characteristics of all systems. As we discussed in Chapter 2, a system consists of input, transformation, and output. Let's look at how the GIS works.

FOR EXAMPLE

Predicting Hurricane Damage

Emergency managers aren't the only ones using GIS to predict potential losses from hurricanes. Insurance agencies use GIS systems as well. For example, the Florida Farm Bureau Insurance Agency uses a GIS system through which they can access information on all their policyholders. Each type of policy is color coded, as is the geographic area they live in. Florida Farm Bureau overlays event information, such as hurricane track and wind speed, against its policyholder points on a map. This way the insurance company can quickly determine which policyholders will have claims, how extensive the claims might be, and what homes to send adjustors to right away.

Figure 4-1

Distribution of Languages Spoken in Brooklyn

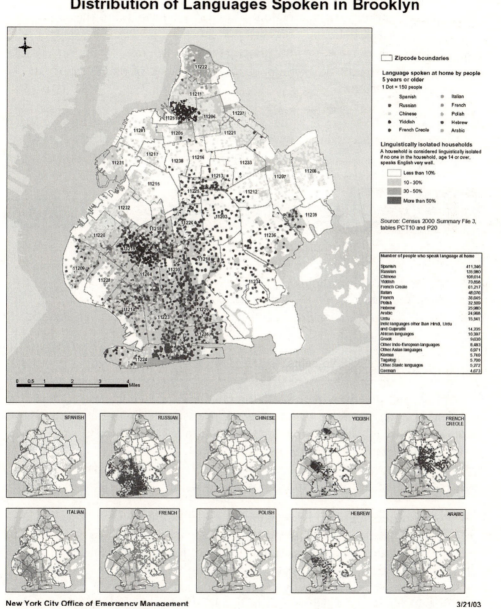

New York City Office of Emergency Management   3/21/03

A map of Brooklyn that shows what languages are spoken in each neighborhood.

▲ **Input:** Input in a GIS system could include a collection of phone listings or census information by geographic area.

▲ **Transformation:** Transformation in a GIS system includes the storage and retrieval of data and analysis.

▲ **Output:** The output in a GIS system is maps and tables. These maps could include risk zones, vulnerable populations, or tables of phone listings in vulnerable areas.

As with every system, GIS is prone to user error during input. The data input must be exact and accurate.

SELF-CHECK

- Define **geocoding.**
- How is **GIS** a system?
- Name the three forms of map data.

4.2 GIS in Emergency Management

Maps provide a very visual representation of an event, phenomenon, or idea. For emergency managers, being able to see the area affected by a disaster supports communication and decision making. The output of a GIS system can be used during all four phases of emergency management. The key is to understand the types of data that could be used and how they contribute to disaster preparedness, response, recovery, and mitigation.

▲ **Preparedness:** You can use a GIS to identify populations and areas at risk for certain hazards. For example, you can identify areas at risk for hazardous spills by matching potential storage facilities for hazardous materials in populated areas to census data. You can also view the areas that are in a floodplain as well as identify appropriate evacuation routes and shelters. Individuals with special needs can be identified by address and assistance with evacuation can be organized.

▲ **Response:** You can use a GIS to help you to respond to an emergency. An area affected by a flood or a chemical spill can be shown on a map. Other information can be shown as well. This information may

FOR EXAMPLE

Red Cross and GIS

Private organizations, such as the Red Cross, are using GIS as well. The Red Cross used mapping software along with population data to be able to respond quickly to the specific needs of Hurricane Katrina and Rita victims. "Using GIS technology, the Red Cross was able to better plan prior to hurricanes Katrina and Rita as well as respond with greater flexibility and precision after the events occurred," says Eric Maier, ESRI (Environmental Systems Research Institute, Inc.) commercial account manager. "ESRI deployed resources to help generate maps and data on wind fields, damaged areas, populations, city infrastructure, streets, and more. This information was provided to Red Cross managers, directors, and senior leadership who make decisions and carry out strategic planning" (ESRI, October 7, 2005).

include the location of critical facilities, including schools, hospitals, nursing homes, parks, shopping areas, business areas, manufacturing areas, and transportation routes. Seeing the location of critical facilities in an area affected by an emergency help emergency managers can determine appropriate evacuation routes or shelter locations. Having the precise location of a school, hospital, park, or business is useful, but other information associated with these sites enables you to make better decisions. Knowing the school enrollment, the number of beds at a hospital by type, or the type of patients in a nursing home could provide you with timely information for use in making evacuation decisions.

▲ **Recovery:** Information from a GIS is also essential to recovery. In the example of a hurricane, a GIS could show you what areas were destroyed and need rebuilding, including the age of housing, as well as where utility lines are, including those where service needs to be restored.

▲ **Mitigation:** Risk analysis occurs both before and after an event. GIS information can be used to first identify the community's vulnerability to hazards. This information can be used for mitigation campaigns. In addition, information such as languages spoken by citizens in specific neighborhoods (see Figure 4-1) can be used to help prepare hazard awareness campaigns. By knowing what languages are common in geographic areas, you can tailor your media messages to that audience by placing the messages in the language they speak and understand.

- How is GIS used in preparedness?
- How is GIS used in response?
- How is GIS used in mitigation?

4.3 Developing and Implementing a GIS

A GIS is a type of computer system that requires building large databases before it is useful. Using a GIS isn't like using other microcomputer applications. With most microcomputer applications, you can use it immediately after the purchase of the hardware and software. A GIS is different. It requires that large spatial databases be created, appropriate hardware and software be purchased, applications be developed, and all components be installed, integrated, and tested before you can begin to use the GIS. Developing a GIS involves investment in five areas: computer hardware, computer software, geographic data, procedures, and trained staff.

▲ **Computer hardware:** Many desktop personal computers Feature dramatic speed with extensive RAM capabilities. To run GIS, you should purchase the fastest computer on the market, with extensive RAM and at least one (possibly two) large monitor (at least 17 inches). A color printer that is capable of printing 17-by-14 inches is essential. A plotter is useful for preparing large 36 inch wide maps. A scanner is useful for including photographs or maps in a GIS.

▲ **Computer software:** Several software companies provide local and state governments with excellent GIS programs. Commercial products include Intergraph's Geo-Media, ESRI products, and MapInfo all have reasonably priced and powerful software. The Census Bureau, in collaboration with EPA, and NOAA distribute LandView software to read Census and other federal agency data. Each of the shell software is fully capable of enabling emergency management agencies to complete complex hazard analysis.

▲ **Geographic data:** Data include relational databases that contain street addresses that can be geocoded or geographic coordinates. The above software can either geocode the databases or create points from the coordinate fields. Census Bureau TIGER street, highway, rail, and water features are available from distributors in common map projections. Feature image data (photos, satellite images, or USGS quad sheets) are also available from either federal or state agencies or commercial distributors in a format that is projected to display an image along with local street and other **vector data.** Vector data is a coordinate-based data layer in a GIS that represents features on a map in the form of a point, a line, or a polygon.

▲ **Procedures:** The manner in which data are stored, analysis is performed, maps are prepared, or files are shared must be established.

▲ **Training staff and technical support:** Training and technical support are critical to efficient and effective program operations. The GIS technical staff person must understand file management, database formatting, and computer-aided graphics drawing programs. If the staff member has these skills, the GIS program can be learned easily. In addition, skills in understanding computer networks will be helpful in ensuring that printers function, scanners work, and server files are available to the staff.

GIS development involves technology that requires management attention. This should be active as opposed to passive management involvement in the project. Past failures of GISs did not result from technical difficulties. Instead, they resulted from a lack of realistic expectations of all parties associated with the project, including GIS technicians, potential users, managers, and officials. You must get involved in planning for the development of a GIS. You may be in a position to facilitate realistic expectations from technical staff, users, and other support staff who might assist in the development of GIS data.

The development of GIS layers must address the following concerns:

▲ What will be the source for each data layer (e.g. shelter locations, schools, hospitals, nursing homes, bridges, streams, or emergency management resources)?
▲ Who will own the data layer?
▲ How will the new GIS layer be integrated with existing data files (e.g. lists of schools, hospitals, nursing homes, etc.)?
▲ Who will be responsible for updates to the data?
▲ How will the cost of the data be allocated?
▲ Will access to the data be made available to the public? How? By whom?
▲ Who will be responsible for archiving and retention of the data layer?

GIS data layers need to be prepared as a team effort with other administrative agencies that are involved in the emergency management system and who may use these up-to-date data layers. Planning and input from a variety of public agencies is critical in facilitating realistic expectations of GIS.

When using a GIS, keep in mind that problems often occur because of the following lessons

▲ The GIS is not integrated with other systems where interaction may be desired.

▲ Staff do not fully understand the technology prior to extensive training.

▲ Development time estimates differ from actual task time.

▲ GIS involves greater uncertainty about costs.

▲ A greater likelihood exists that programmatic changes (to other parts of the emergency management system) will be needed during the development phases.

Management needs to anticipate these problems and take appropriate action. Because the introduction of a GIS affects other elements of the emergency management process, it is an opportunity to introduce fundamental change into the way emergency management operates. You, therefore, must be involved in the adoption of this new technology and help plan, implement, and monitor the process.

A key factor in the success of a GIS is the creation of an "enterprise" or "corporate" database. This is a single, organization-wide data resource for GIS information. In this type of database, all users have access to up-to-date information, and the creation of the data is efficient. Because a GIS can affect an entire organization, its establishment is a question of policy, management cooperation, and coordination, rather than a technical issue.

A GIS is therefore more than a technology issue. It requires data such as databases, images, pictures, and graphics that are fundamental to entire state or local agencies. Know that other agencies, will be interested in data layers, especially those that are maintained by the emergency management unit (shelters, special populations, resources, etc.). You will need to seek out other local or state units that are interested in jointly developing a GIS. These departments could include the departments of planning, public works, public safety, and education.

4.3.1 LandView and MARPLOT Software

Federal agencies have prepared and used spatial data sets for many years. The Census Bureau in collaboration with the EPA and NOAA, distribute mapping software (MARPLOT) and data sets (LandView). The latest data sets for the U.S. are available from U.S. Census Bureau or the EPA for less than $200. Go to either of their Web sites and search for "LandView". LandView for specific states is also available at no cost from http://atlas.lsu.edu.

LandView has its roots in CAMEO (Computer-Aided Management of Emergency Operations) software. CAMEO was developed by the EPA and NOAA to facilitate implementation of the Emergency Planning and Community Right-to-Know Act. This law requires communities to develop emergency response plans addressing chemical hazards and to make available to the public information on chemical hazards in the community.

> ## FOR EXAMPLE
>
> ### Government Resources
>
> The federal government has a wealth of hazard information on the Web available to emergency managers and to private citizens. For example, the National Geophysical Data Center (NGDC) has a collection of databases and data on natural hazards. To view the information, go to www.ngdc.noaa.gov/

The LandView database and MARPLOT map system allows users to retrieve and map Census 2000 demographic and housing data from the 2000 Census; EPA facility air, water, and hazardous waste data; and USGS mapping information. The mapping data comes from the Geographic Names Information System (GNIS), which contains over 1.2 million records that reflect marks such as schools, churches, cemeteries, government sites, and many other places, features, and areas on USGS maps. As with other GIS programs, you can use LandView to create thematic maps of census data. You can also use LandView to locate a street address or intersection on a map based on TIGER road features and address ranges.

LandView allows users to identify and map Census Bureau legal and statistical areas, EPA sites, and USGS GNIS features. You can customize the maps, vary the scale, and search for objects on the map (landmarks, roads, water features, cities, etc.). You can also add information to the maps with MARPLOT. For more information on both products, visit www.census.gov/geo.

SELF-CHECK

- Define **vector data.**
- To develop a GIS, you need to invest in what areas?
- What concerns accompany GIS layers?
- How are LandView and MARPLOT software used?

4.4 Data Representation

GIS represents objects such as roads, land use, and elevation with digital data. These objects can be divided into discrete objects, such as homes and roads, or continuous fields such as rainfall or elevation. There are two methods used to store data in a GIS for both types of objects: vector data layers and raster data layers.

Both vector and raster data layers use longitude and latitude lines.

▲ **Longitude:** Used to describe the east-west position of a point. The position is reported as the number of degrees east (to −180.0 degrees) or west (to +180.0 degrees) of the prime meridian (0 degrees). It is represented by vertical lines running between the north and south poles. Lines of longitude are farthest apart at the equator and intersect at both poles; therefore, they are not parallel.

▲ **Latitude:** Used to describe the north-south position of a point as measured usually in degrees or decimal degrees above or below the equator. Latitude lines are the horizontal lines on a map that increase from 0 degrees at the equator to 90 degrees at both the north (+90.0 degrees) and south (−90.0 degrees) poles.

4.4.1 Vector Data

GIS include graphics that illustrate information about an area. As described earlier vector data layers use geometric shapes such as points, lines (series of point coordinates), or polygons, also called *areas* (shapes bounded by lines), to represent objects.

Figure 4-2

Vector Displays

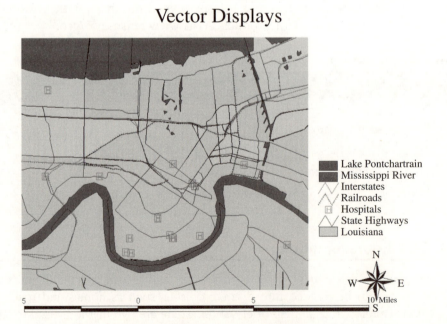

A vector display of the New Orleans area.

A vector data layer is a coordinate-based data structure commonly used to represent map features. Each object is represented as a list of sequential *x,y* coordinates. Attributes may be associated with the objects. For example, Figure 4-2 includes lines such as streets or roads, interstates, railroads, and water features. Hospitals are illustrated points on the map. The polygons include the boundaries of the City of New Orleans, Orleans Parish, Lake Pontchartrain, and the Mississippi River. Additional information on the use of polygons, points, and lines is as follows:

▲ **Polygon (area, parcel):** A polygon is an area feature whose perimeter is defined by a series of enclosing segments and nodes. It is a simple bounded region—simple in the sense that it does not consist of more than one polygon (where a boundary can consist of more than one polygon). Examples of a polygon include the boundaries of a state, urban area, or county (parish). Information about the urban area, county, or state may be attached to the data file that is associated with the graphic image (see figure 4-3).

▲ **Point:** A point is an object on a map that represents a specific location for information. The map object is defined by a single *x,y* coordinate pair. Each point object is represented by a symbol style (e.g., circle, square, triangle, etc.). Figure 4-4 shows the location of cities in Louisiana. The cities would be points on the map. Examples of point data that could be used in emergency management include the locations of special populations, resources, residents, hazard sites, churches, schools, and shelters.

▲ **Line:** A line is a map object defined by a set of sequential coordinates that represents the shape of a geographic feature. For example, a line may

Figure 4-3

Polygon Displays

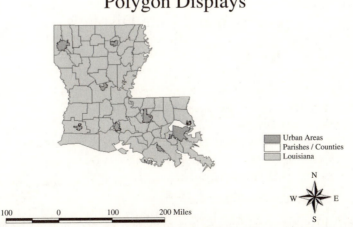

Map of Louisiana counties (parishes) and major urban areas.

Figure 4-4

Polygon and Point Displays

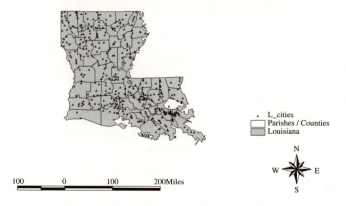

A map of Louisiana counties and cities.

represent street centerlines, railroads, cables, streams, or rivers. Lines join two points. A street map is a collection of thousands of line object segments joined together to provide a visual representation of a community transportation network. For example, Figure 4-5 shows segments of the Louisiana state highway system. Data that is graphically displayed as lines could also include the location of water features by type, including rivers, streams, drainage ditches, or canals.

Figure 4-5

Polygon and Line Displays

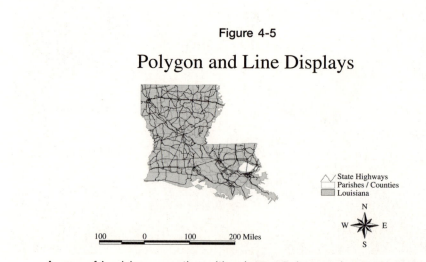

A map of Louisiana counties with primary and secondary state highways.
The highways are shown as line objects.

4.4.2 Raster Data

Raster data consist of rows and columns of cells. Each cell stores a single value. Usually, raster data are images. An image is a graphic representation or description of an object that is typically produced by an optical or electronic device. Some common examples of image data include remotely sensed data, such as satellite data, scanned data, and photographs. Image data such as a photo is also referred to as raster data. The raster image is displayed in a series of grid cells or pixels; each has a certain value depending on how the image was captured and what it represents. For example, if the image is a remotely sensed satellite image, each pixel represents light energy reflected from a portion of the Earth's surface. If, however, the image is a scanned document, each pixel represents a brightness value associated with a particular point on the document. Raster images are sometimes known as *bitmaps*. Aerial photographs, scanned pictures, and satellite images are common types of raster data found in a GIS. Figure 4-6 shows an aerial photo of New Orleans in January 2004.

Figure 4-6

USGS Digital Orthophoto Quad: raster image of New Orleans in January 2004.

USGS Digital Orthophoto Quads were merged to create this image of New Orleans.

Figure 4-7 shows an infrared satellite photo image of New Orleans after Hurricane Katrina. The dark shaded areas of the image highlights flooded and non-flooded areas of the city. Polygons of flooded areas of the city were made by a GIS team from Louisiana State University and used with Lidar elevation contours to determine the depth and extent of flooding.

Figure 4-8 is an image of New Orleans created from the Lidar data that shows land elevations. Note that high ground follows the Mississippi River. Major highways are displayed over the digital raster elevation image. The highways provide landmarks to better understand the high and low areas of the city. There are limitations to image data. The main limitation with image data is that images do not contain attribute information about the features they show.

A United States Geological Survey Quad Sheet is a common map used by emergency managers. These maps appear to be similar to a state transportation road map available from state transportation or tourist agencies. The Quad Sheet maps produced by the U.S. Geological Survey provide additional data beyond

Figure 4-7

Post-Hurricane Katrina satellite infrared image of New Orleans, September 2, 2005.

Figure 4-8

Lidar raster image of New Orleans as prepared by the Center for Public Health Impacts of Hurricanes at Louisiana State University.

roads and waterways, such as wetland areas. The details of local areas are available on a national basis from the U.S. Geological Survey, as well as from many local surveying, mapping, or blueprint vendors. Figure 4-9 is a portion of a 1:100,000 scale USGS Quad Sheet.

Image data can be organized in a number of ways depending upon the particular image format. An image file such as an air photo can contain georeference information so that roads, water features, or schools can be placed at the appropriate location over the image.

4.4.3 TIGER Files

TIGER files are some of the best data layers available for GIS applications in emergency management. They were developed by the U.S. Department of Commerce Census Bureau to assist in the census. Street and water layers were taken from USGS maps and edited to include street and water feature names. The street files also include address ranges. These files thus have been enhanced to allow for geocoding of data files that include street addresses. The TIGER files are the only national source of street files that include address ranges. Although many commercial vendors suggest that their maps are better than the TIGER files, in reality their maps were drawn from the Census Bureau TIGER files. Few commercial vendors have really enhanced these files. If the TIGER files have been enhanced, it has been done by local communities that know the street names and have spent great effort to correct street names, delete streets that are private

Figure 4-9

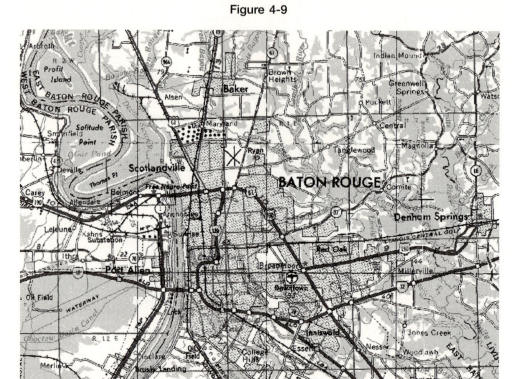

A portion of Baton Rouge, Louisiana, on a USGS Quad sheet.

roads, and add street names to "unnamed street" files. The editing of the TIGER files must be done in collaboration with local officials.

The Census Bureau developed TIGER (Topologically Integrated Geographic Encoding and Referencing System). It is based on the USGS DLG-3 hydrographic and transportation data. Attribute data tied to the topology include feature names; political and statistical geographic area reference codes per county; incorporated places, census tract, and block numbers; and potential address ranges and ZIP codes. These files are at a scale of 1:100,000 as compared to more accurate mapping in the USGS. For more information on the USGS files, see http://www.usgs.gov.

You will need to determine how accurate a specific piece of data is before using it in emergency management. Maps such as the USGS/Department of Commerce TIGER files are approximate files and good for broad views of a local area. They are not suitable for engineering purposes.

With a GIS, you can display image data and feature-based spatial data together. The TIGER street network (feature-based data) can be placed over an

Figure 4-10

TIGER Files

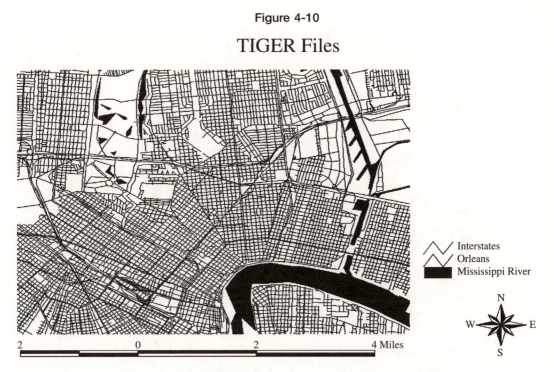

Interstates
Orleans
Mississippi River

N
W   E
S

2   0   2   4 Miles

Road map of New Orleans: source of road files from TIGER.

image (photograph). Combining these types of data is very useful to the emergency manager. See Figure 4-10 for an example of a TIGER file.

Application: Using Flood Zone Maps

Let's take a moment to look at a map and think about how you could use it. Pretend you are the emergency manager for Sulphur, Louisiana, and you know a hurricane is coming. You want to determine what the possible damage could be. You look at the map in Figure 4-11 and see the flood zones displayed on the map. How could you use this information in emergency planning or response?

You could use this type of display in emergency planning or response in several ways. You could determine the potential damage from a flood and easily see who will be affected. A GIS allows the user to select features in a layer (e.g. residents) that intersects with another layer (a flood zone). A list of residents from the flood zone could be created using the GIS. You could then communicate directly with residents in the flood zone in a pending flood. You could see the interstates and plan evacuation routes. You can also attain a list of critical facilities from looking at this map, and you could make special arrangements to evacuate residents in those facilities. For example, there was much outrage in the

Figure 4-11

FEMA A Flood Zones
Sulphur, LA

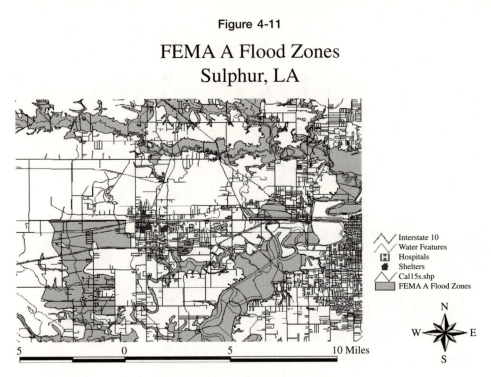

Legend:
- Interstate 10
- Water Features
- Hospitals
- Shelters
- Cal15s.shp
- FEMA A Flood Zones

5   0   5   10 Miles

Flood zones of Sulphur, Louisiana.

aftermath of Hurricane Katrina when it was discovered that some nursing home residents were abandoned by their nurses and caregivers. Evacuation plans for critical facilities must be one of your priorities during a city-wide evacuation. From this map you can also see the location of shelters.

This type of information can be part of a geographic information system and is available to you. Let's once again look at three additional examples of the information that you can receive from a GIS:

▲ A GIS can provide regular maps of the local community and of areas of special interest to emergency management.

▲ A GIS can conduct spatial queries and display the results. Such queries could include, Which households are within a 100-year flood zone? Which schools or nursing homes are within 300 yards of a rail line or major state highway? How many people live within a 100-year flood zone?

▲ A GIS can provide a basis for conducting complex spatial analyses, such as analyses on the area, residents, and businesses that would be vulnerable to a chemical release from a fixed facility or an intersection.

FOR EXAMPLE

Flood Maps

There are several online resources providing maps for your use. One of the best resources is FEMA. FEMA's Map Service Center (MSC) provides online access to National Flood Insurance Program (NFIP) map products. The MSC Web site is designed to provide the latest information and support services to users on flood related data. The Web site address is www.fema.gov/msc/.

SELF-CHECK

- Define **longitude** and **latitude**.
- How are TIGER files used in emergency management?
- What types of vector data are used in emergency management?
- What are the uses of **raster data** in emergency management?

4.5 Geocoding

Many organizations maintain large databases of events by address, such as accident and crime reports, customer records, and tax and parcel records. Addresses are, in fact, the most common form of storing geographic data. With geocoding, you can display the tabular information in a computerized database containing addresses as points on a map and easily find their locations. Address geocoding can allow you to locate fire stations by entering their addresses, show where all students live in relation to the schools they attend, or locate customers and thereby site facilities where the customers are concentrated (See Figure 4-12). As mentioned earlier in this chapter, geocoding was used during Hurricane Katrina to help the Coast Guard rescue stranded flood victims. In this situation, street addresses were of no use to the Coast Guard. This is because the Coast Guard was not familiar with New Orleans, and all the street signs had been destroyed. Longitude and latitude coordinates were the only way the Coast Guard could locate those who called for help.

An address specifies a location in the same way that a geographic coordinate does. But because an address is merely a text string containing the information of house number, street name, direction, and/or zip code, an address needs

Figure 4-12

Geocoding Residents

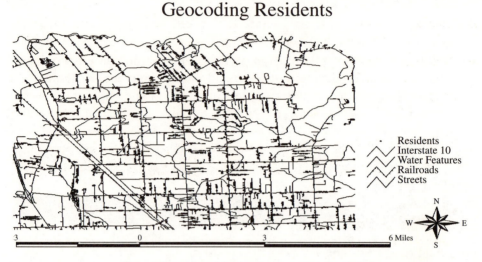

Residents
Interstate 10
Water Features
Railroads
Streets

Geocoding of residents along a street network.

a mechanism to calculate its geographic coordinate for the address and then display the location on a map based on the assigned coordinate. To do so, addresses stored in tabular data files must first be associated with a geographic feature, usually in a street network. The coordinates of a data source can be used to calculate and assign coordinates to addresses if the data source features also have addresses. Geocoding is the mechanism that allows you to use addresses to identify locations on a map.

There are a variety of planning, administrative, and operational activities that use geographic data in the form of addresses. Geocoding enables you to do the following with these data:

▲ Create pin maps to show locations of various events by addresses.
▲ Query and find geographic features using addresses.

FOR EXAMPLE

Evacuating Students

Geocoding is one tool that can be used in evacuating schools. With geocoding, you can match student addresses against a street map of a city. Once the homes of students are located, school assignments and busing plans can be created and analyzed.

▲ Identify and list addresses in a flood zone or within a specific distance of a facility with hazardous chemicals.

▲ Analyze crimes by address. These locations can be mapped and analyzed with other demographic data.

▲ Identify potential impacts of storage facilities for hazardous materials in populated areas by matching the site addresses to a theme containing census data.

SELF-CHECK

- What local organizations could provide accurate residential and business addresses for geocoding?
- Give two examples of how geocoding can be used in emergency management.

4.6 Global Positioning Systems

A **global positioning system (GPS)** is a system to identify and record a geospatial reference point on the Earth's surface using a set of satellites orbiting Earth. This system of 24 Navstar satellites circles Earth every 12 hours at an altitude of 12,000 miles above Earth, constantly transmitting the precise time and satellites position in space. The system created a huge commercial market for hand-held GPS receivers and was used by emergency response personnel, including agencies such as police, fire, emergency, medical, and public works. The unit measures the location to within 30 meters. Drawing its power from flashlight batteries and a small antenna, the unit takes about 10 seconds to find and lock onto radio transmission from at least three Navstar satellites.

GPS uses the triangulation of signals from the satellites to determine locations on Earth. GPS satellites know their location in space, and receivers can determine their distance from a satellite using the travel time of a radio message from the satellite to the receiver. Commercial GPS units vary in price and quality and thus may not provide the accuracy required by a user. Cheaper models may not be able to determine the precise ground position of the GPS unit. GPS products have been developed for use for many commercial applications. They include surveying and mapping, aviation and marine navigation, vehicle tracking systems, and mobile computer and cellular platforms. Following Hurricanes Katrina and Rita, survey teams were dispatched to New Orleans to use GPS to record the extent of flooding at street intersections or in open areas. In addition, the precise locations of residential and commercial buildings in New Orleans were identified using GPS units. High water marks were then measured on these structures in order to verify water depths throughout the city. GPS technology was essential in accurately recording the extent of flooding and the location of high water marks.

GPS technology has many applications. These applications can be broken down into five broad categories:

▲ **Location:** GPS technology determines precise locations. For example, there are now emergency personal locator beacons widely available for less than $1,000. These pocket-sized beacons can be used by anyone. The beacon is capable of pinpointing someone's exact position. The beacon can also send a distress signal to the Air Force, which then routes the information to the state police. A hiker, for example, may want to use a beacon when navigating dangerous terrain. If the hiker gets lost, he or she could send a distress signal and his or her position would be given to the state police. The state police could then send in some rescue personnel to find the hiker. GPS beacons are also now in many cars. If you had an accident in one of these cars, you could send a distress signal and an ambulance would come to your aid.

FOR EXAMPLE

GPS at Ground Zero

The terrorist attacks in New York on September 11, 2001, provided many challenges for emergency managers in the recovery period. One of the challenges was how to remove so much debris quickly and efficiently. The collapse of the World Trade Center left 1.8 million tons of debris. New York City decided to use a GPS tracking system on the trucks that hauled debris away. The GPS-based system enabled staff to locate each truck as it loaded materials at the site. The trucks could be located at all times: during the loading, when they were on the transportation routes, and when they were transferring loads to barges for shipment to the Staten Island disposal site, or to metal recyclers in the area. The Web-based system provided information in near real time, permitting quick correction of any problems. Complete available truck status included time in, time out, whether the truck was loaded or unloaded, type of load, destination, vehicle speed, name of driver, whether the trailer had been disconnected from the tractor at any time, and similar information.(http:// Menard and kneiff, September 2, 2002, GPS world).

▲ **Navigation:** GPS technology enables you to easily travel from one location to another. For example, many cars now have interactive maps on the dash that use GPS technology. Using this program, you can enter in your destination into the computer and the computer will display the best route. Airplanes, ships, and other vehicles have this capability as well.

▲ **Tracking:** GPS systems can be placed on vehicles and cargo, and their movements can be tracked over the Web. For example, emergency managers can track the locations of fire trucks and ambulances over the Web if they are equipped with GPS beacons.

▲ **Mapping:** GPS can be used to survey an area and create maps. State transportation agencies have used GPS to record, in a GIS format, accurate highway elevation centerline data sets. GPS has been used to record the route, distance, and time for school bus routes. GPS has also been used by damage assessment teams following a disaster. They record the location of residential and business structures, which can be combined linked to a damage assessment form.

▲ **Timing:** GPS satellites carry atomic clocks and beam back precise time measurements to receivers here in the United States. Many public safety and utility vehicles are equipped with GPS to provide time and location information to dispatchers. Emergency personnel can thus be directed to deal with emergency situations.

SELF-CHECK

- Define global positioning system (GPS).
- How does GPS work?
- How does a GPS help in emergency preparedness and response activities?

SUMMARY

A thorough understanding of maps and geographic systems is essential to your job as an emergency manager. In this chapter, you learned how to interpret maps. You can use maps in preparing for a disaster and mitigating losses. A GIS is a spatially referenced information system that can support decision making in emergency planning, response, recovery, and mitigation activities. You can also use GPS technology to identify the specific location of a point or area, navigate to a specific location, and track vehicles. In this chapter, you evaluated different GIS and GPS tools and their benefits in emergency management. These tools will help you in every phase of emergency management.

KEY TERMS

Geocoding	A graphic representation, usually in the form of a point on a map, of information in a database that includes street addresses or other location information.
Geographic information system (GIS)	A computer-based information system that provides a means for the capture, storage, manipulation, analysis, and display of geographical reference information for solving complex problems.
Global positioning system (GPS)	A system to identify and record a geospatial reference point on Earth's surface using a set of satellites orbiting Earth.
Latitude	Measurement used to describe the north-south position of a point as measured usually in degrees or decimal degrees above or below the equator.
Line	A map object that is defined by a set of sequential coordinates that represents the shape of a geographic feature.
Longitude	Measurement used to describe the east-west position of a point.
Point	An object on a map in a GIS that represents information for a specific location.
Polygon	An area vector data feature in a GIS that defines a perimeter by a series of enclosing segments.
Raster data	A graphic representation of a geographic area from an optical or electronic device in the form of an aerial photograph, scanned picture, land classification, or ground contour image. The image is represented by rows and columns of cells that may have data values.
Vector data	Coordinate-based data in a GIS that represents features on a map in the form of points, lines, or polygons.

ASSESS YOUR UNDERSTANDING

Go to www.wiley.com/college/pine to evaluate your knowledge of GIS and GPS tools.

Measure your learning by comparing pre-test and post-test results.

Summary Questions

1. The primary purpose of developing a GIS is to support decision making. True or False?
2. Developing a GIS involves investment in which of the following areas?
   (a) Geographic data
   (b) Procedures
   (c) Trained staff
   (d) All of the above
3. Which of the following is not an element of a vector data set?
   (a) Point
   (b) Line
   (c) Polygon
   (d) Cell
4. All vector point objects use longitude and latitude references. True or False?
5. An example of a GIS output would be a map showing address locations in a risk zone. True or False?
6. Which of the following would be an example of using a GIS in an emergency response?
   (a) Showing an area that has been flooded.
   (b) Identify homes or business that have been damaged.
   (c) Pinpointing are closed bridges or streets
   (d) All of the above
7. Emergency managers have found that staff training and technical support are not necessary for effective use of a GIS. True or false?
8. Which of the following is true about GIS?
   (a) GIS requires the use of databases and tables.
   (b) GIS may utilize images and other graphics.
   (c) GIS requires a knowledge of how to store files.

(d) GIS is only used by a central mapping unit and never by other agency personnel.

9. Point data on a map can represent locations such as schools, shelters, businesses, parks, or hazard sites. True or False?

10. A raster file may include a satellite photo of Earth as well as a scanned image. True or False?

11. A GIS can display hazard areas, including areas vulnerable to a wildfire. True or False?

Review Questions

1. How can data be used in a GIS system for emergency response and long-term recovery?

2. Why are GIS used in emergency management?

3. What are the key elements of a GIS, and how are they integrated for decision support?

4. What are the challenges in effectively implementing a GIS?

5. What is geocoding, and how can it contribute to emergency planning?

6. How is geocoding related to a GIS?

7. What is GPS, and how does it enhance emergency response?

8. What is the most important element in effectively using a GIS: people, process, or technology?

Applying This Chapter

1. You are the local emergency manager for a town that was just devastated by a hurricane. You now are in the rescue mode because people need to be taken from their homes to safety. What geographic information system tools can you use to aid in the rescues?

2. You are the local emergency manager of a city that is the target of a terrorist attack. The terrorists plan to release hazardous chemicals in the subway system. Given access to a GIS, what types of maps could be created and how would they be used?

3. You are the local emergency manager of a coastal town that is always vulnerable to hurricanes. How would GIS information be used to predict hurricane damage and plan the recovery?

4. You are the local emergency manager for a town that is home to three chemical companies that work with hazardous chemicals. How does

geocoding assist in identifying potential impacts of disasters on hazardous materials storage facilities in populated areas?

5. You are the local emergency manager for an agency that just installed a GIS system. What challenges do you anticipate in implementing the new system, and how do you plan to overcome those challenges?

6. You are the local emergency manager for a town that was hit by an earthquake. What types of maps do you need and why?

YOU TRY IT

Preparing for an Evacuation

You were just hired as an emergency manager for Newark, New Jersey. One of your concerns is the amount of hazardous waste that the industrial facilities in Newark produce. You want to plan an evacuation of certain areas of the city. How can a GIS help you plan this evacuation?

Creating a Hazard Awareness Campaign

You are an emergency manager for Los Angeles, California. One of your goals is to educate the residents about earthquakes and how they can build homes that are not vulnerable to earthquakes. You also want to educate the residents on what to do if an earthquake does occur. How can a GIS system help you plan your public-awareness campaign?

Managing Relief Supplies

You are the head of FEMA, and Florida has been hit by a hurricane. You are receiving constant calls from the local emergency managers wanting to know where relief supplies are. They are out of food and water. You can answer their questions because you are using a GPS system. How does the GPS system help you answer their questions?

5

DIRECT AND REMOTE SENSING
Describing and Detecting Hazards

Starting Point

Go to www.wiley.com/college/pine to assess your knowledge of direct and remote sensing.
Determine where to concentrate your effort.

What You'll Learn in This Chapter

▲ How direct sensing can be used in emergency management tasks
▲ How weather stations collect data
▲ How water sensors are used in predicting floods and flood patterns
▲ Different purposes of air data sensors
▲ How to evaluate technology for direct sensing
▲ How remote sensing can be used in emergency management tasks
▲ Examples of satellite imaging
▲ How imaging radar works

After Studying This Chapter, You'll Be Able To

▲ Use the data gathered from direct sensing to assist in emergency management tasks
▲ Use weather stations to track weather patterns and the progress of natural disasters such as hurricanes
▲ Compare and contrast different types of water sensors
▲ Examine what hazards can be detected with the use of air data sensors
▲ Analyze what qualities are needed in direct sensing technology tools
▲ Analyze how remote sensing can be used in response to disasters
▲ Analyze what information is available through the use of satellite imagery
▲ Examine how imaging radar works
▲ Analyze the trends in technology and their impact on emergency management

Goals and Outcomes

▲ Assess data obtained from direct sensing
▲ Evaluate where to place different weather stations in a community in order to receive relevant data for the community
▲ Assess what type of water sensors to use and where to place them in a community in order to best predict flooding
▲ Evaluate the usefulness of air data sensors in determining if a chemical or biological attack has occurred
▲ Choose the types of sensors and evaluate where they should be placed within a community
▲ Evaluate information obtained from satellite and radar imaging
▲ Compare and contrast direct and remote sensing
▲ Assess how access to real-time response data affects emergency management tasks

INTRODUCTION

Before you can evacuate a community or adequately mitigate a hazard, you must know that disaster is about to strike. While you can't predict or detect every disaster, you can use sensors to identify vulnerable areas and study trends. With sensors, you can monitor the air, weather conditions, and water at all times. You can detect hazards directly by using tools such as stream gages, and you can detect them remotely through the use of tools such as satellites. In this chapter you will determine what kind of data direct sensing can provide you through weather, air, and water sensors. You will examine how you can use this data in all phases of emergency management, including planning, response, recovery, and mitigation. You will then assess remote sensing and compare it to direct sensing. You will examine remote sensing tools and images and learn how remote sensing can help you in emergency management tasks. Throughout the discussions of direct and remote sensing, you will be presented with real-world scenarios and applications of the technology. This chapter ends with an examination of the trends affecting direct and remote sensing.

5.1 Direct Sensing and Data

Communities vary in their vulnerability to different hazards. An important part of your job is to prepare for the hazards that threaten your community. To do this you must determine what is the biggest threat to your community, and you must monitor the hazards. There are many useful sources of information that are available to you.

Collecting data is critical in emergency planning, response, recovery, and mitigation efforts. Data involves facts that are known. Data is used as a basis for discussion, decision making, calculating, or measuring. For example, one piece of data might be the elevation of a school that is used as a shelter in a community subjected to frequent heavy rains. When data is processed or used in some form of analysis, it can be converted into information. For example, a small community might have six schools constructed or remodeled between 1959 and 1992. When each school is assessed, only four may be suitable as a shelter in a hurricane. Factors such as type of construction, nature and location of windows, type of roof, and the location of the site can be used as shelter-selection criteria. Specific facts or data about each school are assessed to determine if they are suitable as a disaster shelter. The suitable shelters are chosen based on processed data and therefore fall into the concept of information.

Data relating to the actual or potential disaster allows you to understand the hazard. The data also allows you to determine what, if any, steps you can take to reduce losses. You can also use real data as an input to simulate potential disasters. You can simulate floods, hurricane storm surges, earthquakes, or wind. Collecting and using local weather conditions in models allows you to simulate disaster conditions. These simulation models use specific local data. This data includes information on weather conditions, physical terrain, or physical structures.

Data can be obtained by direct contact with the environment as in the case of a **weather station**. A weather station is a sensor that collects information on the temperature, precipitation, wind direction and movement, barometric pressure, and humidity by way of direct contact with the phenomena. Data can also be obtained indirectly or remotely. For example, this can be done with satellites. Methods of collecting data have changed greatly over time because of developments in technology. Today, computerized sensors allow us to see more clearly from the ground, from aircraft, and from satellites. The sensors also allow us to understand the nature of the environment, including winds, soil types and moisture content, water movement, or vegetation type. You can use the information from the direct sensing for emergency planning, response, recovery, or mitigation. Below is an explanation of the role data plays in the phases of emergency managemet.

▲ **Planning:** Data identifies areas that are more vulnerable than others to different types of hazards.

▲ **Response:** Data provides a basis for decisions involving warning for emergencies. Data provides a basis for decisions involving the selection of evacuation routes and shelters.

▲ **Recovery:** Data provides accurate information on the extent of damage in a disaster. Data collected from weather stations, chemical sensors, or stream gage stations identify the high-priority areas affected by the flood. The data-collection stations provide a basis for identifying the areas most affected by the event and in directing responders to areas most impacted by the disaster. In the past, response operational decisions were based on personal observations of emergency management personnel making actual observations in the event. With direct and remote sensing capabilities, you can direct response personnel to critical parts of the disaster without waiting for personal observation of responders.

FOR EXAMPLE

Flooding and Direct Sensing

You can use direct sensing to determine how to mitigate disasters. In the example of flooding, you can use gages to determine the water level of any nearby bodies of water and the level of rainfall. If the readings are high, you may be able to take steps to prevent widespread flooding. For example, you may be able to sandbag an area to prevent flooding.

▲ **Mitigation:** Data identifies the actual impact of a flood, fire, or wind damage. Data collected by the Red Cross provides the basis for determining recovery resources that will be needed by the community in recovery.

SELF-CHECK

- Define **weather station**.
- How has collecting data changed over time, and why has it changed?
- How can data be used to aid in the recovery of a community after a disaster?

5.2 Weather Stations

One of the most common applications of direct sensing is the use of weather stations. Weather stations are one of the key elements in predicting weather patterns. Weather stations help us understand hazardous conditions and have been in use in one form or another since the 1800s. In the early 1800s, temperature was the most common data recorded. By the mid-1800s, weather observations included precipitation, temperature, cloud cover, cloud movement, wind direction, barometric pressure, and humidity. This information came from rudimentary gages and personal observations. These observations were handwritten in logbooks. We now have over 20,000 weather stations that collect, store, and communicate data. Today we have sophisticated gages and data loggers that automatically record the information in digital form for use in our computers. Weather stations typically have the following instruments:

▲ Temperature gages
▲ Barometer gages
▲ Hygrometer for measuring humidity
▲ Anemometer for measuring wind speed and direction
▲ Rain gages for measuring precipitation

There are additional sensors that can be added:

▲ Solar radiation sensors
▲ Snow-depth ultrasonic distance sensors
▲ Soil-moisture sensors

Figure 5-1

The National Oceanic and Atmospheric Administration (NOAA) provides weather data and forecasts for locations throughout the United States.

Manufacturers produce rugged, small-scale, precision data loggers; data acquisition and control systems; and sensors for environmental measurements that are powered by batteries, solar panels, generators, or other sources of electricity. Many companies manufacture meteorological measurement stations. The sensor is the device that measures by direct contact with the environment's air temperature, wind speed, or water level. The reading is then sent to a data logger. The data logger translates the information into digital form that can be saved in a database format. It could also be transferred using landlines to other computers or through telecommunication connections to other sites. The data logger processes the data and can be programmed to store only the information needed. The vendor can help the user choose a system that is customized to provide data in the emergency management information system. Many weather station products are operable down to −55 degrees C. They have minimal power requirements, allowing use in inhospitable environments. In addition, data loggers store data in a memory, which provides a reliable backup even if primary power supplies fail. The direct sensing systems are also capable of transmitting the data directly over phone lines, by radio or microwave signal, or by satellite. Much of the data used by the National Weather Service (NWS) comes from direct sensors. **Direct sensors** are gages and instruments that are in direct contact with phenomena that provide information.

Ski areas, public works agencies, transportation departments, and forestry offices commonly use weather stations equipped with snow-depth sensors for avalanche prediction. Data loggers have also been linked to GPS receivers to record position on Earth's surface.

5.2.1 Data from Outside Weather Stations

In addition to monitoring your community's weather stations, you can access weather information for hundreds of other locations. You may need to track weather patterns in other states. For example, a hurricane can make landfall in several states days apart. You will need to track the progress of the hurricane to determine if your community will be affected. Communities across the country send information to the NWS at regular intervals. The NWS provides weather, hydrologic forecasts, and warnings. With a $700 million annual budget, the NWS collects data in a variety of ways. The data can be used by anyone. Their weather storm warnings provide an excellent example of identifying potential hazards, developing a classification system, and implementing a public notification system. The warning system focuses on flood, tornado, earthquake, and hurricane hazards.

The Emergency Managers Weather Information Network (EMWIN) radio broadcast is used by the NWS and other public and private agencies for disseminating the EMWIN data stream. To receive an EMWIN radio broadcast, hardware and software is needed (for additional information visit www.nws.noaa. gov/oso/oso1/oso12/document/wintip.htm).

5.2.2 Remote Automated Weather Station (RAWS)

Remote automated weather station (RAWS) is a network of weather stations run by the U.S. Forest Service and Bureau of Land Management and is monitored by the National Interagency Fire Center. Most of the RAWS are used to predict fire behavior and monitor fuels. There are 1,500 RAWS in the United States, and they are placed in locations where wild land fires often occur. They collect and store information every 10 minutes, and the data is usually transmitted every hour. However, the units can be programmed to transmit the information anywhere from every half hour to many hours. A geostational operational environmental satellite (GOES) that is operated by National Oceanic and Atmospheric Administration (NOAA) transmits the data to the National Interagency Fire Center (NIFC) in Boise, Idaho. Once the data is received, it is automatically forwarded to other computer systems, including the Weather Information Management System (WIMS) and the Western Regional Climate Center in Reno, Nevada. Each station runs on 8 to 10 watts of power. The battery lasts 3 years and is charged by a solar panel.

Weather is the most important factor in wildfires. Weather plays a role in the destructive force of the wildfire through wind direction, wind speed, and dryness. It also plays a critical role in firefighter safety. RAWS allows you to program parameters for indicators such as wind shifts, humidity changes, or sudden temperature changes. When one of these elements reaches a predetermined crisis level, RAWS can send out a tone to alert firefighters.

Once wildfires have caused loss of ground cover and vegetation, that area is more susceptible to landslides. RAWS can then be set up in those areas or reprogrammed to monitor the amount of rainfall in a given period of time. There are also 40 portable RAWS that can be deployed across the country.

FOR EXAMPLE

Other Uses for RAWS

RAWS can also be set and used to detect hazardous chemicals. There are currently stations set up in various locations to monitor hazardous material levels. A standard RAWS unit costs $12,000.

5.2.3 Case Study: GeoMAC

Often, two or more different types of technology work together and produce powerful results. GeoMAC, short for Geospatial Multi-agency Coordination, is an example of this. After a terrible fire season where 8.4 million acres burned, resulting in over $1 billion in damages, the Great Basin fire coordinators put in a request to build GeoMAC. Developed by Environmental Systems Research Institute (ESRI), GeoMAC is a multilayered GIS system that maps fire conditions against different variables such as weather forecasts, topography, and population centers. The application links GIS technology to the Internet and uses remote sensing data from remote automated weather stations to provide firefighters scattered over vast distances with real-time information on which to base their decisions. These layers of information that include weather variables, population information, and road and infrastructure information allow the emergency management officials to rank fires in terms of the risk they pose and to allocate resources accordingly. All of this information was posted on the Web in real time. ESRI also created a duplicate Web site that could be viewed by the public. This allows the public to track the events and take protective action if necessary. In 2001, GeoMAC's coverage extended from east of the Rocky Mountains all the way to the Pacific Ocean (Wait, P. 2001).

SELF-CHECK

- Define **direct sensor.**
- Define **remote automated weather stations (RAWS)** and give two examples of how they are used.
- What types of instruments do typical weather stations have?

5.3 Water Data Sensors

In an average year, flood damages approach $4 billion. In 2005, however, with flooding caused by Hurricane Katrina, over $200 billion was needed to rebuild the affected Gulf Coast areas. As flooding continues to do damage, communities are constantly looking for ways to mitigate flood losses.

5.3.1 Local Flood Warning Systems

Local flood warning systems are an attractive solution because they are a low-cost way to monitor the water levels. Local flood warning systems detect the amount of water in a specific area and then communicate this information with the local emergency management agency (LEMA). The data is also transmitted to the NWS. The NWS has taken the lead in the development of these systems in cooperation with state and local disaster and emergency services agencies and the U.S. Army Corps of Engineers and FEMA.

The design of local flood warning systems must include instruments that are able to do the following:

▲ Measure and detect water levels
▲ Transmit data
▲ Process and analyze data
▲ Forecast preparation
▲ Forecast dissemination

When the water in a rain or stream gage reaches a predetermined level, a page is sent. Each community may use slightly different equipment. Nevertheless, here is an example of what occurs before a page is sent out.

1. Emergency managers and local officials determine where to place the rain gages. Stream gages are placed in the streams and use a sensor to determine the water depth. Water depth is also referred to as stage. Rain gages use tipping buckets. The depth of the water is recorded and reported.

2. After the water reaches a predetermined depth, the information is transmitted through a VHF radio signal to a repeater site. A repeater is a device that receives communications and amplifies them before sending them out.

3. Two **base stations** receive the information from the repeater. The base station is the final destination for the information from the sensors. The base stations have a decoder to interpret the information. A page is sent to emergency management and utility personnel. Users can also access

the data from Web pages or by using a laptop and dialing in to their station. The information is also sent to the NWS.

There are many communication systems a local flood warning system can use. Systems can use VHF or UHF radio, microwave, satellite, dedicated leased telephone lines, or a combination. The following are some of the more common communications elements:

▲ **Event-reporting sensors:** The sensors are programmed with prerecorded measurements. For example, you may want to only be paged when water depth reaches 2 inches. The sensors then trigger the transmission of signals when the water reaches 2 inches.

▲ **Single-frequency repeater:** The repeater increases the transmission range of event-reporting sensors. Once the repeater received an incoming signal, it regenerates it, amplifies it, and transmits it to a base station.

▲ **Base station:** Data from the repeater is sent to the base station microcomputer. The computer accepts the report, processes it, displays the information, and forwards it to the appropriate computers and personnel. A page is sent. Users can also access the data from Web pages or by using a laptop and dialing in to their station. The information is also sent to the NWS.

5.3.2 Rain and Stream Gages

The first step is to determine where to place the rain and stream gages. The more gages you have, the better the chances of detecting flood-producing rainfall. The number of gages needed depend on the local area. For example, to accurately measure rainfall over a basin, mountainous areas will require more gages than flat lands. The following table suggests the minimum number of gages per river basin area (in square miles):

Table 5-1 Number of Gages per River Basin Area

Number of Rain Gages	River Basin Area (Square Miles)
3	<40
4	100
6	400
8	1,000

Rain gages should be located on ground level and away from obstructions such as trees and buildings. Trees and buildings may cause turbulence and affect the accuracy of the measurements. The gage should be located in an area where it is protected in all directions.

Stream gages measure the stream. In small streams, stream-flow observations trigger alarms when flooding is about to happen or is happening. The location of the stream gages should be based either at the point where flooding would require public notification or where you need information for forecast models. Gages used for alarms should be located at key vulnerable areas that are far enough upstream that you have time to warn downstream inhabitants and locations.

5.3.3 United States Geological Surves (USGS) Stream-Gaging Program

We have seen how local communities use stream gages to monitor their water levels. The USGS has a stream-gaging program that collects this information from stream gages across the country. Data from over half of the 7,292 stations are linked by an earth-satellite-based communications system. This data is available in real time for many agencies to conduct water-resources projects and for the National Weather Service (NWS) to forecast floods. Data from the active stations, as well as from discontinued stations, are stored in a computer database that currently holds mean daily-discharge data for about 18,500 locations and more than 400,000 station years of record. Additional data are added to the database each year. The stream-discharge database is an ever-growing resource for water-resources planning and design, hydrologic research, and operation of water-resources projects.

Funding technology such as the USGS river gages is expensive. The USGS has effectively established relationships with other governmental and private agencies to fund the gage stations. By joining USGS in installing a river gage station, public and private organizations gain access to the desired technology for their operations. Just as the network of stations represents an aggregation, so does the program funding. Operating funds for individual stations in the program may come from a blend of federal funds appropriated to the USGS, funds from state and local agencies, and funds appropriated to other federal agencies. Federal funds are allocated to the USGS for matching state or local agency offerings under the USGS Federal-State Cooperative Program (herein referred to as the Cooperative Program).

More than 50% of the 7,292 stations operated by the USGS are funded through the Cooperative Program. Under that program, the USGS provides up to 50% of the funds, and the state or local agency provides the remainder. Currently, more than 600 state and local agencies participate in the stream-gaging program. The other stations in the program are operated by the USGS. Federal agencies fund these stations. For example, the U.S. Army Corps of Engineers (COE) and the Bureau of Reclamation (BOR) fund the stations. In return, the agencies are provided with the hydrologic data needed for planning and operating water-resources projects. Less than 10% of the stations the USGS operates are fully funded by the USGS.

The USGS stream-gaging program provides hydrologic information needed to help define, use, and manage the nation's water resources. The program provides a continuous, well-documented, well-archived, unbiased, and broad-based source of reliable and consistent water data. Because of the nationally consistent, prescribed standards by which the data are collected and processed, the data from individual stations are commonly used for purposes beyond the original purpose for an individual station. Those possible uses include the following:

▲ Enhancing the public safety by providing data for forecasting and managing floods.
▲ Characterizing current water-quality conditions.
▲ Determining input rates of various pollutants into lakes, reservoirs, or estuaries.
▲ Delineating and managing floodplains.
▲ Setting permit requirements for discharge of treated wastewater.
▲ Designing highway bridges and culverts.
▲ Setting minimum flow requirements for meeting aquatic life goals.
▲ Monitoring compliance with minimum flow requirements.
▲ Developing or operating recreation facilities.
▲ Scheduling power production.
▲ Designing, operating, and maintaining navigation facilities.
▲ Allocating water for municipal, industrial, and irrigation uses.
▲ Administering compacts or resolving conflicts on interstate rivers.
▲ Undertaking scientific studies of long-term changes in the hydrologic cycle.

Data for one or more of these purposes is needed at some point on virtually every stream in the country. With this data, stream flow can be estimated. Estimates and data are needed for both immediate decision making, in the case of flooding, and for future project designs. For example, data and estimates are needed for bridge or reservoir development. A station that supplies data for flood forecasting also provides information that defines long-term trends.

FOR EXAMPLE

USGS Support

The USGS can move staff to any disaster area. During the 1993 Mississippi River floods, USGS field personnel made more than 2,000 visits to stations in the flood-affected areas. They verified that the instruments were working properly. They made repairs as needed. They took direct measurements of the stream flow. Data from these stations were provided continuously to the National Weather Service (NWS) and the Army Corps of Engineers and formed the basis for flood forecasts that allowed people to be evacuated. The Army Corps of Engineers and local agencies used the stream-flow information to protect lives and property and to focus flood-fighting activities where they were most needed.

5.3.4 Using the Stream-Flow Data for Emergency Management

Stream-flow data is needed at many sites on a daily basis. It is needed for forecasting flow extremes, making water-management decisions, assessing current water availability, managing water quality, and meeting legal requirements. These activities require stream-flow information at a given location for a specified time. Operating a station to produce a continuous record of flow best satisfies these needs. The locations of the stations and the periods of operation are dependent on how the data will be used.

More than one-half of the USGS stations provide current information (mostly by way of satellite telemetry) to agencies that operate water-resource systems and forecast floods. The NWS is charged by law with the responsibility of issuing forecasts and flood warnings to help save lives and to help mitigate property damage. The NWS uses data from USGS stations to forecast river stages and flow conditions on large rivers and their associated tributaries. Flood forecasts are issued at about 4,000 locations. These locations are strategically located throughout the nation. The reliability of flood forecasts depends on having reliable current data for precipitation and stream flow. The USGS collects the stream-flow data, and the NWS collects the precipitation data and combines both types of data when making the flood forecasts.

The USGS stream-gaging network is vital. It is vital to the NWS river forecast and warning program. It is vital to the goal to reduce flood damages and loss of life. Without data from this network, this nation would experience increased losses of both life and property. As a national organization, the USGS can move staff from other offices into the disaster areas. Because these hydrologists and technicians were already familiar with the equipment and procedures, they could begin to work immediately upon arrival. This same experience with the real-time use of USGS stream-flow data is repeated several times each year as catastrophic floods strike.

SELF-CHECK

- Define **base station.**
- What steps occur when a rain or stream gage reaches a predetermined level?
- How does an emergency manager determine how many rain gages are needed?
- USGS stream gages provide the public access to water-level information. How could the emergency manager use this information?

5.4 Air Data Sensors

Air sensors could be used for different purposes. Air sensors can determine the quality of the air and the amount of pollution. Sensors can detect a spill of hazardous industrial chemicals in manufacturing plants and alert management and workers. Air sensors can also react to chemical, nuclear, and biological weapons, which are becoming increasingly important during the current fight against terrorism.

5.4.1 Air Sensors and Air Quality

Since the Clean Act became law in 1970, the EPA has used a coordinated system to monitor air quality. The system is a network of thousands of individual air-monitoring stations located across the United States. There are currently 4,000 monitoring stations in the country. These stations collect data on the six key air pollutants:

- ▲ Lead
- ▲ Carbon monoxide
- ▲ Particles
- ▲ Sulfur dioxide
- ▲ Nitrogen dioxide
- ▲ Ground-level ozone (also known as smog)

The EPA also monitors toxic pollutants that cause cancer in key areas of the country that are most vulnerable to these hazards. Monitoring the air has led to better air quality. For example, monitored levels of lead have dropped 98% over the past 20 years.

The EPA plays a big role during disasters as well. For example, the devastation of Hurricane Katrina also had an impact of the air quality in New Orleans and the surrounding areas. The EPA monitored the air quality to determine how to clean up the sites and when it would be safe for the displaced residents to return home. To do this, the EPA used several different methods of gathering data including:

▲ **Fixed site monitors:** These are set up in hurricane-impacted areas, and they continuously monitor fine particle levels.

▲ **Particle pollution measurements:** These are small portable instruments (DataRAM nephelometers) and can be moved daily. They are battery-powered and provide immediate readings. The readouts provide a measure of inhalable particles.

▲ **ASPECT (Airborne Spectral Photometric Collection Technology):** Remote-sensing aircraft known to locate chemical spills that need emergency response. This is done to protect both water and air quality. Data from ASPECT is forwarded to ground-level personnel who evaluate the date and request follow-up monitoring if needed.

▲ **TAGA (Trace Atmospheric Gas Analyzer):** Mobile labs that are buses. The labs gather samples and analyze them for industrial chemicals, including those commonly found in gasoline, such as benzene, toluene, and xylene.

5.4.2 Chemical Sensors

In addition to pollution that comes from everyday chemicals, toxic chemicals and hazardous materials also pose a threat. Chemical sensors can be installed in manufacturing facilities that detect toxic chemicals. The sensor system can be set up so alarms will go off once chemicals have reached a predetermined level. Sensors can also be handheld and portable. Many of the sensors work by using optics. The sensors pass laser beams through the air and detect the chemical signature of the material released. This type of sensor is known as an *active sensor*. These are passive sensors and can pick up on the chemicals' unique pattern of radiation emissions without using lasers. These sensors, however, can only be used when the distance between the sensor and the chemical is short.

You will need to work with your business community to determine which industries and facilities produce hazardous chemicals. You will also need to know the type of chemical produced and the toxicity of the chemical. You must then consider if you only need chemical sensors in the industry for the safety of the employees or if there could be a chemical spill that would affect the community.

5.4.3 Using Air Data Sensors in Cases of Terrorism

The threat of terrorists using chemical, nuclear, or biological weapons has caused several cities to install **remote sensors** in strategic locations. Remote sensors are instruments or gages that can detect phenomena that are not in direct contact with the sensor. Washington, D.C., and New York City in particular are some of the most vulnerable cities in the world. They were targeted in the 9/11 attacks, New York City as a financial capital and Washington, D.C., as a government capital.

Throughout the world, the transportation system is vulnerable to attack. In 1995, the Aum Shrinkyo cult released the toxin sarin on the subway. In 2004, terrorists detonated bombs on the trains in Madrid, Spain, killing close to 200 people and wounding over 1,000. In 2005, terrorists detonated bombs in the London subways, killing 38 and injuring 700.

As a result of these events and the attacks on 9/11, the Washington, D.C., and New York subways have been equipped with sensors. The chemical sensors can immediately detect and identify toxins. However, it takes 2 to 3 hours for the sensors to detect biological agents. Sensors are also placed in Times Square in New York and are frequently checked and constantly monitored. In addition to the subways in Washington, D.C., 20 sensor packages have been placed in the city. The sensors were placed on rooftops, at street level, and on cell phone towers (Munses, F. 2003). Along with the sensors, a communications network was installed. The detection system uses wireless and satellite communications to quickly relay data to first responders. The goal is to have information to responders within 5 minutes of detection.

CNN reported in 2002 that the government has also deployed nuclear sensors around the country that would detect nuclear and radiological sensors. The government has not confirmed or denied this (CNN, 2002).

You will need to determine if terrorism is likely in your community. If it is, you must determine the most vulnerable points before installing sensors. Perhaps the transportation system in your city is vulnerable, or you may have a landmark or monument that is the site of large gatherings. Terrorists might target this site. Hazardous material may be transported through your community. If so, consider installing sensors at key points along the tracks to detect any spill or leak.

FOR EXAMPLE

False Alarm

Chemical sensors can set off false alarms. The subway system in Washington, D.C., was closed for several hours when a false alarm was triggered by cleaning solutions.

SELF-CHECK

- Define **remote sensors** and provide an example of a remote sensor.
- Give an example of where a chemical sensor could be deployed to mitigate an intentional release of a hazardous chemical.
- Chemical sensors can be deployed in an emergency response to a hazardous substance. Provide an example of an accidental release where responders could have used portable chemical sensors.
- What are TAGA and ASPECT and how they are used?

5.5 Evaluating the Technology

You are often faced with choosing technology systems to support operations. A means of evaluating the systems must be in place in order to select an appropriate technology application for operation needs. The following provides a basis for evaluating the technology. These criteria can be used in evaluating a direct sensing technology such as a portable weather system. However, the criteria offered here fit many different technologies in emergency management.

▲ **System flexibility:** Once the system is designed, is it possible to make changes in an easy manner and in a timely basis? Can changes in the type and nature of data be made without totally replacing the sensor? Can alternative communication technology be used without major changes and again replacing the technology?

▲ **Interoperable systems:** Most industry efforts are targeted to the commercial market and are focused on providing a communications infrastructure whose underlying organization is static (placement of routers and sites as hosts). Current systems are designed to carry anticipated loads and provide security. Communication patterns in times of crisis may be unpredictable. It may be impossible to establish and maintain a static routing structure since the host and units are inherently unstable. A self-organizing system may need to be designed.

▲ **Security:** Direct sensing data systems are often in an open environment and subject to tampering by the public. An example is the river-gage system operated by the Corps of Engineers. These units are often found on bridges in public view and easily accessible to anyone. The only security is a simple locking system. Are these direct sensing systems able to communicate data frequently so that if tampering is determined, the data collected is not sacrificed?

▲ **Lack of current relevant information on technology:** A key factor in selecting a data-collection system is the use of current technology. You can examine whether the system is using the most current communication technology and can thus take advantage of current digital transfer technology (wireless communication) and use of direct record communication rather than having to reenter the data after collecting the information from the sensor.

▲ **Financial constraints:** The current weather stations are an example of systems that are reasonably priced, easy to install and maintain, and reliable over a long period.

▲ **Collaboration with other agencies:** Can the system be sponsored by multiple federal, state, and local agencies; educational institutions; and private companies or not-for-profit agencies and therefore be more useful to a wider user group? Many weather stations are located on college campuses and are supported jointly by public agencies and private companies. In some cases, the direct sensing system is collecting information that cannot

---

FOR EXAMPLE

The Value of Real-Time Data

You can have real-time access to sensors through the Internet. This provides you with access to chemical emissions, weather, or flood data. Access to accurate data in a timely manner is essential to understanding the nature and extent of an incident. Public agencies such as the EPA, the USGS, and weather data from the NWS are moving to provide immediate access to information through the Internet.

Field-deployed direct sensors provide you with essential information that might not be available in a disaster. An emergency operations center could have backup power. However, the Internet might not be available during a disaster. Access to the data in a disaster becomes an important consideration.

be shared with other agencies without significant oversight by the sponsoring agency. Collaboration may be inhibited because some state or local agencies may be subject to significant legal and programmatic restrictions and thus unable to share their data with other public bodies.

SELF-CHECK

- What criteria should an emergency manager use when choosing technology? Why?
- A local company has agreed to support the local deployment and ongoing costs for a sensor. Provide an example of a sensor that could be deployed in your community and how it would enhance emergency management.
- Sensors seem costly, very technical, and could easily go out of date. Who could you contact to help answer questions about deploying and operating this ever-changing technology?

5.6 Remote Sensing

You have both direct and remote sensing at your disposal. Data can be obtained directly as in the case of a weather station or a stream gage. Data can also be obtained indirectly as in the case of an aerial photograph, weather radar, or satellite images. The means of collecting the data both directly and remotely have changed due to technology. Remote sensing is the acquisition of information from a great distance. The use of satellites to detect weather patterns is an example of remote sensing. Remote sensing is the collection of data using methods where the sensor is not in direct physical contact with the phenomena. Remote sensing data is critical to the successful modeling and monitoring of many natural processes. These include watershed runoff, weather simulations, land use, and chemical dispersions.

Remote sensing provides either a visualization of the event for operational uses or from a historical perspective for emergency planning, recovery, or mitigation uses. High-resolution photos can show the impacts of flooding, or an infrared image can reveal areas affected by a wildfire or flood. Combined with the image, remote sensing may also provide data to develop a weather forecast or as input in a storm-simulation model. Hurricane models use data collected by remote sensors as inputs into a simulation of the event.

Remote sensing also has a role in emergency response and recovery. Images collected by remote sensors provide real-time observations of the event as it occurs.

FOR EXAMPLE

Remote Sensing Uses in Agriculture

Remote sensing is also used in agriculture. Remote sensing data is used to schedule irrigation. The data can be used to assess plant disease. The data can also be used in modeling plant growth and crop yield and in measuring environmental stresses. Some remote sensing devices are placed on aircraft or satellites in order to monitor agricultural resources over large regions. Other remote sensing devices can be handheld or mounted on a tractor to monitor small field plots. Remote sensing has been used to forecast crop production, making it possible to plan the amount of labor, fuel, and transportation needed for harvest and distribution. Remote sensing can also be applied to developing good livestock-management techniques.

Satellite images are used in a routine manner by the NWS to show weather patterns and as a basis for weather predictions. Satellite images have also been used in floods along the Mississippi, Red, and Missouri Rivers to show areas inundated by heavy rains. Frequently, decisions regarding what communities should be evacuated and routes to be used have to be made. These decisions can be enhanced by the use of satellite photos, radar, and infrared images.

State and local governments are placing an increasing emphasis on mitigation initiatives to reduce the adverse effects of disasters. Governmental agencies use **radar images** collected by satellites to target flood-prone areas. Satellites that use radar are not affected by cloud cover. They can be used to collect data at night and during the most adverse conditions. Radar also clearly distinguishes areas underwater, as well as smoke from fires and the fire's location.

Computerized sensors allow us to see more clearly than ever before from aircraft as well as from satellites. The sensors also allow us to understand the nature of the natural environment relating to winds, soil types, terrain, water movement, or vegetation.

SELF-CHECK

- What is the difference between direct and remote sensing?
- How can remote sensing be used for agricultural purposes?
- Give two examples of how remote sensing can be used in emergency management.

5.7 Satellites

Remote sensing is the gathering of information about Earth from a distance. This can be done from a few meters off the Earth's surface, by an aircraft flying hundreds to thousands of meters above the surface, or by a satellite orbiting hundreds of kilometers above Earth. Airborne remote sensing systems are the most flexible sources of data. Both aircraft and satellites have the capacity to provide you with detailed information.

Satellites have made enormous contributions to regional and global geophysical surveys. Satellite remote sensing, or earth observation, is the use of data from satellite and airborne sensors for the monitoring and management of the environment. Satellite remote sensing is the largest single source of digital spatial data. The attraction of remote sensing data includes its timeliness; potential for uniformity of data formats; and compatibility with many databases and statistical, imaging, and GIS programs. Satellites may be equipped with photographic or nonphotographic sensing devices.

5.7.1 NOAA GOES Satellite

Operating the country's system of environmental satellites is one of the major responsibilities of NOAA. NOAA operates the satellites and manages the processing and distribution of the millions of bits of data and images. The primary customer is NWS, which uses satellite data to create forecasts for the public, television, radio, and weather advisory services.

NOAA's operational weather satellite system is composed of two types of satellites. There is Geostationary Operational Environmental Satellites (GOES) for short-range warning, and there is polar-orbiting satellites for longer-term forecasting. Both satellite systems are necessary for providing a complete global weather monitoring system.

The **GOES satellite** is an airborne remote sensing system that revolves in a fixed spot off Earth's surface and collects continuous observations relating to cloud cover, atmospheric temperature, and moisture in the air. The GOES system provides continuous, dependable, timely and high-quality observations of Earth. The instruments aboard the satellites measure the emitted and reflected radiation of Earth. This helps determine the amount of cloud cover, atmospheric temperature, and moisture in the air. The satellite is a high-altitude satellite that is placed in an orbit above the Earth and set in motion that is parallel to Earth's rotation. Its velocity thus matches that of Earth and it remains above Earth at a fixed point on the surface. The satellite can monitor an entire hemisphere all the time. It can transmit directly to any point on that hemisphere. This type of satellite is especially useful for climatic observations. However, the resolution of the image is coarse since the satellite is at a great distance from Earth.

Figure 5-2

Images from Ft. Collins flash flooding.

You can use GOES images to monitor the intensity of storms, to show the path of a major storm, and to identify the areas that may be affected by a weather pattern. GOES satellites stay above a fixed spot on the surface. Because of this, they provide a constant vigil for the atmospheric triggers for severe weather conditions. Severe weather conditions include tornadoes, flash floods, hail storms, and hurricanes. When these conditions develop, the GOES satellites are able to monitor storm development and track their movements. State and local emergency management agencies use images from the GOES satellite to track the path of hurricanes. Agencies track their potential impact on local communities.

You can use GOES satellite imagery to estimate rainfall during thunderstorms and hurricanes for flash-flood warnings. GOES imagery is also used to estimate snowfall accumulations and overall extent of snow cover. Such data help meteorologists issue winter storm warnings and advisories. Satellite sensors also detect ice fields and map the movements of sea and lake ice. The data from GOES is also used as an input into NWS forecasting and hurricane modeling.

Figure 5-3

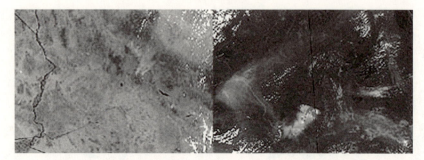

MODIS images showing fires in Arizona and Alaska
(www.nasa.gov/audience/forstudents/postsecondary/features/F_In_Line_Of_Fire.html).

The flooding in Fort Collins, Colorado, in the summer of 1997 caused extensive damage to the community (see Figure 5-2). The storms were viewed on GOES satellites prior to the storm. The following image shows the storm in the Fort Collins area. These images were available to emergency managers and used by weather service personnel to provide warnings to the community.

5.7.2 Polar Orbiting Satellites

Complementing the geostationary satellites are polar-orbiting satellites such as the MODIS (Moderate Resolution Imaging Spectroradiometer). **Polar-orbiting satellites** are airborne remote sensing systems that collect continuous observations such as data transmitted from Earth; high-resolution photos of Earth; images such as cloud cover, smoke, haze, or a storm's path on a specific orbit over the poles. MODIS has been operational since 1999. MODIS has allowed the U.S. Forest Service to keep track of fire activity even as heavy smoke obstructed the view from reconnaissance planes. NASA collaborated with the University of Maryland and the Forest Service to develop a system that generates fire maps within a few hours, and in some cases within minutes, after a satellite overpass (see Figure 5-3).

Figure 5-4 shows a modis image of Hurricane Katrina as it approaches Louisiana and Mississippi on August 28, 2005. Federal, state, and local emergency managers used this image and other similar images of Katrina to understand the vulnerability of coastal communities as the storm approached landfall. The extremely large size of the storm and the areas that would be impacted are clearly shown in the image.

These satellites circle Earth in an almost north–south orbit, passing close to both poles. The orbits are circular and are sun synchronous. Operating as a pair, these satellites ensure that data for any region of the Earth are no more than 6 hours old. A suite of instruments measures many parameters of Earth's

Figure 5-4

MODIS satellite image showing Hurricane Katrina off the Gulf of Mexico
on August 28, 2005.

atmosphere and its surface and cloud cover. As a part of the mission, the satellites
can receive, process, and transmit data from the following:

▲ Search-and-rescue beacon transmitters
▲ Automatic data collection platforms on land ocean buoys
▲ Free-floating weather balloons

The primary instrument aboard the satellite is the advanced very high resolution
radiometer (AVHRR). An AVHRR detects Earth's radiation and can be used for
determining both cloud cover over the earth and the surface temperature.
Figure 5-5 provides an illustration of an AVHRR.

The AVHRR satellite has provided excellent data to both detect and
describe hurricanes. The Southern Regional Climate Center and the Earth Scan
Laboratory at Louisiana State University (LSU) provided images of Hurricane
Andrew as it approached coastal Louisiana. The university researchers in these
units provided timely consultation to support sheltering and evacuation decisions.

Figure 5-5

An advanced very high resolution radiometer (AVHRR).

State of Louisiana officials recognized the value of access to the remote sensing images. The LSU research units continued to provide on site-support to state and local emergency management officials. You can use the images from the AVHRR to:

▲ observe land surface types;
▲ analyze the cloud cover and Earth's surface;
▲ detect smoke and haze;
▲ discriminate between ice and water clouds.

An AVHRR image of Hurricane Andrew can be seen in Figure 5-6.

5.7.3 Landsat

The **Landsat** is a remote sensing satellite program developed by NASA. The first Landsat in a series of seven was developed in the 1970s. It was responsible for opening the new field of remote sensing. The Landsat program is the longest-running enterprise for acquisition of digital imagery of Earth from space. The first Landsat satellite was launched in 1972. The latest Landsat 7 was launched in 1999. The practical applications of this program are far-reaching. Landsat makes it possible to check the health of the Earth. The practical applications include, but are not limited to, the following:

▲ Forecasting agricultural crops accurately
▲ Selecting locations for new power plants that are environmentally safe
▲ Determining the best routes for oil and gas pipelines

Figure 5-6

AVHRR image of Hurricane Andrew on August 25, 1992.

▲ Monitoring pollution
▲ Aiding emergency management in assessing flood damage and plan disaster relief
▲ Determining ice-free shipping routes
▲ Helping urban planners evaluate urban growth

The overall goal of the Landsat program is to provide scientists with a better understanding of natural environmental changes. The images are a unique resource and are archived in the United States and at Landsat receiving stations around the world.

The image of New Orleans in Figure 5-7 provides a broad picture of the metropolitan area prior to the landfall of Hurricane Katrina and after Katrina passed the New Orleans area. Emergency managers used these images in planning,

Figure 5-7

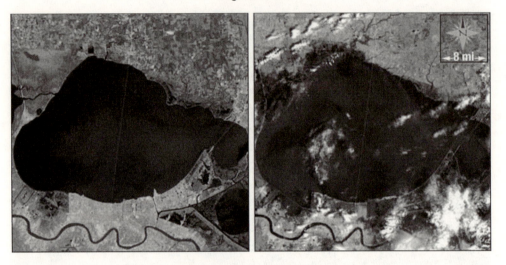

Landsat images of New Orleans.

response, recovery, and mitigation efforts. Local GIS data layers were used with this image for response efforts.

Streets and water features as well as county boundaries may be displayed on Figure 5-7 to show broad relationships. In many cases, the manager needs to show large geographic areas and key points such as interstate highways, rail lines, airports, or waterways. These images are not suitable for close examination of city blocks or buildings. However, they are well suited to show the path of a storm and areas impacted.

5.7.4 Case Example: Long-Term Monitoring of Environmental Change

The three images of the Salt Lake area show the dramatic effects of the Great Salt Lake's high levels in the 1980s. Figure 5-8 shows the Great Salt Lake using a USGS quad sheet (1:500,000 scale).

The Great Salt Lake is a terminal lake. It does not have any outlet rivers running to the ocean. Water leaves the lake only through evaporation. Water leaves behind its dissolved minerals. This makes the lake up to eight times as salty as seawater. The lack of outlets also means the lake responds dramatically to change in inflow. Rainy weather beginning in 1982 brought the highest levels in recorded history. The water peaked in June 1986 and March–April 1987. The lake is shallow for its size. It is only about 40 feet deep. It is 70 miles long and 30 miles wide. Because the lake basin is so shallowly sloped, extra inflow to the lake makes it rise slowly. However, any rise means a large increase in area. Highways, causeways, and parts of Salt Lake City were flooded or threatened in the 1980s. This cost millions of dollars.

Figure 5-8

Earthshots: Great Salt Lake, Utah

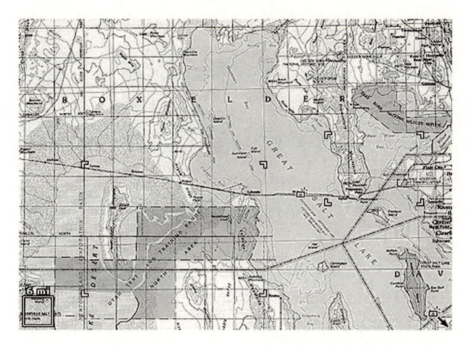

Great Salt Lake USGS 1:500,000 scale map, 1988, USGS.

In 1902, the Southern Pacific Railroad constructed a rail line directly across the lake. It was constructed so engines would not have to climb over the mountains. In 1959 this route was rebuilt by a causeway. The USGS map of the State of Utah (1988) shows the causeway across the center of the Lake (Figure 5-9)

This solid raised roadway divided the lake into two parts. Two 15-foot culverts allowed water to flow under portions of the causeway. The south part of the lake receives most of the lake's inflow from rivers. The south part became higher than the north part. In Figure 5-10, a 1972 Landsat image of Salt Lake, notice that the northern part is a slightly lighter than the southern part. The color difference is caused because the northern part is saltier. This causes different types of algae and bacteria to grow. The algae and bacteria make the north part look a different color.

By July 1984, after 2 years of above-normal precipitation, the south part of the lake was 3.7 feet higher than the north. This is the highest difference it would ever reach. In August of 1984, a 300-foot section of the causeway was replaced by a low bridge, allowing water to flow underneath. Within 2 months, there was no difference between the south and north parts of the lake.

In 1986, Utah began construction of a system to pump excess water west onto the Bonneville Salt Flats. This created the Newfoundland Evaporation Basin.

Figure 5-9

Earthshots: Great Salt Lake, Utah

1972 Landsat image of the Great Salt Lake, USGS.

The effects of this effort are shown in Figure 5-10. Notice the new water body west of the Great Salt Lake.

5.7.5 Imaging Radar

An imaging radar works like a flash camera. It provides its own light to illuminate an area on the ground and take a snapshot picture. However, it does this at radio wavelengths. Instead of a camera lens and film, radar uses an antenna and computer to record its images. In a radar image, one can see only the light that was reflected back toward the radar antenna. In the case of imaging radar, the radar moves along a flight path. The area illuminated by the radar, or footprint, is moved along the surface in a swath, building the image as it does so. The length of the radar antenna determines the clarity of the image. The longer the antenna, the finer the resolution.

The radar image of coastal Louisiana was created by RADARSAT, a satellite radar system. The value of this technology is that you can verify flooding areas after the storm, despite cloud coverage. RADARSAT has been used in the following areas:

Figure 5-10

Earthshots: Great Salt Lake, Utah

1987 Landsat image of the Great Salt Lake, USGS.

▲ **Agriculture:** crop monitoring
▲ **Marine surveillance:** ship detection, marine pollution, iceberg detection, ship routing
▲ **Defense:** surveying territory, identifying targets
▲ **Mapping:** geographical mapping, land use mapping, wetlands mapping, topographic mapping

Radar images are not affected by cloud cover. RADARSAT illuminates the earth with microwaves. This allows detailed observations at any time, regardless of weather or sunlight conditions. The international scientific community uses the multifrequency data. The data is used to better understand the global environment and how it is changing. This satellite data can be complemented by aircraft and ground studies. This gives scientists clearer insights into which environmental changes are caused by nature and which are induced by human activity.

Figure 5-11 was provided by RADARSAT following Hurricane Katrina. It reveals the oil spill along the coast of Louisiana and was used by federal and state officials to detect and respond to the spill. The spill is shown in black in

Figure 5-11

Radar image of Southern Louisiana following Hurricane Katrina, September 2, 2005 (http://katrina.esl.lsu.edu/katrina/).

the lower right-hand corner of the image. As part of FEMA's support of Hurricane Katrina response and recovery efforts, Radarsat and other companies provided high-resolution remote sensing products. See all of these products at www.katrina. lsu.edu

The New Orleans images, including the ones in Figure 5-12, illustrate how high-resolution images can reflect the impact areas of a disaster. An aircraft or satellite produces a high-resolution digital image (orthoimagery). This is illustrated by the images of New Orleans taken prior to and after the Hurricane Katrina landfall on the Gulf of Mexico. These images are photographs of very high resolution. They are used with mapping software GIS. Hurricane Katrina responders used this imagery in rescue efforts. These images may be displayed along with other map layers in the GIS, including interstates and landmarks as reflected in Figure 5-12. The high resolution of these images allowed emergency responders to recognize key landmarks in flooded areas such as parks, schools, health care facilities, and businesses and direct rescue efforts. Digital Globe provided FEMA with high-resolution images of areas impacted by hurricanes in 2005 in an effort to support emergency response and recovery

FOR EXAMPLE

Using Radar Images to Make Decisions

A radar image of Angola State Prison north of Baton Rouge, Louisiana, was taken during extensive flooding on the Mississippi River in the spring of 1997. The radar image showed flooded areas around the prison and provided timely information that local emergency management, public safety, and prison officials used in setting up temporary shelters and a timeline for the movement of personnel at the prison. The radar image was also compared with a similar image taken in a dry period. The image was acquired from and used by state and local emergency management agencies. Information from the images proved invaluable in making decisions relating to the evacuation of the maximum-security prison. Emergency management officials wanted to determine if the floodwaters posed a danger to the prison. The images along with soil analysis from the area helped local officials to determine if additional flooding was possible. This information was used to support the decision that additional housing for the inmates was needed.

efforts to these disasters. Other high-resolution image products used by emergency responders in Hurricanes Katrina and Rita in 2005 are at www.katrina.lsu.edu.

Figure 5-12

Digital Globe images of New Orleans.

March 9, 2004; August 31, 2005; New Orleans, LA: Before and After Hurricane Katrina. Maps prepared by LSU World Health Organization Collaborating Center LSU CADGIS Research Laboratory Louisiana State University Images Source: http://digitalglobe.com/press/images_media.shtml

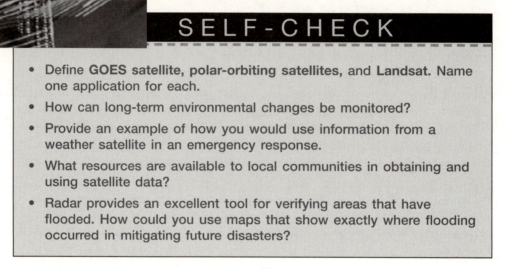

5.8 Using and Assessing Data

Image map products can be produced easily, can include recognizable landmarks, and can offer a clearer view of an area. Image maps such as photos can provide you with a broad view of an area and provide information on potential losses. The satellites may also provide detailed information on the intensity of storms, including winds, rainfall, and potential storm surge.

Remote imaging data can display data on arid or flooding areas. The images can illustrate before and after characteristics of the area to identify the vulnerability of the site to flooding or drought. Remote sensing images provide an excellent background for displaying roads, water features, city boundaries, and flood zones. The viewer can observe the general features of the area and then zoom in to examine specific areas of interest.

Remote sensing data can be a valuable tool. However, the data quality, accessibility, and information presentation varies with the type of data. The following provides an evaluation checklist for the many alternative remote sensing providers and the use of the data for emergency management activities.

▲ Data Quality:
  ▲ Accuracy, precision, completeness, age, timeliness, and source
  ▲ Relevance of the data to the user
  ▲ Who collects the data, when, how it is imputed in the system, and how the data will be used
  ▲ Who and how the data will be used should influence what data is collected, who and how it will be loaded into the system, and who will manipulate the data for users

FOR EXAMPLE

Using Data

During the Mississippi and Missouri River floods in the 1990s, federal agencies, including FEMA, used satellite images to monitor rising waters and guide response, recovery operations, and mitigation efforts. The same images provide information on the extent of the area subject to damage for use in mitigation and planning efforts.

▲ **Accessibility:**
  ▲ Public agencies may restrict access to some remote sensing images because of the sensitivity of work that is done at specific sites
  ▲ Availability and possible access restrictions

▲ **Information Presentation:**
  ▲ Format of the data may limit the user in presenting information
  ▲ Format for output
  ▲ Data flow diagrams
  ▲ Definition of the data item
  ▲ Name of the file the data item is stored
  ▲ Abbreviation that can be used as a column heading for reports
  ▲ Range of values

SELF-CHECK

- What criteria do you use to assess data?
- What is meant by **accessibility of data?**

5.9 Trends in Technology

Critical hazard information from remote and direct sensing sources is now more available to you. This is a result of our use of computer networks, the Web or Internet, radio communication, or direct links to sensors. During Hurricane Katrina, FEMA made governmental and commercial remote sensing images available to emergency responders. Images from GOES, Landsat, and MODIS; along with commercial images, including RADARSAT, provide critical information throughout the recovery process. In addition to the images, USGS system of stream-monitoring gages provide timely information on water levels in streams, lakes, and rivers, and on the weather. More widespread use of sensors will give you valuable information in a crisis. Access to this information by way of the Web or our networks makes this all possible. The increasing use of direct and remote sensors can have significant impacts, including the following:

▲ **Information overload:** The increasing attention to technology may inadvertently result in information overload. If a communication system is highly centralized, even a limited emergency can result in communication bottlenecks. Subnetworks may need to be created to divert communication from the operations center. A planned distributed computing capability can be designed by examining elements of the emergency management system. Who needs to communicate directly and frequently and with whom?

▲ **Data integration:** Many organizations have been struggling to cope with increasing demands for timely and accurate data to support ongoing decision making. As a result, large centralized systems have been adapted to more distributed databases. Maintaining linkages and integration of the data is critical in times of crisis. In the future, data will include more databases (relational), digital libraries, and multimedia databases maintained in a distributed environment. Distributed data sets also provide an opportunity for agencies that create or obtain data as well as to maintain it. Documentation on the source of data and data types will be critical to ensure that information is used for its intended purpose.

▲ **Real-time response data:** In a disaster, complex computing may not be possible for those directly involved in the response. In disasters, a rear support team can be organized to carry out high-performance modeling and analysis. Dependable networks should be designed to allow for detailed analysis to occur even during stressful events. Links between support staff and operations units must be maintained in a secure environment.

FOR EXAMPLE

Landsat Data

Landsat data is available through the Web. The Earth Observation Satellite Company is under contract with the U.S. government to market the Landsat data. General information on Landsat 7 is available through the Landsat Gateway Web page at http://landsat.gsfc.nasa.gov/

SELF-CHECK

- What is meant by **data integration?**
- Why is real-time data so important to emergency response?
- What is meant by **information overload** and what are its consequences?

SUMMARY

Direct and remote sensing tools are among the most important tools for any emergency manager. Computerized sensors allow you to continuously monitor the natural and built environment. Computerized weather stations provide an ongoing means of collecting, recording, and transmitting data for use in emergency planning and response. Direct sensors can be linked to information systems that provide hazard warnings on a local or regional basis. For those areas not covered by direct sensors, field-deployed sensors can provide essential information for areas where data is not available.

Remote sensing tools are critical as well. Remote sensing images are well suited for display and analysis along with road, water feature, railroad, and other layers in a GIS. High-resolution images provided by aircraft or satellites allow emergency responders to see flooded areas and direct rescue efforts.

In this chapter, you assessed how to use weather stations and water and air sensors to protect your community. You analyzed how to best evaluate the technology tools you choose to use. You assessed remote sensing capabilities provided by satellites and determined how satellite images can be used in all phases of emergency management. Finally, you examined ways to assess the quality and value of the data you receive from these tools. With this knowledge, you will be able to use direct and remote sensing information in all phases of emergency management to protect lives and property.

KEY TERMS

Base station	Final destination for the information from the sensors. Information is accepted, processed, displayed, and forwarded to the appropriate computers and personnel.
Direct sensors	Gages and instruments that are in direct contact with a phenomena that provide information.
Event-reporting sensors	Programmed with prerecorded measurements that trigger the transmission of warning signals.

Geostational Operational Environmental Satellites (GOES)	An airborne remote sensing system that revolves in a fixed spot off Earth's surface and collects continuous observations relating to cloud cover, atmospheric temperature, and moisture in the air.
Landsat	A remote sensing satellite program developed by NASA.
Polar orbiting satellites	An airborne remote sensing system that collects continuous observations such as data transmitted from Earth; high-resolution photos of Earth; images such as cloud cover, smoke, haze, or storm path on a specific orbit over the poles.
Radar images	Data collected by remote sensing collecting observations at any time, regardless of weather or sunlight conditions. Data reveals environmental conditions such as flooded areas, oil spills in the water, or wetlands mapping.
Remote automated weather stations (RAWS)	A network of weather stations run by the U.S. Forest Service and Bureau of Land Management and monitored by the National Interagency Fire Center.
Remote sensors	Instruments or gages that can detect phenomena that are not in direct contact with it.
Single-frequency repeater	Increases the transmission range of event-reporting sensors by regenerating, amplifying, and transmitting to a base station.
Weather station	A sensor that collects information on the temperature, precipitation, wind direction and movement, barometric pressure and humidity by way of direct contact with the phenomena.

ASSESS YOUR UNDERSTANDING

Go to www.wiley.com/college/pine to evaluate your knowledge on direct and remote sensing.
Measure your learning by comparing pre-test and post-test results.

SUMMARY QUESTIONS

1. Data relating to an actual or potential disaster allow the emergency manager to do which of the following?

   (a) Understand the hazard

   (b) Determine what steps can be taken to reduce losses

   (c) Use the data to simulate potential disasters

   (d) All of the above

2. Today, computerized sensors allow us to see more clearly from the ground, aircraft, and satellites. True or False?

3. Sensors allow us to understand the nature of the natural environment, including winds, soil types, moisture content, water movement, or vegetation type. True or False?

4. Data collected from sensors may be used to do which of the following?

   (a) Identify the high-priority areas affected by floods

   (b) Identify the areas most affected in a disaster

   (c) Determine how to direct personnel in a cleanup operation

   (d) All of the above

5. Weather stations are an example of a remote sensor. True or False?

6. Weather stations usually collect data for each of the following, except:

   (a) temperature.

   (b) humidity.

   (c) wind speed.

   (d) hazardous chemicals.

7. The USGS stream-gaging program provides information for which of the following?

   (a) Enhancing the public safety by providing data for forecasting and managing floods

   (b) Characterizing chemicals in a water feature

   (c) Defining the boundary of a water feature

   (d) All of the above

8. Stream-flow data are needed for making water management decisions and measuring water quality. True or False?

9. Once a direct sensing system is designed, it is neither important nor practical to make changes. True or False?

10. Field-deployed direct sensors provide emergency managers with essential information that can help in a disaster response. True or False?

11. Satellites provide a basis for collecting remote sensing data. True or False?

12. Satellites are the only means for collecting remote sensing data. True or False?

13. Radar imaging remote sensing is affected by cloud cover. True or False?

14. High-resolution images from an aircraft provide a means of assessing the impact of a disaster following the event. True or False?

REVIEW QUESTIONS

1. How can information from direct sensing be used in emergency planning?

2. What does a weather station measure?

3. What are the primary instruments on a weather station, and what is their purpose?

4. What sensors does a typical weather station employ and how do these stations help emergency planning?

5. What are the primary types of water data sensors, and how can they be integrated into a flood warning system?

6. What are the primary substances that can be detected by air data sensors?

7. How is the technology application evaluated and selected, and what are the key factors to be considered?

8. What are the aspects of remote sensing that make it attractive?

9. How will the trends in technology development affect the evaluation and use of information?

10. How can satellite images be used in emergency response and recovery?

11. What is imaging radar, and how is it used?

Applying This Chapter

1. You are the emergency manager for a community that was taken by surprise last year by a massive flood. What equipment do you install to help with detection?

2. You are the emergency manager for Yellowstone National Park, a large park with many trees and natural resources. One hazard that concerns you is wildfires. What equipment would you install to detect wildfires? Why?

3. You are the emergency manager for a state emergency management agency. You receive information from local emergency management agencies and from national information sources every day. How do you integrate this information?

4. You are the emergency manager for a midsized city. Five hundred thousand dollars of funds were just approved for the purchase of technology for the agency. How do you determine what types of technology you should purchase?

5. You are the emergency manager for a town that was just hit hard by a hurricane. What types of direct and remote sensing information do you need to aid in the recovery and why?

6. You are the emergency manager for a town that contains many chemical facilities. You have received reports from each facility detailing what chemicals they store and in what quantities. How do you assess the data? What qualities do you look for in the data?

7. You are the emergency manager for a town that is in the path of a hurricane. Weather analysts are claiming that your town may be struck within the next 72 hours. What satellite images do you want to see and why?

8. You are the emergency manager for a town that is prone to flooding in some areas. Part of the town sits on a lake. How do you determine where to place water sensors, and how do you know how many gages you need?

9. You are the emergency manager for a town on the coast. How do you determine where to place weather stations, and how do you determine how many you need?

10. You are the emergency manager for New York City. The federal government has told you that many terrorists have discussed plots involving releasing chemical/biological weapons in the subways. What sensing tools do you use to combat this threat? Where do you place the tools?

YOU TRY IT

Fighting Terrorism

You are the emergency manager for New York City. Write a paper on how you would choose direct and remote sensing tools to combat the threat of terrorism. Include in your paper how you would choose the technology, what technology you would choose, and how it would be evaluated.

Analyzing Information

You are the emergency manager for a city that was just hit with a massive flood. What kind of images do you want and why? What information will you look for in the images?

Chemical Sensors

You are in charge of safety at a large chemical company. This chemical company runs the risk of being attacked by terrorists or having an accidental leak. What kind of equipment do you install and why?

6

EMERGENCY MANAGEMENT DECISION SUPPORT SYSTEMS
Using Data to Manage Disasters

Starting Point

Go to www.wiley.com/college/pine to assess your knowledge of emergency management decision support systems.
Determine where to concentrate your effort.

What You'll Learn in This Chapter

▲ Components of a management information system
▲ Characteristics of useful information systems
▲ Examples of federal, state, and local information systems
▲ How data is organized
▲ How to use a hazardous chemical (Tier 2) database structure
▲ Qualities of databases that should be considered when evaluating databases
▲ Useful emergency management databases
▲ Examples of public federal data sources that provide access to data that is useful to emergency managers

After Studying This Chapter, You'll Be Able To

▲ Use emergency management information systems to make well-informed decisions during a crisis
▲ Examine the characteristics of a relational database and its application to emergency management
▲ Examine how emergency managers can use FEMIS, NEMIS, and CAMEO for managing hazards
▲ Use metadata to sort information and support emergency management efforts
▲ Examine the components of a hazardous chemical (Tier 2) database structure
▲ Compare and contrast different databases on the basis of data quality, accessibility, and information presentation
▲ Use public and federal data sources to support emergency management efforts

Goals and Outcomes

▲ Evaluate management information systems based on quality, timeliness, completeness, and performance
▲ Assess how to use the information in FEMIS, NEMIS, and CAMEO to support emergency management tasks
▲ Design data tables to quickly access and sort information
▲ Evaluate the design of the hazardous chemical (Tier 2) structure
▲ Evaluate databases based on data quality, accessibility, and information presentation
▲ Select public and federal data sources to support your daily emergency management tasks

INTRODUCTION

As an emergency manager, you will be asked to make many decisions. Some of the decisions will be easy day-to-day decisions. Other decisions will be difficult ones made during a crisis. As a decision maker, you need to have data and information available to you instantly.

▲ **Data** is a fact or things that are known.
▲ **Information** is data that is processed or used in some form of analysis.

During this chapter, you will examine how decision support systems and their databases, if correctly designed, will give you the information you need to make the best decisions. You will also examine what characteristics are necessary for useful information systems. You will assess different federal, state, and local information systems. You will then assess data and what qualities should be considered when data is inputted. You will evaluate databases, including a hazardous chemical database (Tier 2) structure. Finally, you will assess public federal data sources and emergency management databases and how they can help you in your daily tasks as well as during a crisis.

6.1 Emergency Management Information Systems

You must be able to make quick, well-informed decisions in a crisis. You must also be able to make quality decisions when preparing for emergency situations. Information about community resources, vulnerable populations, as well as the hazards is fundamental to effective response. In the past, managers maintained lists of local and regional contacts, paper maps and layouts of critical resources, and charts showing when to make contacts. Today, we can store this information and much more electronically. We can also store it in ways that support effective decision making.

You can store records in many forms. Records may be maintained to ensure that agency activities are effective. Agency digital records are data. They are created and stored. They can be sorted, merged, retrieved, displayed, and used to make decisions or calculations. When data is processed in such a way as to enable the organization to make decisions, it is referred to as a decision support system or a **management information system.** A management information system is a set of digital databases that may be sorted, merged, retrieved, displayed, and used to make decisions or calculations.

A management information system must include the following:

▲ Inputs: data, storage processes, or procedures
▲ Transformation: methods of sorting, merging, accumulating, and retrieving the inputs/data

> ### FOR EXAMPLE
>
> ### Using a Management Information System
>
> One way to use a management information system is to determine where vulnerable populations are located. For example, if a town is prone to flooding, you could use a management information system to determine who lives in the flood zone as well as what businesses are located in the flood zone. You can then use this information to help residents take mitigation measures, evacuate, or even just to warn them.

▲ Outputs: information that allows you to make decisions about evacuations, disaster declarations, and evacuation zones

The idea behind information systems is that they provide a systematic way to collect, manipulate, maintain, and distribute information throughout an organization. This provides unlimited opportunities to collect, explore, and display information relating to disasters, risks, or the community.

Computer-based management information systems are critical in emergency management. These systems allow you to record, select, sort, and save population, chemical, or weather data about a community. The systems allow you to process the data. You can sort, calculate, or retrieve specific data. Individual facilities with hazardous chemicals and local communities can use an information system to comply with or monitor federal and state requirements. Information systems allow you to access data that will enhance planning, response, recovery, and mitigation efforts.

A systems view of an organization suggests that it has several elements:

▲ Inputs: information, equipment, and computer programs
▲ Transformation: the manipulation of the data using the program
▲ Outputs: decisions and actions based on lists, messages, reports, or maps from the information system

SELF-CHECK

- Define **management information system.**
- What components must a management information system include?
- Why are information systems an important tool for emergency managers?

6.2 Evaluating Information Systems

There have been many cases in recent years where decisions were made with inaccurate information. For example, there have been intelligence failures within the United States government. There has also been debate about when information and what information was available to emergency planners during Hurricane Katrina. Your decisions are only effective if you have accurate information. You rely on the advice and counsel of the people you work with. However, you also base decisions by assuming your data is reliable. Your information system must be clear, accurate, reliable, and complete. It must be able to provide you with all the information you need. Below is a list of the qualities of useful information.

6.2.1 Quality

Quality consists of several factors, including, accuracy, clarity, and the medium through which the information is communicated. If the details do not accurately reflect current conditions, then any decision made using the information may be adversely affected. Clarity refers to the meaning and intent of the information. It must be clear to the decision maker. Finally, the information must be presented in a neat and orderly way. It must be presented in a way that assists the decision maker. Providing the decision maker with a massive computer printout instead of several pages of summary information is inappropriate. In addition, the quality of the system includes the cost in comparison to other similar systems. As a part of the quality consideration, there are other questions you should ask: Does the program conform to any state or national standards? Does the system use custom data format (databases, graphics, maps, or images)? Does the system allow the user to import common format database, spreadsheet, text, image, or map files?

6.2.2 Timeliness

Many day-to-day decisions are time sensitive. Decisions on how to respond to situations must be made quickly. Timely information has several ingredients. First, it should be provided when it is needed to support making a decision. Another key ingredient of timely information is currency. Ideally, data would be provided to decision makers as change occurs. Changes in the weather could drastically influence the dispersion of hazardous chemicals. Information systems should provide for an easy means of updating data, even real-time changes as it occurs. Information should be up-to-date when it is given to the decision maker. Finally, the information should be provided as often as needed or at an appropriate frequency.

6.2.3 Completeness

Information must be complete to be of value. The data must allow the decision maker to make an accurate assessment of the situation and to arrive at a suitable decision. Where appropriate, decision makers should have access to current information and to past history and future plans. Conciseness and detail are part of completeness. Information should be presented to the decision maker in as concise a form as possible. However, there should be sufficient detail to provide the decision maker with enough depth and breadth for the current situation. Finally, only the relevant information should be provided. This is to avoid information overload.

6.2.4 Performance

Performance of information systems has the following variables:

- ▲ **Capacity:** The amount of work that the system can perform or the number of users at the same time.
- ▲ **Productivity:** The extent that data input is required and the types and quality of outputs from the system.
- ▲ **Consistency:** The number of breakdowns in the operation of the system.
- ▲ **Cycle time:** The time it takes the system to perform functions.
- ▲ **Flexibility:** How easily is the system able to switch from one process to another, and must the user perform numerous steps to move from one function to another?
- ▲ **Security:** What protection does the system provide to restrict unauthorized users?
- ▲ **Responsiveness:** Can the system be changed based on user input?
- ▲ **Reliability of the product:** Does the system require frequent support?

FOR EXAMPLE

First Reports

During a crisis, first reports are often wrong. For example, in Hurricane Katrina, the first reports were that New Orleans was "spared" and that the levees were not breached. During the terrorist attacks on September 11, 2001, the early reports were that tens of thousands were killed and that the state department in Washington, D.C., had been bombed. This is why it is important for you to have the most accurate up-to-date information and a strong communication network in place. Without accurate information, you will not be able to make effective decisions.

SELF-CHECK

- Considering the quality of information, what is meant by the term clarity?
- How would access to real-time information assist in the evaluation and decision-making process?
- Why is it important to balance the level of detail versus conciseness?
- What variables must be considered when evaluating the performance of information systems?

6.3 Accessing Federal, State, and Local Information Systems

The following are illustrations of information systems, which are being used at the national, state, or local level. These systems provide information that is critical to the emergency management community. The following explains how specific information systems may be created to support emergency management at the national, state, or local level. The Internet address of the information system is provided, where available.

6.3.1 The National Emergency Management Information System (NEMIS)

NEMIS is an information system that was designed to support FEMA. NEMIS automates vital functions and tasks. These tasks include providing disaster assistance for individual victims; support of infrastructure and mitigation programs for state and local government recovery efforts; and support for direction, control, and administrative activities at both the headquarters and field levels of operations. NEMIS builds on existing FEMA information technology capabilities.

NEMIS drives standardization in FEMA. Because of NEMIS, FEMA has establishing agency-wide standards for personal computer configurations, operating systems, relational databases, and GIS software. It helps FEMA work with other agencies and states. NEMIS provides timely and accurate information to all users.

NEMIS is able to provide resources for all hazards. It provides cross-disaster information and analysis capabilities to improve prevention and mitigation efforts. NEMIS improves the timeliness and accuracy of disaster response. NEMIS improves the efficiency and thoroughness of recovery operations. It provides states the ability to use key functions through remote access to FEMA's networks. This reduces the need for separate state systems and improving standardization and compatibility of operations. NEMIS empowers FEMA's workforce by automating tedious, error-prone, and costly manual procedures.

6.3.2 Federal Emergency Management Information System (FEMIS)

FEMIS is an automated decision support system that makes it possible to pre-plan for emergencies and to coordinate operations and make decisions during an emergency. It was developed in the mid-1990s at the Pacific Northwest National Laboratory. The FEMIS software package includes a GIS, relational database management, electronic mail, and several simulation models. It can be modified to accept additional data such as data from sensor devices. FEMIS is unique and significant is several respects:

- ▲ It was developed as a partnership between FEMA and the U.S. Army as part of the Chemical Stockpile Emergency Preparedness Program.
- ▲ It addressed public concerns about U.S. capabilities in dealing with far-reaching emergency situations.
- ▲ It brings together all levels of government and all relevant agencies to work jointly to plan, coordinate, and manage emergency situations.
- ▲ While it was originally developed and specifically designed to address accidental chemical releases, it has been expanded to included oil refineries and potential oil spills.

FEMIS is an integrated system that provides planning, coordination, response, and exercise support for emergency management. It is an automated decision support system that integrates all phases of emergency management. FEMIS provides for:

- ▲ resource tracking
- ▲ task lists
- ▲ contact lists
- ▲ event logs
- ▲ status boards
- ▲ hazard modeling
- ▲ evacuation modeling

The program was designed to support the Chemical Stockpile Emergency Preparedness Program planning and operations.

The electronic plan is a central feature of FEMIS. It provides a framework for acquiring, displaying, and analyzing agency information. FEMIS includes model animation to predict the consequences on a community. Evacuation modeling is also included. The program uses several commercial off-the-shelf software, including Oracle, ArcInfo and ArcView, Microsoft Project, and Novell GroupWise.

6.3.3 (CAMEO) Computer Aided Management of Emergency Operations

CAMEO is computer software for chemical emergency planners and responders. CAMEO was developed by the Environmental Protection Agency (EPA) and National Oceanic and Atmospheric Administration (NOAA). It was developed to help government and industry plan for and mitigate chemical accidents. It was also developed to comply with the Emergency Planning and Community Right to Know Act of 1986. CAMEO is one of the most widely used information and decision support systems. It is used for chemical emergency response, planning and regulatory compliance, planning and response to natural hazards. More recently, it was used to prepare and respond to threats of terrorism. CAMEO does the following:

▲ Provides safety and emergency response information on 4,700 hazardous chemicals
▲ Tracks chemical inventories in the community and on transportation routes
▲ Automates chemical inventory reporting
▲ Provides a basis for conducting hazards analysis and off-site consequences analysis
▲ Included with CAMEO is the Arial Locations of Hazardous Atmosphere (ALOHA) air dispersion model and Mapping Applications for Response, Planning, and Local Operational Tasks (MARPLOT) mapping application
▲ CAMEO is used for Chemical Emergency Response, Planning, and Regulatory Compliance

Users of CAMEO include the following:

▲ local emergency planning committees (LEPCs)
▲ fire departments
▲ state emergency planning commissions (SERCs)
▲ emergency planners
▲ chemical facilities
▲ health care facilities
▲ universities

CAMEO is a suite of separate, integrated software applications: CAMEO, MARPLOT, LandView, and ALOHA. CAMEO also includes many databases and other applications. The purpose of this suite of software is to assist front-line chemical emergency planners and responders in planning for and responding to hazards and disasters. The addition of LandView was to bring the extensive data from the Census Bureau. This helps you better understand the characteristics of your community. Although LandView can be run independently from CAMEO, it is linked to each of the CAMEO components.

ALOHA is an atmospheric dispersion model. It evaluates releases of hazardous chemical vapors. ALOHA allows the user to estimate how far downwind a chemical cloud is likely to travel. The estimate is based on

▲ toxicological/physical characteristics of the chemical;

▲ atmospheric conditions at the time;

▲ specific circumstances of the chemical release.

Graphical outputs, including a cloud footprint, can be plotted on maps. This can be done using MARPLOT. These graphical outputs can show vulnerable locations such as schools, hospitals, and facilities storing hazardous materials. This information, combined with information from CAMEO, can be used to evaluate the hazardous potential of the chemical release.

MARPLOT is the mapping application component of the CAMEO suite of software. It allows users to see their data (e.g., roads, schools, factories, etc.), display this information on computer maps, and print this information on area maps. The areas contaminated can be overlaid on these maps to determine potential impacts. The maps are created from the U.S. Bureau of Census TIGER/line files. These maps can hurriedly be manipulated to show potential hazard areas.

A vital element of CAMEO is the chemical database. It contains a chemical database of more than 4,700 chemicals, 70,000 synonyms, trade names, and other labeling conventions. CAMEO provides a powerful search engine that allows users to find chemicals instantly. Each chemical is linked to a response information data sheet (RIDS). RIDS details the chemical-specific information on fire and explosive hazards, health hazards, firefighting techniques, cleanup procedures, and protective clothing.

6.3.4 Other Decision Support Information Systems

Governmental agencies at all levels and private businesses are using the Internet to link agencies involved in responding to disasters and provide decision support tools to keep track of information in a disaster. Several commercial applications allow multiple agencies to send requests for services or supplies, track progress on these orders, and then record the communication for billing or reimbursement purposes. In the future, we will likely see greater use of the

Internet in linking our systems. We will use the Internet to build more powerful tools. These tools will support information sharing and decision making. The Internet provides a means for real-time access to data that might be at a distance. It allows for the sharing of comprehensive information with decision makers.

For example, one company, E Team, sells decisions support systems to communities that have been affected by disasters. To understand E-Team's capability, let's examine their role in the September 11, 2001, terrorist attacks. The terrorist attacks posed several unique challenges. The attacks were unprecedented in both their lack of forewarning and their scope. The Emergency Operations Center (EOC) of New York City was one of the casualties. It was housed in the World Trade Center building #7. An alternate solution to the EOC had to be deployed quickly. Something had to be in place to coordinate and manage the response. New York City had purchased the E Team software. It was not scheduled to be installed until September 17, 2001. However, within hours of the collapse of the EOC on September 11th, E Team installed a fully operational decision support system over the Internet. The system allowed for 150 federal, state, and nonprofit agencies to collaborate. They were able to relay status, order resources, report incidents, and manage logistics of response and cleanup. Seventeen hundred individuals were trained on the system and were able to use the system in as little as 15 minutes. Even volunteers at the site were able to use the software from wireless command posts. They could enter this list of rescuer needs, ranging from gloves to dump trucks, and the requests were routed to the appropriate parties. Incorporated in the E Team software was also mapping software that provided information showing destroyed, damaged, and unstable buildings, emergency center locations, power outages, debris-removal routes, and asbestos plume paths. Finally, the software provided incident reporting, asset tracking, action planning, and other logistics support.

FOR EXAMPLE

E Team Customers

The E Team sells decision support systems. E Team customers include federal agencies, state governments, city and county governments, nonprofit organizations, and private corporations. E Team has played a role in many disasters and security settings. The E Team has been used in hurricanes, the 2004 tsunami, and in wildfires. In addition, it has been used in security situations such as the Salt Lake City Olympics and the 2004 presidential inauguration.

SELF-CHECK

- Define **FEMIS** and **NEMIS.**
- How can NEMIS be used to assist state-level emergency management activities?
- Which suite of software has the purpose to assist front-line chemical emergency planners and responders?
- How can the Internet be used to link agencies and information?

6.4 Using Data

Decision support systems provide a means for the emergency manager to get correct information quickly. Information and decision support systems are based on data. As an emergency manager, you have to make many decisions. Some are daily decisions such as who to meet with and what supplies you need. Some decisions affect many people and businesses, such as when to evacuate or how to enforce building codes. You cannot make these decisions in a vacuum. You make these decisions, however, based on data. Data is a fact that is known. Data is something that is used as a basis for discussion, decision making, calculating, or measuring. For example, data might be the number of hours it takes to drive from point A to point B at 60 miles per hour, or the elevation of a school that is used as a shelter in a community subjected to frequent heavy rains. When data is processed or used in some form of analysis, it can be converted into information. For example, a small community might have six schools constructed or remodeled between 1959 and 1992. When each school is assessed as to factors affecting shelter location, only four may be suitable as a shelter in a hurricane. Specific facts or data about each school are assessed to determine if they are suitable as a disaster shelter. The suitable shelters are thus the result of processed data and therefore fall into the concept of information.

6.4.1 Databases

We organize data into blocks and categories and then collect and store it in a database. The CAMEO system combines data relating to a list of facilities with chemicals, a separate list of their hazardous chemicals, another list of contacts at each facility, and finally a list of accidental releases from each facility. Each type of information is linked to create a related data set or a database. A database is thus a collection of related information that is organized so that it provides a foundation for procedures and making decisions. The CAMEO program is an example of a related database.

Databases do not have to be stored in a computer. Libraries, for example, used to keep a filing system of index cards for each one of their books. This was a database. As technology has progressed, however, most databases have become computerized. Databases include tables, fields, and records. A table is a set of data arranged in rows and columns reflecting individual records and fields. A record is a collection of fields or a row of a table representing one record entry. A field is a subdivision or a record; it contains a single piece of data. For example, you might have a table of hazardous chemicals that your city produces. A record details the chemicals and related information on the chemicals that a particular company in your city produces. A field could be the amount of chemicals the facility produces in a year.

In this example, we used a relational database. A relational database uses the contents of a particular field as an index. For example, you can look up chemicals by their name or properties or amounts. A relational database is comprised of a number of related tables. Each table is made up of rows of data (records), and each record contains information organized into columns (fields). When tables are related, they contain a common element or field. The common fields allow for matching of information between tables.

6.4.2 Data Dictionary (or Metadata)

The most costly and time-consuming part of developing a useful information system is the design of the data tables. The system should allow the user to sort or find information quickly and accurately with ease of effort. After systems are designed, support staff often tell the manager that the information system cannot provide the requested need. Planning can prevent this problem and ensure that the system is responsive to the user's needs. Time should be taken in setting up the database to identify how and by whom the system will be used. The types of data should be outlined before a system is selected. In addition, the system should be easily adapted to reflect the special needs of the user. A critical part of any database is documentation or creating a data dictionary.

For the information in a database to be useful to the manager, users must have confidence in the quality of the data. A data dictionary or **(metadata)** should be developed and maintained for each data set used. Metadata can broadly be defined as data about data. It refers to searchable definitions used to locate existing information. Metadata has become a crucial concern as the Web has emerged as a major research tool. Metadata may determine how accessible a particular Web site is to researchers. Every Web site is indexed based on metadata tags. For example, if you wanted to look up information on Hurricane Katrina, you could look it up under "Hurricane Katrina" or "2006 Hurricanes." Or you could look it up under "Hurricane" AND "Louisiana" or "Hurricane" AND

"Mississippi", and so on. The data dictionary includes information as to where the data was obtained, when, how the data was formatted, and if the data has been altered. In addition, the nature of the database must be identified so that users fully understand what is included in the database (data dictionary). The following are elements of a data dictionary:

▲ Name of each table and fields in a table
▲ Definition of each field
▲ Name of the file where the data item is stored
▲ Typical format for output
▲ Range or type of values for a record
▲ Description of data flow
▲ Identification of user input screens

The Census Bureau provides metadata in TIGER/line files (see Figure 6-1). The Census TIGER database is a seamless national file. There are 19 record types or layers in a GIS. These records include: coordinate points, geographic codes, census feature class codes, address ranges, zip codes, legal entities, statistical entities, landmarks, and other features. Each layer has a database file associated with the map feature. The information on each layer was developed by the Census Bureau to help them to collect accurate information in local communities.

Figure 6-1

Census Tiger road files of Baton Rouge, Louisiana.

FOR EXAMPLE

The U.S. Geologic Survey (USGS) and the Census Bureau

The USGS gives map layers to the Census Bureau. These map layers included road features for a GIS. The Census Bureau edits the road files and added the road name, a road classification code, local zip code, and county code information and many more details about local roads throughout the United States. The metadata file is provided by the Census Bureau to users of their map files to ensure that the mapping files are used correctly and with an understanding of the quality of the road data. A good example of why metadata is important is that when one places the road files over a high-resolution photo image, roads do not appear in the proper location. The USGS road files and the Census Bureau editing was based on USGS quad sheet information at a scale of 1:24,000. Today, many high-resolution photos have a resolution of 1:10,000 or less. When you place the road layer files over the high-resolution photos, they do not lay in the proper place. The roads are almost in the correct place. However, the high-resolution image reveals errors in the map files. Most local government jurisdictions use the Census road files but take the time to move them to the correct location. Metadata explains these details. This type of information allows you to fully understand the limitations that come with the data.

SELF-CHECK

- Define database.
- What is the most costly and time-consuming part of developing a useful information system?
- Define **metadata** and list reasons why it is important.

6.5 Working with Hazardous Chemical (Tier 2) Database Structure

The Environmental Protection Agency (EPA) provides a computer-based means of recording, storing, and using hazardous chemical inventory records either by state or local government units or reporting facilities that have hazardous chemicals. This Tier 2 program is an excellent example of an information decision support system. An example of a database structure can be shown in the Tier 2 database. It is in the CAMEO and Tier 2 programs. The Tier 2 hazardous chemical database is maintained at both the state and local level. Data records are loaded or edited in a database. This is done by a facility with hazardous chemicals, a local community, or a state agency that maintains these records on an annual basis. The database is updated annually at the state and local level from facility reports due in March of each year. Individual facilities can keep their records up-to-date on an ongoing basis to reflect changes of the use of hazardous chemicals.

All counties collect and store information related to the hazardous chemical inventories in their jurisdiction. State and local chemical inventory databases are used by the emergency management community to understand the nature of chemical hazards in a community, region, and state. According to the EPA, the following information must be provided:

▲ The chemical name or the common name.
▲ An estimate of the maximum amount of the chemical present at any time during the preceding calendar year and the average daily amount.
▲ A brief description of how the chemical is stored.
▲ The location of the chemical at the facility and an indication of whether the owner of the facility elects to withhold location information from disclosure to the public.

The tables in this case provide an example of the type of information that reflects the facility with the hazardous chemical, the characteristics of the substance, and its location. Each field in the three tables provides information to support the emergency planning and community right to know program at the national, state, and local level. For databases that already exist such as the local Tier 2 Chemical Inventory, it is critical to understand why the data was collected and what is included in it. The key, then, is to clarify the hazard that the data reflects and how to use the information that it contains. The tables in this case provide an example of the type of information, including:

▲ the facility or site where the hazardous chemical is stored or used;
▲ the name and characteristics of the hazardous substance;
▲ where the hazardous chemical is located.

Each field in the three tables provides information to support the emergency planning and the community-right-to-know program at the state and local level.

6.5.1 Example of a Tier 2 Database

Let's look at an example of a Tier 2 database. In this particular example, there are three tables:

▲ **Facilities**: this table includes a set of public, private or nonprofit organizations (facilities) reporting hazardous chemicals

▲ **Chemicals:** this table includes a set of hazardous chemicals stored or used at each facility

▲ **Locations:** this table provides a specific location of hazardous chemicals at each facility

The data in each of the Tier 2 tables can be sorted. You may want to only look at a few of the records and can sort the data by the following:

▲ Facilities in a single city in your county.

▲ Facilities in a specific ZIP code.

▲ Facilities in a single county.

▲ Facilities of a specific type reflected in the SIC (Standard Industrial Classification Code). For example, select records that are just gas stations, gasoline refineries, chemical facilities, or chemical distribution sites.

Because new data is loaded in this database each year, you might want to sort the data by year. The table has many different types of information to serve your needs. You can search for information about chemical facilities in different ways.

Table 6-1 Facilities

Field Name	Description
IDNUM	Identification Number
Name	Facility NAME
FADDR	*Address of the facility*
FCITY	City of the facility
FSTATE	State of facility
FZIP	Zip code
FMAIL	Mailing code
FMCITY	Facility name
FMSTATE	Facility state
FMZIP	Facility ZIP

FPORC	Parish/county
FSIC	SIC (Standard Industrial Code)
DUN_BRAD	Facility identification number
CEN_TRAC	Census track name
ONAME	Owner's name
OPHON	Owner's phone
OADDR	Owner's address
OCITY	Owner's city
OSTATE	Owner's state
OZIP	Owner's zip
C1_NM	Contact name
C1_TIT	Contact title
C1_PH	Contact phone number
C1_PHA	Contact phone number—alternate
C2_NM	Contact #2 name
C2_TIT	Contact #2 title
C2_PH	Contact #2 phone
C2_PHA	Contact #2 phone number—alternate
R_DATE	Report date
R_YEAR	Report year

The chemicals table is linked by a common field with the facilities table. You can thus search for specific chemicals such as chlorine or ammonia and get the name and address of the facility with those chemicals. Because the data tables are linked, you can get a list of all chemicals at a single facility or a list of just extremely hazardous substance (EHS) chemicals by each facility. Chemicals at a facility can be listed by the name of the chemical, by the chemical abstract number (CAWS), by state (liquid, gas, or solid), or if it is a fire or reactive hazard. Because each of the tables has a common field, they can be linked. These related tables are thus a relational database. Such databases make up the foundation of an information system such as CAMEO or Tier 2.

Table 6-2 Chemicals

Field Name	Length Field Description
IDNUM	Identification of the Field
CAS	CAS Number (Chemical Abstract Number)
LA_CODE	Louisiana Code for the Substance
CH_NAME	Chemical Name
TR_SECR	Trade secret (Yes or No)
CS_PUR	Is this a pure substance?
CS_MIX	Is the substance pure or a mixture?
CS_SOL	Is the substance solid?
CS_LIQ	Is the substance a liquid?
CS_GAS	Is the substance a gas?
CS_EHS	Is the substance EHS? (extremely hazardous substance)
EHS_NAME	Name of EHS
PH_FIRE	Is the substance a fire hazard?
PH_PRRE	Is the substance a pressure hazard?
PH_REAC	Is the substance a reactive hazard?
PH_IMAC	Is the substance an immediate risk to the health and safety of the public and workers?
PH_DECH	Is the substance a delayed risk?
A_MAX	The maximum number of days the substance is on site
A_AVG	The average number of days the substance is on site
N_DAYS	Number of days the substance is on site

You can search for chemicals stored by amount, type of storage, or location. You could also search for all the facilities that have large quantities of a specific chemical or type of chemical (EHS).

Table 6-3 Locations

Field Name	Description
IDNUM	Identification of the record that matches a specific chemical for a Facility
Amount	Amount of the Substance Stored
Units	Amount units (mass or volume)
Type	Type of storage
Pressure	Code reflecting the amount of pressure at which chemical is stored
Temp	Temperature at which the chemical is stored
LOCATION	Text describing the location of the chemical

6.5.2 Tier 2 Database Reporting Model

There are inputs and reviews along the way toward the creation of the Tier 2 database. The creation and accuracy of the database depends on the thoroughness of employees at the following locations:

▲ **Facility:** Employees complete the initial input of the data either in electronic form or on paper. The tables along with paper forms are sent to both a state Tier 2 reporting agency and the Local Emergency Planning Committee (LEPC). The local fire department or emergency management agency could receive the facility inventory reports.

▲ **State agency:** Employees receive the paper or electronic forms from the facility. Reviews the completeness of the data and stores the data. The state does a quality-control check on the data and sends the local agency a summary of the reporting facilities for review by the LEPC.

▲ **LEPC:** Receives the paper or electronic forms from the facility. Reviews the completeness of the data and stores the data. The LEPC may also receive the same information from the state Tier 2 reporting agency in a digital format compatible with CAMEO and Tier 2. The LEPC reviews the list and provides feedback to the state Tier 2 agency and facility.

FOR EXAMPLE

Not Reporting Chemicals

Companies who do not accurately report their chemical stockpiles and production are subject to fines and penalties. For example, in 2002 the EPA settled a complaint that VTC (now doing business as PolarFab LLC) in Bloomington, Minnesota, for alleged failure to disclose the storage of hazardous chemicals. The company had to pay a penalty of $36,800 and agreed to perform six environmental projects with a total cost of over $100,000.

SELF-CHECK

- What decision support function does the Tier 2 database provide?
- Why is it an advantage to use relational databases in decision support?
- What is a key factor in the creation and accuracy of databases?

6.6 Evaluating Databases

Databases and information systems are not all the same. Some are limited in information. The data could be old and out of date. The accuracy of the data could be very questionable. You have probably had the experience of looking for something in a database and not being able to find it. It can be a frustrating experience when you cannot find the information you need. For many information systems, it is very difficult to get the data that you need. Others are well-designed, user-friendly, and provide the needed information and details on the source of the information.

If you are involved in the input of data into a database, there are several things to keep in mind. You will need to understand:

▲ What data will be collected
▲ The purpose of the data
▲ Who will collect the data
▲ Who will input the data
▲ How the data will be used
▲ Who created the data

FOR EXAMPLE

The Coast Guard and Databases

Following Hurricane Katrina, the U.S. Coast Guard worked with FEMA to locate and remove boats that were blocking waterways. The list included over 4,500 boats of all sizes. The coast guard worked with state wildlife agency staff to identify boat owners and potential contact information. Once a boat was identified in the state wildlife agency database, location coordinates were added to the record. The coast guard could then arrange for salvage contractors to move the boat to a safe location and let the owner of the boat know its status. Accurate information on boat ownership helped the coast guard to manage this response.

▲ How the data will be placed into the system
▲ Who will manipulate the data for users

Any errors that are made in collecting and inputting data will lead to inaccurate information and faulty conclusions. For example, a facility might leave blank the amount of chemicals stored at their site. If you do not know the volume of a chemicals produced or stored at a facility, then you cannot properly plan for an accidental release. When evaluating a database, you will need to consider the following:

▲ **Data quality:** Accuracy, precision, completeness, age, scope of the information, timeliness, and source.
▲ **Accessibility**: Availability and possible access restrictions.
▲ **Information presentation:** Format of the data may limit the user in presenting information.

SELF-CHECK

- When inputting data into a database, what are the important factors to consider?
- What should be considered when evaluating the usefulness of a database?
- Why is accessibility of data important?

6.7 Using Emergency Management Databases

National databases and information systems are available from many federal, state, and local public agencies for public access, use, and dissemination. These databases provide essential information on local communities. The information is useful in risk assessment and hazards analysis. Envirofacts provides an excellent illustration of a national database. It has extremely useful hazardous chemical information for local communities in the United States. Envirofacts includes several environmental data sets available to you from the EPA on a national basis. It provides public access to sets of related databases. The system allows the user to select records by geographic area, by EPA program, or by chemical.

Other databases that are useful are in Hazards United States (HAZUS), developed by FEMA. HAZUS was a comprehensive hazard modeling and vulnerability assessment tool for many natural hazards. In 1997, FEMA began distribution and training for HAZUS. This natural hazards modeling and GIS program allowed the user to model earthquake hazards. Today, the model has expanded. It now provides for modeling of floods, wind, and coastal hazards in the United States. Within Hazards United States Multi-Hazard (HAZUS-MH) are extensive databases that provide the location of police and fire stations, EMS, schools, and hospitals. In addition, it provides a comprehensive count of buildings for commercial, industry, educational, governmental, and residential property. The database provides the count of buildings by type of property, type of construction, value of the property, as well as the value of the contents. The building inventory database is summarized by block. It provides a good basis for examining the impact of hazards on a community. FEMA recognized that this national database would need updating and provided tools for editing and updating all the data in HAZUS-MH. Emergency managers from small to large communities should examine this resource. They should ensure that the data accurately reflects the local community. Accurate building inventory data in HAZUS-MH will enable you to accurately determine the potential impacts of disasters on their community. The list below is a sample of one data table from HAZUS-MH for schools. Note what information is included in the database. Think about how you could use this information in different emergency management tasks. The information on schools includes:

▲ Name of school
▲ Identification number
▲ Address
▲ City
▲ State
▲ Zip code
▲ Contact

▲ Phone number

▲ School class

▲ Description (primary school)

▲ Year built

▲ Cost

▲ Number of stories

▲ Building type (masonry)

▲ Design level

▲ Foundation type

▲ First-floor height

▲ Generator (Yes/No)

▲ Number of students

▲ Shelter capacity

▲ Kitchen (Yes/No)

▲ Latitude

▲ Longitude

▲ County code

▲ Comment field

FEMA designed the database as a resource to emergency managers.

Additional helpful emergency management databases include the following:

▲ **Superfund: Comprehensive Environmental Response, Compensation, and Liability Information System (CERCLIS; www.epa.gov/superfund/index.htm)**. This database contains general information on hazardous waste sites and potential hazardous waste sites being assessed under the Superfund program. This data include location, contaminants, and cleanup actions. National Priorities List (NPL) sites are shown in a standardized site progress profile format. Information in this format includes current status of cleanup efforts, what cleanup measures have been reached, and how much liquid and solid-based media have been treated.

▲ **Hazardous Waste Reports: Resource Conservation and Recovery Act Information (RCRAInfo; www.epa.gov/rcraonline/)**. The data in RCRAInfo consist of information about generators, transporters, treaters, storers, and disposers of hazardous waste, which are required to give activity reports to state-level regulators. State regulators provide this information to regional and national EPA offices. Data includes permit status, compliance and violation information, cleanup activities, and information on related laws and regulations.

▲ **Emission data by media: toxic release inventory program (www.epa. gov/tri/).** The Toxic Release Inventory contains information on more than 650 chemicals that are being used, manufactured, treated, transported, or released into the environment. Manufacturers of these chemicals are required to report to state and local governments the locations and quantities of chemicals stored on-site. States give this information to the EPA. EPA compiles this data in an online, publicly accessible computerized database. This database includes basic facility information and chemical reports, tabulation of air emissions, surface water discharges, releases to land, underground injections, and transfers to off-site locations.

▲ **Aerometric Information Retrieval System (AIRS; www.epa.gov/enviro/ html/airs/airs_query_java.html).** This is a computer-based repository for information on air pollution in the United States. Information from this system is used to track compliance with requirements of various regulatory agencies and report air emissions estimates for pollutants regulated under the Clean Air Act. AIRS makes available information specifically relating to industrial plants and their components and, in so doing, provides valuable information about industrial facilities and the chemicals they release into the air. In addition, information is available on management of operating permit applications and renewals.

▲ **Water quality: Permit Compliance System (PCS).** PCS is the national database used to track compliance with National Pollutant Discharge Elimination System (NPDES) permit requirements. Information is provided on facilities that have been issued permits to discharge specific levels of wastewater into lakes, rivers, and streams. The following specific data is available: permits issued and when they expire, how much the company is permitted to discharge, the actual monitoring data, enforcement, compliance schedules, and compliance monitoring.

▲ **Envirofacts:** Provides an illustration of a public access national environmental database system. Users have access to data on facilities regulated by EPA. Records from EPA databases may be selected by location and downloaded to the user's system. Envirofacts also contains a grant information database, three integrating databases, and mapping applications. These are:

- **Grants Information.** Grants Information and Control System (GICS), which is updated bi-weekly.
- **Facility Index System (FINDS).** Integrates EPA facility information in the five facility based Envirofacts data systems.
- **Latitude/Longitude Info (LRT).** Integrates latitude and longitude coordinates for EPA-regulated facilities.
- **Master Chemical Integrator (EMCI).** Integrates chemical information in Envirofacts data systems.

- **Maps on Demand (MOD).** Contains SiteInfo, ZipInfo, CountyInfo, BasinInfo, and Facility Density Mapper.

Envirofacts (see Figure 6-2) contains data that is available under the Freedom of Information Act. No enforcement, budget-sensitive, or proprietary business information is contained in this database. The Envirofacts overview is highly recommended for new visitors to this site. The Envirofacts database is available on the Internet. Access to selected data in Envirofacts is provided through the online query forms provided at this site. These forms execute predefined queries for the types of facilities selected by filling out the form. A description of the software required for accessing the database is provided for users who want to query the database using other methods.

The information at this site describes the structure and content of the EPA program system databases included in Envirofacts. This description provides complete documentation of the database. It can be used to become familiar with the data available in Envirofacts. It is also essential information for users who write and execute their own queries.

Figure 6-2

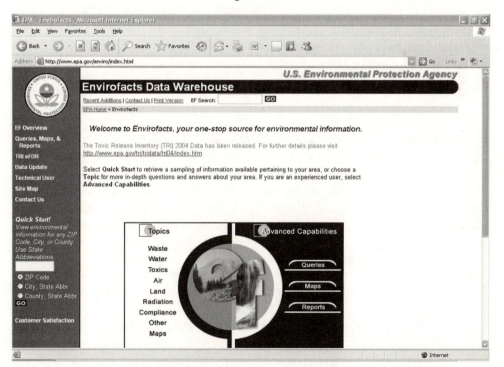

Opening screen for Envirofacts.

FOR EXAMPLE

Applying for Grants

Funding from state and federal agencies is available for training emergency response personnel in how to use information from hazards databases or services provided by governmental agencies such as the National Weather Service. Other funding supports training in the use of database systems such as CAMEO or HAZUS-MH.

SELF-CHECK

- What database illustrates a public access national environmental database system?
- What type of information would you want in a database for your community?
- How would you use the Toxic Release Inventory System (TRIS)?
- What database provides hazard modeling for natural disasters?
- How could the databases within HAZUS be used for vulnerability assessment?

6.8 Obtaining Data from Public Federal Data Sources

You can obtain useful data from many federal agencies. The following federal agencies collect, store, use, and provide access to data sets that are useful to the emergency management community. Take a look at the type of information that is available from these agencies and assess the data using the evaluation criteria previously noted.

▲ **Army Corps of Engineers (www.usace.army.mil/index.html.** Includes information on resources inside and outside the corps, programs, emergency operations, and organizational elements.

▲ **United States Department of Agriculture (www.usda.gov).** Includes information on USDA program missions, agencies, and programs, USDA's news and current information, Government Information Locator Service, and Topical Guide to Agricultural Programs.

▲ **Department of Commerce (www.doc.gov).** Includes information concerning the department's role in expanding U.S. exports, developing innovative technologies, gathering and disseminating statistical data, measuring economic growth, predicting the weather and monitoring stewardship.

▲ **Department of Energy (www.doe.gov).** Includes technical information as well as scientific and educational programs for technology, policy, and institutional leadership relevant to achieving efficiency in energy use.

▲ **Emergency Managers Weather Information Network (www.nws.noaa. gov/oso/oso1/oso12/document/wintip.htm).** Radio broadcast is one method used by the NWS and other public and private agencies for disseminating the EMWIN data stream. The NWS broadcasts the EMWIN data stream by radio only in the Washington, D.C., and Norman, Oklahoma, areas. Elsewhere, other public and private agencies downlink from a satellite and then retransmit by radio or other means. To receive an EMWIN radio broadcast, hardware and software is needed.

▲ **Environmental Protection Agency (www.epa.gov).** Access to EPA documents describing environmental information, as well as a number of links from the EPA and related organizations. Also the EPA's Public Information Center is available to provide assistance in accessing environmental information.

▲ **National Oceanic Atmospheric Administration (www.noaa.gov).** NOAA monitors and predicts changes in Earth's environment in order to ensure and enhance sustainable economic opportunities.

▲ **Nuclear Regulatory Commission (www.nrc.gov).** The NRC offers a variety of programs to make agency, licensee, and nuclear industry information available to the public. It includes improved standard technical specifications, occupational radiation exposure information, and plant information.

▲ **Occupational Safety and Health Administration (www.osha.gov).** The mission of OSHA is to save lives, prevent injuries, and protect the health of America's workers.

▲ **U.S. Geological Survey (www.usgs.gov).** The USGS is the nation's largest earth-science research and information agency. Access to USGS fact sheets, general information and contacts, public issues, education, grant information, and Internet resources.

▲ **Integrated Risk Information (IRIS; http://www.epa.gov/iris/).** IRIS is a reference document that contains U.S. EPA health risk assessment information used in determining safe levels of human and environmental exposure to chemicals. The effects of chronic and acute exposure to carcinogens on human health are detailed, and the regulatory status of over 450 chemicals is provided. Evaluations of the data are included and assist with comparison of information.

> ## FOR EXAMPLE
>
> ### Watershed
>
> You can use the EPA site (www.epa.gov/surf) to search and determine the watershed in your area. The EPA provides a search engine to help you find data from EPA databases concerning water quality in your community.

▲ **NASA Images Catalog (http://rsd.gsfc.nasa.gov/rsd/images).** NIX (NASA's Image eXchange) is a meta-search engine. It pulls images from across NASA's Web space. This Web space includes NASA's space centers and research centers. Not all of NASA's imagery resides in NASA's databases. As a result, some of NASA's imagery collections aren't searchable through NIX. The user can link with some of these external collections. The NASA Multimedia Gallery is one of these external links that includes a photo gallery, video gallery, and the arts gallery. NASA's Scientific and Technical Information Program (STI) sponsors NIX.

▲ **Registry of Toxic Effects of Chemical Substances (RTECS; http://library.dialog.com/bluesheets/html/bl0336.html).** RTECS is prepared by the National Institute for Occupational Safety and Health. RTECS is a reference document that provides an annual compendium offering toxicity data on over 100,000 substances. Extracted from scientific literature worldwide, the information presented includes specifics on mutagenicity, carcinogenicity, reproductive hazards, and acute and chronic toxicity of hazardous substances.

▲ **NIOSH Pocket Guide (www.cdc.gov/niosh/npg/default.html).** The Guide to Chemical Hazards from the National Institute for Occupational Safety and Health. The NIOSH pocket guide contains critical industrial hygiene data for approximately 675 chemicals regularly found in the workplace. The information presented includes exposure limits and IDLH (immediately dangerous to life and health) concentrations. It also includes incompatibilities and recitatives, personal protection, and recommendations for respirator selection. The guide has been proven helpful in recognizing and controlling occupational chemical hazards. It offers data compiled from a number of sources. Two of the sources are NIOSH criteria documents and Current Intelligence Bulletins (CIBs). It includes references in the field of industrial hygiene, occupational medicine, toxicology, and analytical chemistry. Updated more frequently than the hard copy, *NIOSH Pocket Guide,* the electronic pocket guide offers fast, easy access to industrial hygiene data by using databases. It allows the user to identify substances and avoid confusion or interpretation error. Searches can be done using chemical name, formula, CAS or RTECS numbers, and synonyms or trade names.

SELF-CHECK

- In decision support, why would it be important to have access to the Integrated Risk Information database?
- What weather information source can be downloaded from a satellite?
- What database provides recommendations for protection from chemical hazards?

SUMMARY

As you have learned, it is critical for you to have up-to-date and accurate information to plan, mitigate, and respond to disasters. In obtaining accurate information, you will need to use and rely on databases. Before you use databases to make important decisions, you will also need to evaluate them. In addition, there are many federal and state databases that are available to you to help you make well-informed decisions. The idea behind management information systems is that they provide a systematic way to collect, manipulate, maintain, and distribute information throughout an organization. Management information systems provide a way for you to get the right information quickly and thus support decision making.

KEY TERMS

Data	A fact or things that are known.
Federal Emergency Management Information System (FEMIS)	An automated decision support system that makes it possible to preplan for emergencies and to coordinate operations and make decisions during an emergency.
Information	Data that is processed or used in some form of analysis.
Management information system	A set of digital databases that may be sorted, merged, retrieved, displayed, and used to make decisions or calculations.

Metadata

Data about data, and includes information on where the data was obtained, when, how it was formatted or altered, geospatial references if available, purpose of the data, and ownership.

National Emergency Management Information System (NEMIS)

An information system that was designed to automate and support vital emergency response and recovery operations by the federal government.

ASSESS YOUR UNDERSTANDING

Go to www.wiley.com/college/pine to evaluate knowledge of emergency management decision support systems.
Measure your learning by comparing pre-test and post-test results.

Summary Questions

1. A management information system includes which of the following?
   (a) Data
   (b) Means of sorting the data
   (c) Information to support decisions
   (d) All of the above

2. The idea behind an information system is to provide a systematic way to collect, manipulate, maintain, and distribute information in an organization. True or False?

3. Which of the following best describes a quality requirement for an information system?
   (a) Accuracy of the data
   (b) The data is in a specific format
   (c) The data is timely
   (d) All of the above

4. The performance of an information system is best characterized by
   (a) capacity, productivity, and consistency.
   (b) completeness, clarity, and concision.
   (c) timeliness, high quality, and dependable.
   (d) All of the above

5. Management information systems provide a means for the emergency manager to get the right information quickly. True or False?

6. Data can be processed into information. True or False?

7. Which of the following is included in metadata?
   (a) Name and definition of each field in the database
   (b) The Census Bureau phone number
   (c) Only geospatial information
   (d) Zip codes

8. When evaluating a database quality consideration, include accuracy, precision, completeness and age. True or False?

9. What is information?

(a) Data

(b) Data that has been processed

(c) Specific types of data

(d) Data about data

Review Questions

1. Why is data so important to the emergency manager in preparedness and response?

2. What are the qualities of useful data?

3. Why is it so important to take the time to plan what goes into an information system?

4. Under what circumstances would you want to use a hazardous chemical (Tier 2) database?

5. What qualities do you need to consider about data before inputting information into a database?

6. Give an example of how information presentation can be limited by the format of the data.

7. What are the factors that comprise data performance?

Applying This Chapter

1. You are the emergency manager for a small town that has areas that are prone to flooding. You do not have a database that helps you mitigate flooding. What types of information would you want in the database and why?

2. You are the emergency manager for a town that is vulnerable to hurricanes. You are reviewing data in the emergency management database. As you review the data, how do you determine if it is useful?

3. You are the emergency manager for a city that has tons of hazardous waste trucked on its interstates every year. What public resources do you have to prevent and respond to a hazardous chemical accident?

4. You are the emergency manager for a community where the majority of the population is 60 or over. What equipment and databases do you use to reduce deaths due to breathing problems? What information do you make available to the public?

5. You are the emergency manager for a community that is home to industries that use toxic chemicals in their manufacturing process. What are

the most important databases to use when working with these facilities and why?

6. The list below is a sample of one table from HAZUS-MH for schools. Note what information is included in the database. How could you use this information to enhance emergency preparedness, response, recovery, and mitigation activities?

- Schools
- Identification number
- Name of school
- Address
- City
- State
- Zip code
- Contact
- Phone number
- School class
- Description (primary school)
- Year built
- Cost
- Number of stories
- Building type (masonry)
- Design level
- Foundation type
- First-floor height
- Generator (Yes/No)
- Number of students
- Shelter capacity
- Kitchen (Yes/No)
- Latitude
- Longitude
- County code
- Comment field

7. FEMA designed the database to be a resource to emergency managers. What data fields would be useful in determining if a school would make a good emergency shelter for a local community?

YOU TRY IT

Information

You are the emergency manager for a town that has just suffered from a massive landslide. You are trying to make decisions about the resources you need and how they should be deployed. Reports are coming in from all over the field. Your employees are generating dozens of different reports. How would you like the information presented to you, and what type of information do you need?

Creating a Database

You are the emergency manager for a community that is prone to flooding but does not have a database on the water levels. You decide to create a database. What fields do you need and why?

Evaluating Databases

You are the emergency manager for a community that does not currently have a database. You meet with the information systems team that is going to design and implement a database. What qualities do you tell them are important in the database architecture and design?

7

HAZARDS ANALYSIS AND MODELING
Predicting the Impact

Starting Point

Go to www.wiley.com/college/pine to assess your knowledge of hazards analysis and modeling.
Determine where to concentrate your effort.

What You'll Learn in This Chapter

▲ How to use hazard modeling to simulate real disasters
▲ Different components of the SLOSH model
▲ How to read the output of the ALOHA chemical dispersion model
▲ Types of models for evacuations, fires, and drought
▲ Characteristics to consider when evaluating hazard models

After Studying This Chapter, You'll Be Able To

▲ Examine ways to use the results of modeling
▲ Examine the strengths and limitations of the SLOSH model
▲ Examine the conditions that make ALOHA chemical dispersion model results unreliable
▲ Compare and contrast the analysis Levels 1, 2, and 3 of HAZUS-MH
▲ Examine under what circumstances to use OREMS
▲ Analyze what hazard models your office needs based on a careful evaluation of the strengths and disadvantages of each model

Goals and Outcomes

▲ Evaluate the output of hazard models and how to use the output results to prepare for potential disasters
▲ Evaluate how to use the SLOSH model for planning, response, recovery, and mitigation efforts
▲ Select the optimal conditions for using the ALOHA chemical dispersion model
▲ Evaluate how to mitigate disasters using HAZUS-MH
▲ Compare and contrast the models for fires, evacuations, and drought
▲ Select which hazard models to use based on your community's hazard vulnerability analysis and the quality, cost, usability, completeness, and timeliness of the models

INTRODUCTION

You may not be able to predict the future, but with the help of computer modeling programs, you can predict how a hazard will affect your community. In this chapter, you will examine the strengths and limitations of the SLOSH hurricane model in terms of planning, response, recovery, and mitigation efforts. You will also examine the use of the ALOHA model in chemical dispersion incidents. You will assess the strengths and limitations of another modeling program, HAZUS-MH. You will also assess when to use additional models for other disasters such as fires and drought. You will then evaluate each model. You will consider how you can use these programs to mitigate disasters, prepare for disasters, and enhance your response to disasters.

7.1 Modeling and Emergency Management

What if you could predict the future? What if you knew a hurricane was coming and would cause thousands of people to be displaced, lose their homes, and be in danger of losing their lives? Would you try to save them? Would you warn them? Would you evacuate? Answering these questions is the purpose of hazard modeling. **Hazard modeling** is a simulation of a real system or replication of a potential hazard event. Before you can determine how a disaster will affect your community, you must first determine what hazards your community is vulnerable to. Modeling as a part of the hazards analysis process provides a means of simulating the nature and extent of a disaster. With modeling, you can simulate a disaster using computers and graphics. This let's you see how a specific storm, chemical incident, fire, landslide, or tornado could affect the community. Because modeling is associated with complex mathematical formulas, assumptions, and high-powered computers, it is often left to the experts. Today with advancements in computer technology, you can provide the data inputs for the models, run the model, and interpret the output of the models. The key is for you to understand what is needed in the hazard model, what the limitations of the model are, and how to use the results in emergency management activities.

Many hazard models are currently being adapted to run on computers, including laptops, that are available in emergency management offices. Emergency management staff and managers can thus utilize them. Some are easy to use, but at the same time they are very capable of providing an accurate representation of a hazard event. For example ALOHA is widely used because it provides a very accurate representation of a chemical spill and can be run in a short time period. As with any model, it does require training and practice, but many local emergency responders find this model a great asset in both planning and response to hazardous chemicals. Many local hazardous materials teams are well trained in planning for and responding to hazardous chemical spills; the ALOHA chemical dispersion model is often used by these teams to prepare for and respond to spills in their community. It shows the size of the area in which chemicals will be dispersed during a hazardous materials chemical incident.

7.1.1 The Technology behind Modeling

A model of a natural or technological hazard is a simulation or replication of a potential event. It is a "simplified representation of the real system" (Drager 1993). In the real world, a disaster is very complex. There are many factors involved. Wind velocity, the surface roughness, air temperature, and surface features all contribute to the effects of natural events such as hurricanes. These factors also affect man-made disasters such as chemical accidents. You can build these factors into a hazard model as data inputs, although the model itself is a set of mathematical equations and formulas.

With this inherent complexity, all models must make simplifying assumptions. Therefore, the attempt to exactly model a disaster is only an approximation. The accuracy of the model's estimation of an event is determined by the assumptions contained within the model along with the data and specifications made by the user. The user thus could provide key inputs based on weather conditions, local geography, and, in a chemical spill, data concerning the chemical and incident scenario. All these factors are used in chemical dispersion modeling. The key is to provide accurate data inputs. For example, if you enter a population of one million for your city when the population is only half a million, your results will be inaccurate. Or, you may enter information into the computer indicating that most people live in low-lying areas when they do not. In this case, the model for a hurricane will simulate a worse disaster than you will have in reality.

Computer models that simulate disasters require a variety of data sets. As an example, flood-modeling programs require information on the type of soil, land use characteristics, and elevation points in the study area. These models also require weather information, such as precipitation readings. In many cases, the data is very accurate and meets engineering quality standards. However, some data sets may be less accurate, thus affecting the accuracy of the model output. Complete sets of data that are used in a model are very difficult to obtain. They may require extensive time and expense to prepare.

If the agency sponsoring a modelling project is willing to put in the time and expense, the model is able to replicate a specific disaster event. Unfortunately, agencies are often unable or unwilling to allocate resources to the modeling efforts. Using approximate and not exact data will provide outputs that are less accurate. In flooding models, for instance, much of the data may have been prepared at a scale that could have errors by as much as 200 feet. You should discuss the quality of the data with those who are running the model. You should ensure that the use of a model is consistent with the data used in the program. Given the limitations of the data used in a model, current modeling technology allows the user to predict close approximation to the real event.

Even with the limits of the technology, modeling still provides the best working estimate of the potential impact of a disaster. The outputs from models may provide the basis for determining vulnerability zones to floods or chemical releases. They can be used in response plans and procedures. Modeling provides a tool to help establish priorities for evacuation plans or land use planning.

Drager et al. (1993) noted that modeling attempts to quantify elements of the real world. For example, they looked at models for the evacuation of a building. They determined that with all the assumptions, the best route for a person from a building will depend on the time when he or she starts to escape. The models are usually based on assumptions such as that a person will behave rationally and follow the best route. The fact that in modeling human behavior, most models seriously underestimate total evacuation time. This is because the last people who leave the building seldom followed pre-defined evacuation plans (Drager 1993). An understanding of the assumptions used and how these assumptions were made are critical. You must have this understanding to be able to use the model as a managerial tool. Drager stresses that "the primary condition for performing an evacuation analysis is that the critical questions with respect to the system to be analyzed are raised. This process requires skill of the analyst as well as suitable calculation tools" (1993).

Mathematical Models

In addition to the need to understand the assumptions made in a model, it is also helpful to know which type of model was used. The mathematical models used at the National Hurricane Center include statistical, dynamic, and combination (statistical and dynamic together) models.

▲ *Statistical models* forecast the future by using current information about a hurricane and comparing it to historical knowledge about the behavior of similar storms. The historical record for storms over the North Atlantic begins in 1871, while the record for storms for the East Pacific extends back to 1945.

▲ *Dynamic models* are designed to use the results of global atmospheric model forecasts in different ways to forecast storm motion and intensity. Global models take current wind, temperature, pressure, and humidity observations and make forecasts of the actual atmosphere in which a storm exists. Because of their mathematical simplicity, dynamic models ignore the behavior of historical storms.

▲ *Combination models* can be constructed to capitalize on the strengths of each. Because of their simplicity, statistical models were designed first for storm forecasting. Combination models were developed as global models and were used in making forecasts in tropical regions.

FOR EXAMPLE

Use of Models

As computers have become more powerful, global models have improved and pure dynamic models became more precise. This is particularly true when storms approach regions close to the continents where the state of the atmospheric environment is adequately observed and well known. Over oceanic areas far removed from land, combination models are still the best performers.

7.1.2 Understanding the Results of Modeling

Detailed scientific results from complex models are often not understood by the public (Kirkwood 1994). Kirkwood states that in many cases, the public does not understand or have sufficient scientific knowledge to evaluate risks from hazards. He further explains that new technology is very often presented as being too complex for those outside the scientific community to understand. The fact is that the public cannot know what it cannot understand. There are two implications to Kirkwood's observations. First, you must communicate with the public in direct, nontechnical language. You must take into account the public's lack of technical knowledge. Attempts to gain public acceptance of risks and hazards could be aimed at increasing the level of technical knowledge of the public. Local news outlets can also partner with local officials to inform the public of hazards and risks. Storm warnings that may be based on complex models can also be expressed in graphical form to illustrate the technical basis of the weather model outputs.

Kirkwood also believes that the public has a simplistic view of risk and that decisions are based on a "rule of thumb." The key for you is to provide enough information to the public so that each person can weigh the risks and make decisions. Public education and partnering with the local media are long-term investments in community education. Both the emergency management community and the media have an interest in understanding the science behind the hazard models. An increased understanding of hazards by the public can lead to more informed decisions concerning sheltering, evacuations, and long-term actions to reduce vulnerability. A word of caution here: You cannot assume that simply modeling a disaster will make your community better prepared. You must take the lessons you learned from the simulation and apply them in planning and mitigation. You must also have the support of government officials in order for your efforts to be effective. You must also have the budget needed to take the necessary preparation measures.

SELF-CHECK

- Define **hazard modeling**.
- The outputs from models can provide what types of information?
- What's the advantage of using a combination model?

7.2 Using a Hurricane Model (SLOSH)

Different types of disasters are modeled with different programs. One of the models used for hurricanes is called **SLOSH** (sea, lake, and overland surges from hurricanes). The SLOSH model is used by the National Weather Service (NWS) to calculate potential surge heights from hurricanes. SLOSH was developed for real-time forecasting of surges from actual hurricanes and as a planning tool for evacuation and shelter decisions by state and local entities.

The SLOSH model is used to examine the impact of hurricanes along the Gulf and Atlantic coasts. It is based on information from past storms and is used to determine the effect of a storm as it reaches land. Outputs show the inundation area of a storm as it reaches land and the depth of the water in these areas.

The SLOSH model is based on generalized assumptions and data to model all storms within all basins. The model has been adjusted based on comparisons of computed and observed meteorological and surge-height data for numerous historical hurricanes. It is based on information about many storms rather than a single storm event within a basin.

The model is designed for different Atlantic and Gulf Coast basins. It includes the topography of the following:

▲ Inland areas
▲ River basins and waterways
▲ Bays and large inland water bodies
▲ Significant natural and man-made barriers, such as barrier islands, dunes, roadbeds, floodwalls, levees, and so on
▲ A segment of the continental shelf

The SLOSH model simulates inland flooding from storm surge and permits overtopping of barriers and flow through barrier gaps.

7.2.1 SLOSH for Planning, Response, Recovery, and Mitigation

The SLOSH output footprint, wind calculations, and water depth can be used to examine the vulnerability zones to hurricanes. Variables used in the model include the direction, severity of the winds, and speed of the storm. As a result of the use of the model, you should be able to determine the areas that may be affected by specific types of storms. As a planning tool, it presents a realistic description of the results of an event and provides the basis for conducting drills or capability assessment efforts in the community.

When SLOSH is used in a planning mode for a specific basin, as many as 1,500 simulated hurricanes may be computed. As many as 150 storm tracks are modeled for a specific basin. These tracks represent the five categories of hurricane intensity, as described by the **Saffir-Simpson Hurricane Scale**; different paths of the storm track (west, west-northwest, northwest, north-northwest, north, north-northeast, northeast, east-northeast, and east); forward speeds of 5 and 15 miles per hour; and numerous landfall locations.

The characteristics of the simulated hurricanes are determined from an analysis of historical hurricanes that have occurred within the basin. The parameters selected for the modeled storms are the intensities, forward speeds, directions of motion, and radius of maximum winds.

When you work with SLOSH, you will need to input the following data concerning the location and nature of the hazard:

- ▲ Latitude and longitude of storm positions at 6-hour intervals for a 72-hour tract
- ▲ The lowest atmospheric sea level pressure in the eye of the hurricane at 6-hour intervals
- ▲ The storm size measured from the center to the region of maximum winds, commonly referred to as the "radius of maximum winds." Wind speed is not an input parameter since the model calculates a wind field for the modeled storm by balancing forces according to weather input parameters.

SLOSH output for a modeled storm consists of a tabulated storm history containing hourly values of storm position, speed, direction of motion, pressure, and radius of maximum winds; a surface envelope of highest surges; and for preselected grid points, time-history tabulations of values for surge heights, wind speeds, and wind directions. The model also provides a two-dimensional snapshot display of surges at specified times during a simulation.

The maximum storm surge is the highest water level reached at each location along the coastline during the passage of a hurricane. Maximum surges along the coastline do not necessarily occur at the same time. The time of the maximum surge for one location may differ by several hours from the maximum surge that occurs at another location.

Figure 7-1

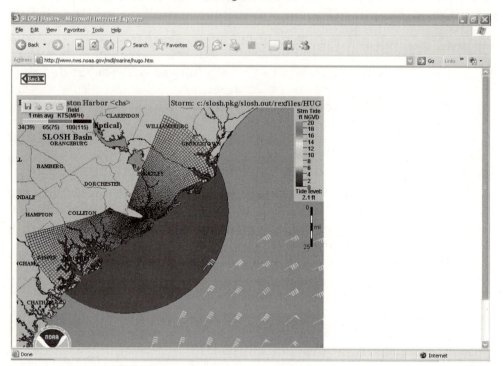

SLOSH model showing a MEOW for a basin.

This maximum surge is called a *maximum envelope of water* (MEOW). As many as 90 MEOWs are developed for a basin study area. Each MEOW represents a different combination of hurricane intensity, direction, and forward speed. The MEOW shows the peak surge heights for each grid cell within the basin, independent of where the hurricane actually crosses the coastline. See Figure 7-1 for an example of the SLOSH model showing a MEOW for a basin.

When SLOSH is used in a planning mode, the MEOW displays from the study do not predict the limits of inundation from a single storm. They rather delineate the areas that are threatened by storm surge from many potential storms.

MEOWs can thus be used in a community vulnerability analysis to identify the areas, populations, and facilities that are potentially vulnerable to flooding associated with hurricanes. MEOWs can also be used to do the following:

▲ Determine evacuation zones
▲ Determine evacuation scenarios for local areas
▲ Quantify the population at risk under a range of hurricane intensities
▲ Identify major medical institutional and other facilities that could be vulnerable to storm surge

Verification of SLOSH is performed in a "hindcast" mode, using the real-time operational model code and storm parameters and an initial observed sea surface height occurring approximately 48 hours before the storm landfalls or affects the basin. This is a good method for correcting the model, but hurricanes are a

FOR EXAMPLE

Hurricane Pam

In 2004, FEMA, the National Weather Service, Louisiana State University researchers, the state of Louisiana, and private contractors developed the parameters of a simulated hurricane exercise. The goal of the exercise was to improve state and local emergency response plans and provide better coordination to the National Response Plan. The National Weather Service used SLOSH and other hurricane models to simulate Hurricane Pam. This simulated storm had sustained winds of 120 miles per hour, up to 20 inches of rain in parts of southeast Louisiana, and a storm surge that topped levees in the New Orleans area. According to the disaster exercise, more than 1 million people had to evacuate. The simulated hurricane destroyed 400,000 buildings. If this scenario sounds familiar, it is because it is close to what happened a year later during the real Hurricane Katrina. Unfortunately, federal, state, and local officials had not finalized emergency response plans from this exercise when Hurricane Katrina hit the Gulf Coast communities. The SLOSH model outputs and other hurricane storm surge models clearly showed when evacuation routes should be closed and the impacts that powerful storms would have. Local and state officials adapted their evacuation plans and had a real test in the fall of 2004. More lessons learned from these real storms resulted in changes as to how the evacuation of New Orleans would occur in future storms. When Hurricane Katrina hit, more people evacuated New Orleans than ever before. The models had helped state and local officials more clearly understand how to get people out of the vulnerable city.

The use of Hurricane Pam also shows that hazard models cannot guarantee that a community will be risk-free. Effective emergency management requires collaboration between many government agencies at all levels and between the public, private, and nonprofit sectors. Hazard models are tools that provide information for decision making, especially public policy decisions. Unfortunately, the hazard models could not ensure that all residents vulnerable to a hazard could be evacuated. The model could only show that extensive flooding in the city of New Orleans was a possibility and that planning to get all residents out should be initiated.

rare meteorological event for any given region. You must be careful in assuming that the model is an actual representation of a specific storm.

7.2.2 Strengths of SLOSH

SLOSH has several strengths. It is run by experts from the National Hurricane Center. SLOSH is provided to the public and to public officials on a timely basis prior to a storm making landfall. With SLOSH, you can receive graphic displays that show the path of the storm and that show coastal areas that could be impacted by the impending storm. Also, public officials and the public can use the outputs to help make decisions concerning when to evacuate and what routes to take.

7.2.3 Limitations of SLOSH

SLOSH requires considerable expertise usually limited to staff from the National Hurricane Center and the National Weather Service. When this model is run for evacuation planning, the Army Corps of Engineers and the National Hurricane Center run many hurricane scenarios. As a result, the process takes extensive planning and a great deal of time. Unfortunately, the evacuation planning using SLOSH for Southeastern Louisiana was in process when Hurricane Katrina hit in 2005. SLOSH can also be used in an operational mode or real time. The National Hurricane Center uses the latest weather data from a specific storm and provides the outputs as part of their public information. SLOSH outputs are not directly provided to either the public or local or state officials. The information provided on a specific storm is usually limited to the path, intensity of the storm, wind speeds, and forward movement of the storm. Public warnings do not give anticipated storm surge values from SLOSH.

THE SAFFIR-SIMPSON HURRICANE SCALE

The *Saffir-Simpson Hurricane Scale* was intended as a general guide for use by public safety officials during hurricane emergencies. It does not reflect the effects of varying localized coastline configuration, barriers, or other factors, which can greatly influence the surge heights that occur at differing locations during a single hurricane event.

▲ **Category 1:** Winds of 74 to 95 miles per hour. Damage primarily to shrubbery, trees, foliage, and unanchored mobile homes. No real damage to other structures. Some damage to poorly constructed signs. Storm surge 4 to 5 feet above normal. Low-lying coastal roads inundated, minor pier damage, some small craft in exposed anchorage torn from moorings.

▲ **Category 2:** Winds of 96 to 110 miles per hour. Considerable damage to shrubbery and tree foliage. Some trees blown down. Major damage to exposed mobile homes. Extensive damage to poorly constructed signs. Some damage to roofing materials of buildings; some window and door damage. No major damage to buildings. Storm surge 6 to 8 feet above normal. Coastal roads and low-lying escape routes inland cut by rising water 2 to 4 hours before arrival of hurricane center. Considerable damage to piers. Marinas flooded. Small craft in unprotected anchorages torn from moorings. Evacuation of some shoreline residences and low-lying inland areas required.

▲ **Category 3:** Winds of 111 to 130 miles per hour. Foliage torn from trees; large trees blown down. Practically all poorly constructed signs blown down. Some damage to roofing materials of buildings; some window and door damage. Some structural damage to small buildings. Mobile homes destroyed. Storm surge 9 to 12 feet above normal. Serious flooding at coast, and many smaller structures near coast destroyed; larger structures near coast damaged by battering waves and floating debris. Low-lying escape routes inland cut by rising water 3 to 5 hours before hurricane center arrives.

▲ **Category 4:** Winds of 131 to 155 miles per hour. Shrubs and trees blown down; all signs down. Extensive damage to roofing materials, windows, and doors. Complete failure of roofs on many small residences. Complete destruction of mobile homes. Storm surge 13 to 18 feet above normal. Major damage to lower floors of structures near shore due to flooding and battering waves and floating debris. Low-lying escape routes inland are cut by rising water 3 hours before hurricane center arrives. Major erosion of beaches.

▲ **Category 5:** Winds greater than 155 miles per hour. Shrubs and trees blown down; considerable damage to roofs of buildings; all signs are blown down. Very severe and extensive damage to windows and doors. Complete failure of roofs on many residences and industrial buildings. Extensive shattering of glass in windows and doors. Some complete building failures. Small buildings overturned or blown away. Complete destruction of mobile homes. Storm surge possibly greater than 18 feet above normal. Major damage to lower floors of all structures less than 15 feet above sea level. Low-lying escape routes inland cut by rising water 3 to 5 hours before hurricane center arrives.

SELF-CHECK

- Define **Saffir-Simpson Hurricane Scale**.
- What types of input information are needed for the SLOSH model?
- What does the term *MEOW* mean, and why is it important?
- What groups are responsible for managing the SLOSH system?

7.3 Using the ALOHA Chemical Dispersion Model

Chemical storage facilities have always posed a security and emergency response challenge for governmental agencies. An accidental release of chemicals from a storage facility or a railway car transporting waste would require you to track the chemical's gas cloud, or plume. You would need to track the plume to determine its potential impact on the nearby population. In light of the terrorist attacks of September 11, you should also be prepared for an intentional release with the potential for a big impact (Tomaszewski, 2005). The tool that you have to help you predict the potential impact of such an event is ALOHA.

ALOHA stands for aerial locations of hazardous atmospheres. It was developed by the Environmental Protection Agency (EPA) and the National Oceanic and Atmospheric Administration (NOAA). Its purpose is to simulate airborne releases of hazardous chemicals. The National Safety Council distributes ALOHA and provides technical support. The ALOHA plots a "footprint." The footprint represents the area within which the ground-level concentration of a pollutant gas is predicted to exceed individual exposure levels. Several exposure levels are provided by EPA and used in ALOHA. These allow the user to determine the area at which the modeled airborne pollutant could become hazardous to people. ALOHA plots a footprint that represents the zone where the ground-level pollutant concentration is predicted to exceed permitted or recommended exposure levels. ALOHA allows the user to specify different exposure levels, such as levels for children, older adults, and adult male workers.

ALOHA uses the Gaussian model, which is a computer model. It is used to calculate air pollution concentrations and was developed in 1981 by Roland Draxler of NOAA. The model assumes that a cloud of pollutants or chemicals is carried downwind from its emission source by a mean wind. The model also assumes that concentrations in the cloud, or plume, can be approximated by assuming that the highest concentration occurs on the horizontal and vertical midlines of the plume. The distribution has Gaussian or bell-shaped concentration profiles in the vertical and horizontal planes. ALOHA uses the Gaussian model

Figure 7-2

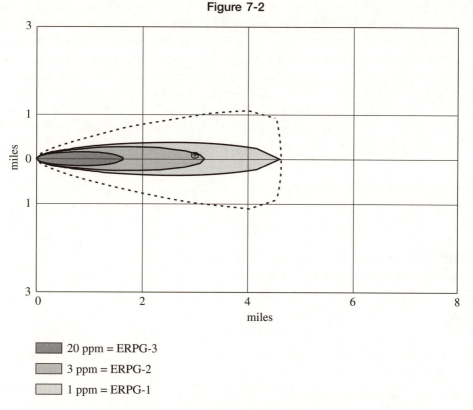

20 ppm = ERPG-3
3 ppm = ERPG-2
1 ppm = ERPG-1

ALOHA footprint for a chlorine tank release.

to predict how gases that are about as buoyant as air will disperse in the atmosphere. According to this model, wind and atmospheric turbulence are the forces that move the molecules of a released gas through the air, so as an escaped cloud is blown downwind, "turbulent mixing" causes it to spread out in the crosswind and upward directions. According to the Gaussian model, any crosswind slice of a moving pollutant cloud looks like a bell-shaped curve, high in the center and lower on the sides.

7.3.1 Model Outputs

ALOHA plots a footprint. ALOHA footprints can be automatically scaled and displayed on a grid or scaled to a user-selected scale in ALOHA's Footprint window.

On ALOHA's footprint plot, the shaded area represents the footprint itself (see Figure 7-2). Dashed lines along both sides of the footprint represent uncertainty in the wind direction. The wind rarely blows constantly from any one direction. As it shifts direction, it blows a pollutant cloud in a new direction. The "uncertainty lines" around the footprint enclose the region within which the gas cloud is expected to remain about 19 out of 20 times. The lower the wind speed, the more the wind changes direction. So as wind speed decreases, the uncertainty lines become farther apart. They form a circle when wind speed is very low. A curved, dashed line leads from the end of one uncertainty line, across the tip of the footprint, to the end of the other uncertainty line. This line represents the farthest downwind extent of the footprint, if the wind were to shift to rotate the footprint toward either uncertainty line.

7.3.2 Strengths of ALOHA

ALOHA has several strengths, is available without cost, and is easy to use. The following are also features of ALOHA:

▲ It may be used with heavy gases or neutrally buoyant gases.
▲ It provides easy-to-understand estimates of the source strength.
▲ It can simulate releases from tanks, puddles, and pipes.
▲ It can calculate indoor air infiltration.
▲ It contains an extensive chemical library that is user expandable.
▲ It estimates gas cloud area and concentration over time under varying environmental conditions.
▲ It can be used with real-time input of weather data provided by the user or directly from a meteorological station.
▲ It plots toxic cloud footprints onto area maps.
▲ It has an easy-to-use graphic interface and display.
▲ It includes mapping program, called MARPLOT that uses digitized mapping data or other mapping images. Also enables customized overlays showing area facilities and vulnerable populations.
▲ It is a available for Windows or Macintosh platforms.

7.3.3 Limitations of ALOHA

ALOHA or any other model is only as accurate as the information you give it to work with. But even when you provide the best input values possible, ALOHA, like any model, can be unreliable in certain situations. It cannot model some types of releases at all.

ALOHA's results can be unreliable when the following conditions exist:

▲ **Very low wind speeds.** ALOHA's footprint accurately depicts a pollutant cloud's location only if the wind direction does not change from the value that you entered. Generally, wind direction is least predictable when wind speed is low.

▲ **Very stable atmospheric conditions.** Under the most stable atmospheric conditions, there is usually very little wind. There is almost no mixing of the pollutant cloud with the surrounding air. Gas concentrations within the cloud can remain high far from the source. The cloud spreads slowly, and high gas concentrations may build up in valleys or depressions and remain for long periods of time. This occurs even at distances far from the release point. ALOHA does not account for buildup of high gas concentrations in low-lying areas.

▲ **Wind shifts and terrain steering effects.** ALOHA assumes that wind speed and direction are constant (at any given height) throughout the area downwind of a chemical release. ALOHA also assumes that the ground below a dispersing cloud to be flat and free of obstacles. In reality, though, the wind typically shifts speed and direction as it flows up or down slopes, between hills and down into valleys, turning where terrain features turn. In urban areas, wind flow around large buildings forms eddies and changes direction and speed. This significantly alters a cloud's shape and movement. Through streets bordered by large buildings can generate a "street canyon" wind pattern that constrains and funnels a dispersing cloud.

FOR EXAMPLE

NOAA Office of Response and Restoration and ALOHA

Hurricanes Katrina and Rita have passed, but the NOAA Office of Response and Restoration (http://response.restoration.noaa.gov/) will be on the scene for a year or more responding to the challenges faced in cleaning up the hazardous chemical and oil spills generated by the storms' destructive powers. Since the passage of the hurricanes, NOAA, along with the EPA, U.S. Army Corps of Engineers, and the U.S. Coast Guard, has been working to assist in coordinating response and restoration efforts by positioning NOAA-trained "Scientific Support Teams" (www.incidentnews.gov/) in each of the joint federal-state agency command posts established in Alexandria and Baton Rouge, Louisiana; Mobile, Alabama; and Austin and Houston, Texas. NOAA and EPA staff utilized many models, including ALOHA, to examine the potential impacts of large and small tanks containing hazardous materials. Models such as ALOHA could help responders work safely during cleanup operations. Simulations of breaches from tanks could be run quickly and could show responders graphics of danger zones.

TERMS USED IN ALOHA

The following are some important terms and phrases used in the ALOHA model:

▲ **Level of concern or output concentration:** A level of concern (LOC) is a threshold concentration of an airborne pollutant. It is usually the concentration above which a hazard may exist. ALOHA plots a "footprint" that represents the zone where the ground-level pollutant concentration is predicted to exceed the LOC at some time after a release begins.

▲ **Immediately dangerous to life or health (IDLH) level:** This is the default LOC in ALOHA. An IDLH has been established for about one-third of the chemicals in ALOHA. You may choose to use the IDLH, when a value is available, as your LOC. You can also choose another threshold concentration.

▲ **Threshold limits:** The American Conference of Governmental Industrial Hygienists (ACGIH) publishes recommended occupational exposure limits for hazardous chemicals. The TLV, or threshold limit value, is the maximum airborne concentration of a given hazardous chemical to which nearly all workers can be exposed during normal 8-hour workdays and 40-hour workweeks for an indefinite number of weeks without adverse effects.

▲ **TLV-TWA:** The maximum allowable time weighted average concentration for an 8-hour day and 40-hour work week. TLV-TWA values are obtained either from industrial experience, from experimental human and animal studies, or from a combination of both. If a TLV-TWA level has been established for a chemical that you select, this value will be displayed on ALOHA's text summary window.

▲ **Stability class:** The atmosphere may be more or less turbulent at any given time. It depends on the amount of incoming solar radiation as well as other factors. Meteorologists have defined six "atmospheric stability classes," each representing a different degree of turbulence in the atmosphere. When moderate to strong incoming solar radiation heats air near the ground, causing it to rise and generating large eddies, the atmosphere is considered "unstable," or relatively turbulent. Unstable conditions are associated with atmospheric stability classes A and B. When solar radiation is relatively weak, air near the surface has less of a tendency to rise and less turbulence develops. In this case, the atmosphere is considered "stable," or less turbulent. The wind is weak. The stability class would be E or F. Stability classes D and C represent conditions of more neutral stability, or moderate turbulence. Neutral conditions are associated with relatively strong wind speeds and moderate solar radiation.

FOR EXAMPLE

Summary of Release Scenario

SITE DATA INFORMATION:

- Location: Anywhere, USA
- Building Air Exchanges per Hour: 0.86 (sheltered single storied)
- Time: June 20, 2005, 1000 hours EDT (user specified)

CHEMICAL INFORMATION:

- Chemical Name: CHLORINE   Molecular Weight: 70.91 g/mol
- ERPG-3: 20 ppm ERPG-2: 3 ppm   ERPG-1: 1 ppm
- DLH: 10 ppm
- Carcinogenic risk—see CAMEO
- Normal Boiling Point: $-29.3°F$ Ambient Boiling Point: $-29.3°F$
- Vapor Pressure at Ambient Temperature: Greater than 1 atm
- Ambient Saturation Concentration: 1,000,000 ppm or 100.0%

ATMOSPHERIC INFORMATION: (MANUAL INPUT OF DATA)

- Wind: 12 mph from East at 3 meters   No Inversion Height
- Stability Class: D   Air Temperature: 76°F
- Relative Humidity: 50%   Ground Roughness: open country
- Cloud Cover: 0 tenths

SOURCE STRENGTH INFORMATION:

- Leak from hole in horizontal cylindrical tank
- Tank Diameter: 3 feet   Tank Length: 8 feet
- Tank Volume: 423 gallons   Tank contains liquid
- Internal Temperature: 76°F
- Chemical Mass in Tank: 1.98 tons   Tank is 80% full
- Circular Opening Diameter: 4 inches
- Opening is 1.02 feet from tank bottom
- Release Duration: 1 minute
- Max Average Sustained Release Rate: 55.9 pounds/sec (averaged over a minute or more)
- Total Amount Released: 3,353 pounds
- Note: The chemical escaped as a mixture of gas and aerosol (two-phase flow).

FOOTPRINT INFORMATION:

- Model Run: Heavy Gas
- Red LOC (20 ppm = ERPG-3) Max Threat Zone: 1.8 miles
- Orange LOC (3 ppm = ERPG-2) Max Threat Zone: 3.6 miles
- Yellow LOC (1 ppm = ERPG-1) Max Threat Zone: 5.4 miles

▲ **Concentration patchiness, particularly near the source.** No one can predict gas concentrations at any particular instant downwind of a release. This is because concentrations result partly from random chance. Rather than showing exact concentrations, ALOHA shows you concentrations that represent averages for time periods of several minutes. It uses the laws of probability as well as meteorologists' knowledge of the atmosphere to do this.

Avoid using ALOHA's Gaussian model to predict how a large heavy gas cloud will disperse. Large gas clouds that are denser than air ("heavy gases") are not buoyant and disperse in a very different way. They are affected by gravity and other forces besides wind and turbulence. As they move downwind, they remain much lower to the ground than neutrally buoyant clouds and flow like water.

Also, be aware that ALOHA cannot take into its modeling processes fires, chemical reactions or solutions, particulates, and terrain.

SELF-CHECK

- What is meant by the **immediately dangerous to life or health (IDLH) level?**
- Define **stability class.**
- What is meant by the term footprint in **ALOHA?**
- What conditions can cause ALOHA modeling to be less reliable?

7.4 Assessing HAZUS-MH Models

In addition to programs that modeling chemical releases and hurricanes, we also have a software program that models potential losses from earthquakes, floods, wind, and coastal hazards. It is **HAZUS-MH** (Hazards United States—Multi Hazard). It is an emergency planning and response software package. Officials at all levels of government have long recognized the need to more accurately estimate the escalating costs associated with natural hazards (FEMA 1997). The Hazard Mitigation Act of 2000 requires that local jurisdictions complete a comprehensive hazards analysis as a part of their hazard mitigation plan in order to qualify for FEMA mitigation funds. HAZUS-MH provides needed tools to estimate the adverse economic impact of a flood, wind, or coastal hazard in a community. This mapping and modeling software utilizes the power of geographic information systems (GIS) and hazard modeling to estimate associated social and economic losses. It also characterizes the nature and extent of the hazards.

HAZUS-MH enhances our capacity to determine the potential damage from inland and coastal flooding, hurricane winds, earthquakes, and chemical hazard events (FEMA 2003). Local, state, and federal officials can improve community emergency preparedness, response, recovery, and mitigation activities by enhancing their ability to characterize the economic and social consequences of flood, wind, and coastal hazards (O'Connor 2003). HAZUS-MH provides three levels of analysis (www.fema.gov/plan/present/hazus/hz_levels.shtm):

▲ **Level 1 analysis:** This can be thought of as an initial screen that identifies areas and communities that are most at risk. A Level 1 analysis uses national average data to produce approximate results. This is also referred to as an "out of the box" estimate or a "default" estimate.

▲ **Level 2 analysis:** This requires work on your part. You must enter additional data and hazard maps. You may also work with GIS professionals and urban and regional planners to do this. The system then produces more accurate risk and loss estimates.

▲ **Level 3 analysis:** This the most accurate estimate of loss. It usually requires the involvement of experts such as structural and geotechnical engineers. This analysis modifies loss based on the specific conditions of a community.

Figure 7-3 shows HAZUS-MH flood risk zones around the East Baton Rouge Parish:

HAZUS-MH includes database tools to facilitate the collection and editing of local building stock information for use in HAZUS-MH. Having accurate local building information makes the damage assessment in HAZUS-MH more accurate. INCAST is a software application to facilitate the collection, verification, and editing of local building data. FIT is a utility that converts locally edited data from INCAST concerning local building information for use in the HAZUS flood module. It is intended for use for a Level 2 or 3 analysis.

Once vulnerability zones are created for the hazard, HAZUS-MH calculates damage estimates. It creates a total damage estimate by occupancy for residential, commercial, industrial, agricultural, religious buildings, education buildings, and government buildings for the hazard zone. These calculations include damage to buildings and building contents possibly impacted by the hazard.

Damage calculations in HAZUS-MH are determined from databases included in the software. The building inventory databases were created from information provided by the Census Bureau and business information sources. Figure 7-4 provides an example of the type of building inventory database and shows the total number of buildings as well as the number of buildings by Census block for the following categories:

▲ Residential buildings
▲ Commercial buildings

Figure 7-3

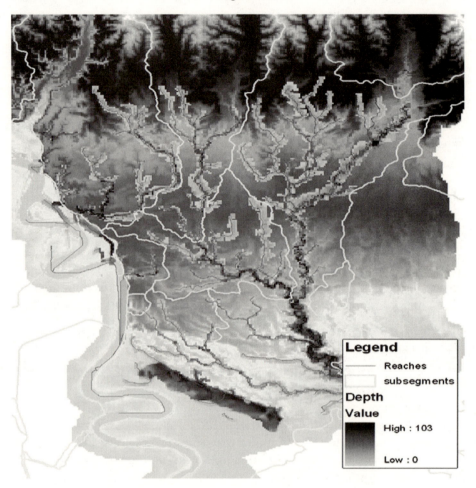

East Baton Rouge Parish with HAZUS-MH flood risk zones.

▲ Industrial buildings
▲ Agricultural buildings
▲ Governmental buildings

Additional databases in HAZUS-MH provide information on the value of buildings and their contents by Census block as well as the number of structures by the type of construction (wood, steel reinforced, brick, concrete, and manufactured housing) and the square footage of the structures by type of occupancy (residential, commercial, etc.).

It is important that many local offices and units understand the nature and extent of earthquake, flooding, wind, and coastal hazards. HAZUS-MH increases understanding by providing a tool to share map layers with anyone interested

Figure 7-4

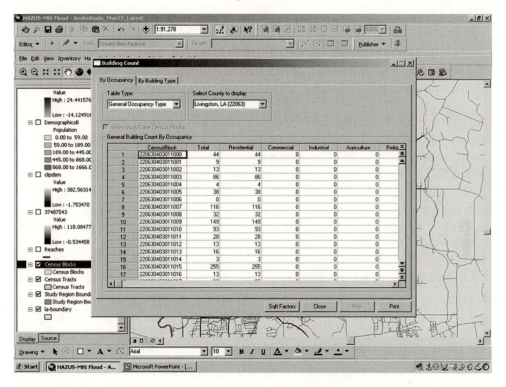

HAZUSMH building count by type of occupancy.

in viewing the HAZUS-MH study results. Having the capability to share many mapping layers from HAZUS-MH allows others associated with hazard mitigation to examine risks and view estimated losses through too is such as flood-depth grids, wind fields, earthquake zones, high-resolution photos, street and water features, critical infrastructures (schools, shelters, bridges, and government buildings), and political boundaries.

7.4.1 Strengths of HAZUS-MH

HAZUS-MH is a robust program with many capabilities and strengths. HAZUS-MH provides local government jurisdictions with an exceptional tool in preparedness, response, and the hazard mitigation process. The ease of use and the quality of the data provided with the program enable the user to generate information on where to expect losses in the community and considerable information on the nature of these losses.

FEMA has created a powerful tool for the assessment of hazard-related losses. The tool allows the user to execute a local analysis in a reasonable period of time and estimate losses to the jurisdiction. It provides a basis for examining the economic impact of flooding and using loss estimates in establishing hazard

> ## FOR EXAMPLE
>
> ### HAZUS-MH Updates
>
> FEMA issues regular updates to HAZUS-MH, which are available at no cost. FEMA releases new versions of the software on an ongoing basis.

mitigation priorities at the local level. By allowing users to establish a regional study area, the program facilitates a broader examination of hazard mitigation. Counties can work together to examine risks and concentrate more local analysis in HAZUS-MH to specific geographic areas. As the program gains broad use, local jurisdictions will find help and overcome many technical problems that users are encountering today. HAZUS-MH is thus a powerful hazard mitigation tool. It is a tool that makes a significant contribution in informing local decision makers as to the impacts of hazards in their community.

7.4.2 Limitations of HAZUS-MH

As with all robust programs, using HAZUS-MH effectively requires training. You will also need to work with experts to produce accurate estimates of losses in your community. Difficulties in using HAZUS-MH will be overcome as local officials become more skilled in utilizing the power of GIS and the HAZUS-MH hazard models. Training scenarios will likely be prepared to help users anticipate common problems in using the models. Feedback to FEMA on difficulties in using the program will also result in system changes.

One of the biggest concerns by raises local users is the quality of the data in HAZUS-MH, especially for building counts and their characteristics. Studies to demonstrate the validity of building counts and the economic values associated with the structures have helped in assuring local officials of the validity of the data. For jurisdictions where major population shifts have not occurred since 2000, local officials can be more confident in the economic loss analysis for residential properties provided by HAZUS-MH.

SELF-CHECK

- Describe the **HAZUS-MH model.**
- What level of HAZUS-MH requires input from the local emergency manager?
- What type of outputs does HAZUS-MH provide?
- What is the primary limitation of the HAZUS-MH model?

7.5 Additional Models

In addition to the models we have already discussed, there are additional models that you may use in mitigation and planning. These include fire, drought, and evacuation models.

7.5.1 Fire Modeling

Due to air quality regulations and requirements, the USDA Forest Service has had to become more active in smoke modeling and emission tracking. It is their job to understand the impact of fire on air quality and visibility. The National Fire Plan, which was developed in 2000 after a dry season with many forest fires, requires the enhancement of fire behavior models. Fire planners use these models to increase the effectiveness and safety of fire operations.

Four regional fire, weather, and smoke modeling centers have been established. These provide weather and smoke modeling support to Forest Service, state, and other partners. Weather models and fire behavior models are used together to provide greater detail of anticipated fire spread, better planning for the response and safety of firefighters and the public, and a better allocation of fire-suppression resources. These centers have high-speed computing capabilities.

FOR EXAMPLE

The National Interagency Fire Center

The National Interagency Fire Center in Boise, Idaho, is the nation's primary logistical support center for wildland fire suppression. The center is the home to federal wildland fire experts in areas such as fire ecology, fire behavior, technology, aviation, and weather. For further information see www.nifc.gov. For more information on the National Fire Plan, visit www.fireplan.gov.

7.5.2 Evacuation Modeling

OREMS (Oak Ridge Evacuation Modeling System) was developed by Oak Ridge National Laboratories. It is a microcomputer-based model developed to simulate traffic flow during an emergency evacuation that may be undertaken in response to a natural or man-made calamity. Examples of man-made disasters include nuclear reactor failure, release of toxic gases, and dam failure–related flooding. Natural disasters that may require evacuation include hurricanes, earthquakes, and forest fires. OREMS is being developed by the Center for Transportation Analysis at Oak Ridge National Laboratory (ORNL) for FEMA and the U.S. Army.

One of the key factors used in evaluating the effectiveness of evacuation as a protective action option is the estimate of time required for evacuation—that is, the time associated with clearing an area at risk to areas considered safe. Once evacuation is identified as a viable protective action strategy, considerable planning and analysis is required to develop an evacuation plan that best serves the population at risk.

OREMS allows the user to experiment with alternate routes, destinations, traffic control and management strategies, and evacuee response rates. For a given situation, OREMS can help identify evacuation or clearance times, traffic operational characteristics, bottlenecks, and other information necessary to develop effective evacuation plans. Detailed information on traffic operational characteristics can also be obtained at user-specified time intervals between the beginning and end of an evacuation. For more information on how this model has been used see www.ornl.gov/info/ornlreview/v35_2_02/responding.shtml.

For more information on evacuation modeling, write to
Center for Transportation Analysis
Oak Ridge National Laboratory
P.O. Box 2008; MS 6206, 4500N, H-16
Oak Ridge, TN 37831-6206

For more information on OREMS see www.cta.ornl.gov/cta/One_Pagers/OREMS.pdf.

To get the software, see emc.ornl.gov/CSEPPweb/data/html/software.html.

7.5.3 Drought Modeling

In the last few decades, interest in drought planning has increased. In 1980, only three states had drought plans. Today, 38 states either have drought plans or are in the process of developing plans. The National Drought Mitigation Center at the University of Nebraska, Lincoln, is sponsored by the U.S. Bureau of Reclamation. It was established in 1995. Its activities include the following:

▲ Maintaining an information clearinghouse
▲ Drought monitoring
▲ Drought planning and mitigation
▲ Advising policy makers
▲ Research
▲ Conducting educational workshops for U.S., foreign, and international organizations

This center helps people and organizations plan for droughts. This planning is based on three components: monitoring and early warning, risk assessment, and mitigation and response.

These components complement one another and create an integrated institutional approach. This approach addresses both short-and long-term drought management issues. For further information on National Drought Mitigation Center activities and modeling efforts, see http://enso.unl.edu/ndmc.

SELF-CHECK

- For fire modeling, what two types of models are used together to provide greater detail?
- What types of disasters would OREMS be applied to?
- What are the three components of drought modeling?

7.6 Evaluating Hazard Models

As with any technology or tool, you have to evaluate the pros and cons of using a hazard model and investing and allocating resources for it. When deciding what model(s) to use, you will want to evaluate the models. You can use the following as a framework for identifying the critical elements of a hazard model.

Quality:

▲ Do the results accurately reflect the event simulated under specified conditions?
▲ Do the damage assessments accurately reflect the residential, commercial, industrial, agricultural, government, and educational structures in the community?

Usability:

▲ Does the model require extensive training to use?
▲ Does the model require expertise that is readily available at the local level?
▲ Are limitations of the model stated in a clear, straightforward manner?
▲ Are results expressed in an easy-to-understand manner?
▲ Will you have to format the results before you can use them?
▲ Are results outlined to easily understand the intended use?
▲ Is the information presented in an orderly arrangement and in a form that assists you?

Timeliness:

Many day-to-day decisions are time sensitive. Decisions on how to respond to situations must be made quickly. Timely information has several ingredients:

▲ Is the information provided when it is needed for making preparedness, mitigation, and response or recovery decisions?

FOR EXAMPLE

Accuracy of Data

Regardless of what model is used, it will only provide valid and useful results to support decision making if data used in characterizing the hazard (ALOHA or HAZUS-MH flood, wind or earthquake) or in estimating the adverse impacts accurately. ALOHA clearly provides the user with choices in setting up a chemical-release scenario and provides options for selecting exposure values. HAZUS-MH provides extensive data sets for all local communities in the United States, but the information about local property is limited. Users of HAZUS-MH should double-check local data to ensure that the damage calculations are appropriate for their area. Where the user has local knowledge of a community, you could compare building counts in a portion of the community with what is in the HAZUS-MH building inventory data set.

▲ Is the information resulting from the model output current? Information should be up-to-date when it is provided to the decision maker.

▲ Is the information from the model updated as needed? When conditions change, is information provided as often as needed or at an appropriate frequency?

Completeness:

The results of the model must be complete to be of value to decision makers. Conciseness and detail are two additional aspects of completeness.

▲ Does the model give you enough information to make an accurate assessment of the situation and to arrive at a suitable decision?

▲ Do you have access not only to current information, but also to past history?

▲ Are the results of the model presented to you in a concise form but with sufficient detail to provide you with enough depth and breadth for the current situation?

▲ Is sufficient relevant information provided to you without information overload?

SELF-CHECK

- What are the critical elements of evaluating a model?
- How does the accuracy of the input data affect the validity of a model's output?

SUMMARY

Understanding the impact different hazards could have on your community is essential in forming your planning and mitigation efforts. In this chapter, you evaluated the strengths and limitations of different hazard models. Specifically, you evaluated the SLOSH hurricane model. You also examined the ALOHA chemical dispersion model. In addition, you assessed what qualities you should consider when you evaluate hazard models. These qualities will guide you in selecting the models you will implement in your community.

KEY TERMS

Aerial Locations of Hazardous Atmospheres (ALOHA)	A chemical dispersion model developed by the EPA and NOAA as a guide for emergency responders to track a chemical-release plume and determine its potential impact on nearby populations.
Hazard modeling	Simulation of a real system or replication of a potential hazard event.
HAZUS-MH model	Suite of hazard models developed by FEMA to describe the nature of hazardous conditions for earthquakes, wind, coastal, and flooding hazards and their economic and social impacts.
Immediately dangerous to life or health (IDLH) level	The IDLH is an exposure limit to hazardous chemicals established to provide guidance to industry and emergency response personnel.
Saffir-Simpson Hurricane Scale	Scale developed as a general guide for use by public safety officials during emergencies to communicate and describe the nature and intensity of hurricanes.
Sea Lake, and Overland Surges from Hurricanes (SLOSH)	A model used by the National Weather Service to calculate potential surge heights from hurricanes.
Stability class	A classification system used in dispersion modeling to describe wind speed, atmosphere turbulence, and solar radiation.

ASSESS YOUR UNDERSTANDING

Go to www.wiley.com/college/pine to assess your knowledge of hazards analysis and modeling.

Measure your learning by comparing pre-test and post-test results.

Summary Questions

1. A hazard model is a simulation or replication of a potential hazard event. True or False?

2. The accuracy of a model's estimation of a hazard event is determined by
   (a) the assumptions contained within the model.
   (b) data provided by the user.
   (c) specifications made by the user.
   (d) all of the above.

3. Modeling provides an excellent working estimate of the potential impact of a disaster. True or False?

4. The outputs from a chemical dispersion model may provide the basis for determining emergency planning vulnerability zones. True or False?

5. Hazard modes are often presented as being too complex for those outside the scientific community to understand. True or False?

6. Both the emergency management community and the public media have an interest in understanding the science behind hazard models. True or False?

7. SLOSH was only developed for operational forecasting of hurricane storm surges and not as a planning tool. True or False?

8. SLOSH model outputs are not provided for distribution to the general public. True or False?

9. A Category 1 storm is classified by the Saffir-Simpson Scale as the most intense and severe hurricane storm. True or False?

10. ALOHA is not a reliable chemical dispersion model under very low wind speeds or very stable atmospheric conditions. True or False?

11. Having accurate local building information for a community would enhance the building damage assessment performed by HAZUS-MH. True or False?

12. HAZUS-MH building inventory databases include which of the following?
    (a) Residential buildings
    (b) Hospitals
    (c) Banks
    (d) All of the above

13. HAZUS-MH provides local government jurisdictions with an exceptional tool for preparedness, response, and hazard mitigation. True or False?

Review Questions

1. What are the strengths of the ALOHA chemical dispersion model?
2. What conditions are necessary for use of the ALOHA chemical dispersion model?
3. What are the limitations of the SLOSH model?
4. What qualities do you consider when selecting a hazard model for use in your office?
5. What does level of concentration mean in the ALOHA model? What does stability class mean?
6. Why is it so important to understand that a hazard model is just a representation of an event?
7. Why is usability so important with the HAZUS-MH model?
8. What is OREMS?

Applying This Chapter

1. Your community is prone to hurricanes. What model do you use and why? What information do you want from the model?
2. Why do you need to be able to predict and monitor a chemical plume resulting from a chemical accident?
3. You are the emergency manager for a city that has several chemical plants. An onsite chemical release on-site occurred. You are told that the chemicals are above the IDLH threshold levels. What does this mean?
4. You are the emergency manager for a city that has a nuclear power plant. You want to be prepared for an evacuation in case of a chemical dispersion caused by either an accident or by terrorists. What models do you use and why?
5. You are the emergency manager for an area that is prone to wildfires. What models do you use and why?
6. You are the emergency manager for Tucson, Arizona, a town that can be affected by drought. What model do you use to prepare for drought and why?
7. How can you use hazard models to design training for staff members?

YOU TRY IT

Earthquake Modeling

You are the emergency manager for a city that is prone to earthquakes. You want to prepare and mitigate for earthquakes, so you decide to use HAZUS-MH for a Level 3 analysis. What resources are available to you as a public or private organization to get help in using this modeling software to understand local vulnerabilities?

Using Models

What is the best use for models and why? At what stage in the emergency management process should you use emergency management models? Write a paper outlining your answers to these questions.

Hurricane Modeling

You use SLOSH hurricane model outputs as information for updating the emergency preparedness plan for your community or your organization. What are the limitations to this model?

8

WARNING SYSTEMS
Alerting the Public to Danger

Starting Point

Go to www.wiley.com/college/pine to assess your knowledge of warning systems.
Determine where to concentrate your effort.

What You'll Learn in This Chapter

▲ Different components of warning systems
▲ Different ways to detect disasters
▲ Issues to consider when issuing warnings
▲ Types of warning systems
▲ Myths of public response to warnings

After Studying This Chapter, You'll Be Able To

▲ Examine the composition of warning systems and their subsystems
▲ Examine different ways to detect and manage disasters
▲ Assess how organizational issues affect the process of issuing warnings
▲ Examine the advantages and disadvantages of each type of warning system
▲ Analyze the myths of public response to warning systems

Goals and Outcomes

▲ Evaluate the organizational and technical obstacles to implementing a warning system
▲ Evaluate the role of detection, management, and response in warning systems
▲ Evaluate the potential public response to warnings
▲ Select national and local resources to help monitor disasters
▲ Select the types of warning systems that best serve your community

INTRODUCTION

Warning the public of a disaster is one of your most critical functions as an emergency manager. Warning, however, is a complex function. In this chapter, you will examine the qualities of warning systems. You will then examine ways disasters are detected and managed. After a disaster has been detected, you must decide what criteria to use to warn others. You must decide what warning system to use. You will examine different types of warning systems and analyze the advantages and disadvantages of each. You will end the chapter by examining the myths of public response to warnings and how to ensure that the public has all the information it needs to respond appropriately to a warning.

8.1 Warning Systems

Issuing warnings is one of the most important tasks you have. Warnings allow people to protect themselves, their families, and their property. If a warning is issued early enough, people will also have time to prepare for a disaster. The warning process includes disaster assessment and dissemination (Quarantelli 1990, 1).

▲ **Assessment:** This is the phase when information is gathered, decisions are made, and the message is formulated.

▲ **Dissemination:** This is the phase when information is relayed to those who will assist with the issuance of the warning. Information is relayed to and received by the public, which then hopefully acts in accordance with the warning.

Warnings provide three pieces of key information:

1. When a disaster may occur
2. How long a disaster could last
3. What the impacts of the disaster could be

A **warning system** is "a means of getting information about an impending emergency, communicating that information to those who need it, and facilitating good decisions and timely response by people in danger" (Mileti and Sorensen 1990). The most effective structure for a warning system is that of an integrated system. An integrated system has two qualities that make it unique.

1. The system is to ensure preparedness and effective response.
2. The integration requires that sound relationships among these subsystems be developed and maintained (Mileti and Sorensen 1990).

FOR EXAMPLE

Warning Times

The ability to give people enough time to respond to a warning varies widely depending on the type of hazard, the technology used to detect the hazard, and the circumstances surrounding the hazard. For example, earthquake and tsunami warnings may be issued only minutes before impact. Hurricane warnings, on the other hand, can be issued days before impact, although there is always a chance that the storm will weaken or change course between the time the warning is issued and impact.

The warning system is composed of three separate subsystems: the detection, management, and response subsystems.

▲ **Detection:** Detection includes the monitoring of the natural, technological, and civil environments. Detection includes collecting information for analysis. The National Weather Service (NWS) has many detection systems for different hazards. The collection of this weather data would be viewed as the "inputs" for the warning system.

▲ **Management:** Management integrates the information from the detection subsystem. Examples include the federal NWS Severe Weather Warning systems. Local and regional weather centers along with emergency management officials receive the information. They then analyze the information. They determine if a warning is justified. This is the transformation part of the warning system.

▲ **Response:** Individuals respond to a warning message. They bring their own interpretations of the warning and determine what appropriate action is required. The warning message and the individual response are both outputs of the warning system.

We will now further examine detection, management, and response.

SELF-CHECK

- Define **warning system.**
- Name the three subsystems in warning systems.
- List the key pieces of information that warnings provide.

8.2 Detection and Management

Effective response to a disaster includes the timely warning of the local community and the region of a potential hazard. Detecting disasters is a difficult process. It cannot always be done accurately. For example, alerts about terrorist activities are based on human intelligence that may or may not be accurate. Industrial accidents resulting from mechanical or human error are difficult to predict. We can, however, predict severe weather. We can predict floods, hurricanes, tsunamis, and other types of severe weather. Once a disaster is set in motion, we can detect it. We can then warn the population to take protective action. There are different services and detection equipment we can use to detect hazards. Let's first examine how detection works at a local level before we look at what is in place at the national level.

8.2.1 Case Study: Detection at a Local Level

In 1997, Fort Collins, Colorado, had several days of heavy thunderstorms. As a result, sections of Fort Collins flooded. The flooding caused a freight train to detail and crash into two residential trailer parks. Five people were killed. Colorado State University sustained extensive damage. The flooding had a huge financial impact on all of Fort Collins.

After this experience, the emergency managers wanted to install a flood warning system. After being awarded a $250,000 grant from FEMA, the city developed and installed a complete system. The system provides real-time information on rain, storm water runoff, and weather conditions. The NWS uses the data and other information to issue flash flood and severe weather advisories.

The flood warning system consists of 54 gauge sites, 38 automatic rain gauges, 35 water level gauges, and five automatic weather stations. These stations report information to radio and computer base stations. The software program that the emergency managers use is DIADvisor. This program determines when gauges exceed a predetermined level and automatically sends a page to emergency management personnel. Figure 8-1 shows a smaller flood warning system from another Fort Collins that is prone to flooding, Fort Collins, Texas.

Here are the steps that occur before a page is sent out:

1. Emergency managers and local officials determine where to place the rain gauges. The location of these gauges depends on local weather patterns, potential for flooding, city projects, environmental factors, land availability, and the proximity of other gauges. Stream gauges are placed in the streams and use a sensor to determine the water depth. Water depth is also referred to as *stage*. Rain gauges use tipping buckets. The depth of the water is recorded and reported.

Figure 8-1

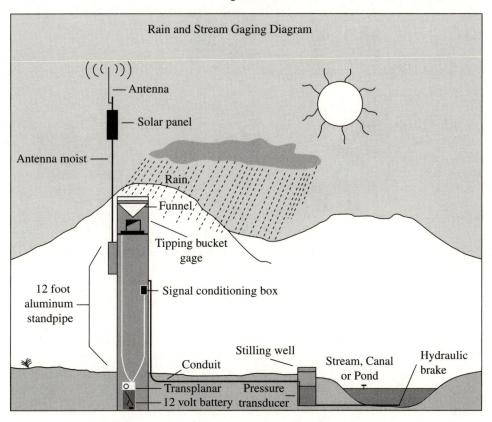

Illustration of the Fort Collins, Texas, flood warning system.

2. A solar-powered 12-volt battery powers this particular system.

3. The tipping bucket rain gauge is on top of a 12-foot-tall pipe.

4. A conduit runs from both gauges through a conduit to a sitting well.

5. After the water reaches a predetermined depth, the information is transmitted through a VHF radio signal to a repeater site on top of a tall grain tower. A repeater is a device that receives communications and amplifies them before sending them out.

6. Two base stations receive the information from the repeater. The base stations have a decoder to interpret the information. A page is sent to emergency management and utility personnel. Users can also access the data from Web pages or by using a laptop and dialing in to their station. The information is also sent to the NWS. See Figure 8-2 for an illustration of the process.

Figure 8-2

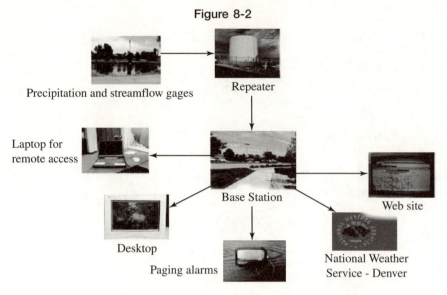

The Fort Collins ALERT system.

ALERT

The Fort Collins flood warning system is an example of ALERT (automated local evaluation in real time). As you can see, it uses remote sensors strategically placed in different locations to transmit data to a central computer in real time. ALERT was developed by the NWS in the 1970s and is used by many federal and local agencies. There are many manufacturers of ALERT software and hardware. All hardware and software is designed to meet the same end result, so they are all interchangeable regardless of who the manufacturer is. Competition helps keep costs low. For more information, visit www.alertsystems.org.

8.2.2 National Weather Service

Just as the Fort Collins station sends information to the NWS, hundreds of locations also send information to the NWS at regular intervals. The NWS has 4,700 employees at 122 weather forecast offices. In addition, the NWS has 13 river forecast centers and 9 national centers. The NWS has other support offices around the country. The NWS provides weather and hydrologic forecasts and warnings. With a $700 million annual budget, the NWS collects data in a variety of ways. The data can be used by anyone. Their weather storm warnings provide an excellent example of identifying potential hazards, developing a classification system, and implementing a public notification system. The warning system focuses on flood, tornado, earthquake, and hurricane hazards. It provides an excellent model for state and local governments. It is also a model for non-profits and the private sector. Complementing this system is the Emergency Alert System (EAS). Backing up this warning system is a set of sensors that monitor weather patterns. These sensors include National Oceanic and Atmospheric Administration (NOAA) satellites, local airport radar, United States Geologic Survey (USGS) river gauge and weather sensors, and offshore weather monitoring stations. In addition, NWS uses trained volunteers to collect weather data information.

The NWS provides current hourly reports for weather conditions for each state. State forecasts are provided twice daily for each state. Other forecasts include the following:

▲ Local forecasts: City specific and covers 1 to 3 days; not all sites issue this.

▲ Zone forecasts: Twice daily for individual county/zones in every state.

▲ Information reports: Past and current record reports, public information statements, recreational reports, and additional state information reports.

▲ Climate data: Historical comparisons, running totals for precipitation, and so on. Issued daily for each state.

▲ Coastal, river, and hydrologic information: Various hydrologic reports. Select water-related recreation reports.

▲ Other weather statements: Additional details on current conditions. Can give more detailed information on any current severe weather in each state.

▲ Watches, warnings, and advisories: For tornados, severe thunderstorms, floods, flash floods, winter storms, marine warnings, and severe weather incidents.

Extreme weather and water events cost more than $11 billion dollars annually. In 2005, the damage skyrocketed due to Hurricane Katrina. The services provided by the NWS help you predict and track severe weather patterns. Visit www.nws.noaa.gov for more information.

National Weather Service—NOAA Weather Radio Network

The NWS Weather Radio Network provides an excellent example of a well-designed warning system. This network provides ongoing communication with public agencies, the public, and private businesses. The means of communication is adapted to suit the target audience.

The NWS was an early contributor to the emergency warning system. Today the NWS receives weather data from ground-based weather sensors and remote sensing data systems. The data is assessed and distributed to a broad group of users, including the public, public agencies, and private organizations. These warnings include the following:

▲ Hurricane and tropical storm advisories

▲ Tsunami watches/warning

▲ Local marine forecasts

The NWS also has the Emergency Management Weather Information Network (EMWIN). The EMWIN supplements other NWS dissemination services. It provides a low-cost method for receiving NWS information on a wireless data system. EMWIN presents the information directly on your computer in a user-friendly graphic display. Simple mouse clicks retrieve the latest weather and flood warnings, watches, forecasts, statements, observations, and other data in text format, along with a subset of weather graphics, including the national radar summary and some satellite imagery. Users set alarms to be alerted to particular information, whether for their local area or adjacent areas. Visit www.nws.noaa.gov for more information.

8.2.3 Case Study: Detection at a National Level

The United States is served by two tsunami warning centers: the Pacific Tsunami Warning Center and the West Coast/Alaska Warning Center. The Pacific Tsunami Warning Center is also an international warning system, and 26 nations are participating members. The West Coast/Alaska Warning Center is a regional warning center. NOAA and the NWS operate both centers.

A tsunami may originate from two sources: a distant source or a local source. If the source is local, there is little time to prepare. If an earthquake occurs along a coastal region and lasts for several minutes, the earthquake is the warning. If a tsunami originates from a distant source, the Pacific Tsunami Warning Center and the West Coast/Alaska Warning Center can detect a tsunami hours before it reaches land. When a tsunami is detected, tsunami watches and warnings are issued. When a tsunami watch or warning is received, coastal offices of the NWS activate the EAS. All broadcasters receive the tsunami EAS message at the same time. NOAA's Weather Radio also activates the All-Hazard Alert Broadcast units.

FOR EXAMPLE

Working with the National Weather Service

If your community is under threat from severe weather, the NWS will warn you. One of the first people to convey the seriousness of Hurricane Katrina to New Orleans Mayor Ray Nagin was Max Mayfield of the National Hurricane Center, which is run by the NWS (Thomas, 2005).

This system alerts people living in isolated areas. Warnings to the general public can be issued in less than 15 minutes.

The warning systems designed to detect tsunamis and save lives and property have three components (see Figure 8-3).

1. The equipment to detect earthquakes and ocean wave activity and scientists to analyze data
2. Communications equipment to issue warnings
3. Local emergency response teams to mobilize quick evacuations

Another key element in reducing losses is education. Many coastal areas have marked evacuation routes to guide people to higher ground. Local officials conduct community meetings and workshop, and distribute tsunami education information. The NWS has a community program called Tsunami Ready. Through this program, the NWS recognizes communities that have put extra effort into enhancing their tsunami warning system. Communities do this through awareness activities and widespread use of weather radio receivers.

SELF-CHECK

- What information do National Weather Service forecasts provide?
- What components does a tsunami warning system have?
- How does the National Weather Service warn for hazards in your community?
- What detection system is or could be used in your community?

8.3 Issuing Warnings

Before your organization is faced with the need to issue warnings, you must make some decisions. It is critical to coordinate with other organizations to ensure that warning have the desired individual and organizational actions. To do this, you must do the following:

▲ Understand the roles and responsibilities of other organizations.

▲ Establish clear lines of authority.

▲ Identify procedures that will be followed in a crisis.

Figure 8-3

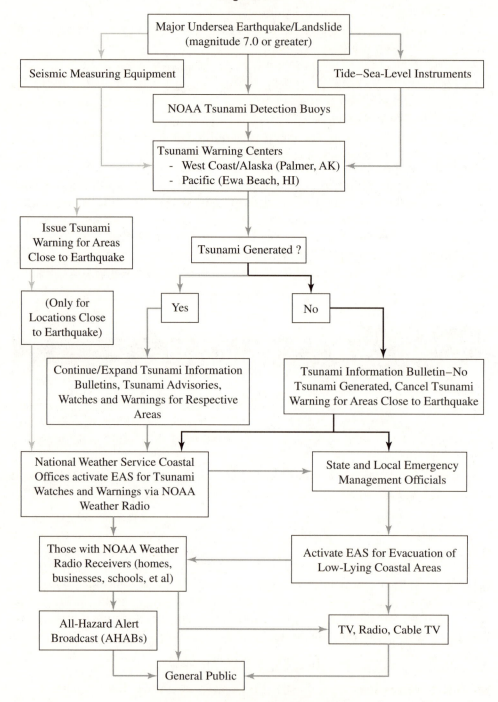

Diagram of tsunami warning system.

Coordination with others might present other issues, including technical, organizational, and societal issues.

8.3.1 Technical Issues

With a warning system, you must become technically and scientifically informed in order to make sound warning decisions. As an example, you must understand the differences between tropical depression and a hurricane. It is critical that you build technical competence in warning systems so as to understand what actions should be taken in an emergency. You can take other actions to ensure that effective decisions are made from the scientific information received, including the following:

▲ Identify local experts who can provide advice and consultation on a disaster and appropriate actions for warnings for various hazards. Members of the local emergency preparedness committee often include those with knowledge of chemical and natural hazards as well as terrorism. Identify volunteers who can provide advice on the disaster.

▲ Contact the nearby NWS office for detailed and up-to-date information.

▲ Contract for expertise from a private company, government agency, and university.

▲ Examine monitoring and detection issues. Is the entire community covered by a warning system, or are there gaps in coverage in the community? For example, if you are using sirens, you may not have sirens placed in rural areas of your community.

▲ Examine communication hardware issues. Does the system require specialized technology that may not be present in some homes or businesses? For example, if a weather radio is the only way someone may receive a warning, then most people will not hear it.

8.3.2 Organizational Issues

Warning systems are perceived from different points of view. The detecting organization such as the NWS, the community emergency manager, and the public may have all different perceptions. How they perceive the effectiveness of the system affects their role. Many organizational issues impact the operational success of a warning system (Mileti and Sorensen 1990). Each issue varies based on the scope of the system and if it is a national, regional, state, or local focus. The first question you have to ask is how the warning system is activated. You need to know what rules govern the process. In determining the rules, the following list of questions needs to be considered:

▲ Interpretation dilemmas. How do organizations ensure that the correct information is not distorted or lost in the system?

FOR EXAMPLE

Chemical Processing Facilities and Warnings

The Mississippi River corridor between Baton Rouge and the city of New Orleans has many chemical processing facilities. Chemical facility representatives established a warning system for the metropolitan Baton Rouge area utilizing real-time Internet communications. The system was designed to provide immediate notification and warning of a chemical release from a facility in the Baton Rouge area. The system was designed by a company in Baton Rouge. It links chemical facilities and local emergency management operations. The system can send an electronic message to selected users or to all users on the system and activates an alarm on the receiving end of the electronic (e-mail) communication. The receiving units must respond manually to confirm receipt of the "emergency warning message." This secure system provides real-time warning to the emergency management agencies in the Baton Rouge area. The city of Baton Rouge and other local entities can then determine if further warning is required for the chemical release. (See www.i-notification.net/ for more details on this use of technology.)

▲ Recognition of the event, the hazard, and the magnitude of the event. How do you verify that an incident is an emergency and avoid unnecessary false alarms? This is important, as a series of false alarms will lead people to ignore the real alarm.

▲ Sorting of relevant information in an event. For example, if there is a terrorist attack 100 miles away and another one 200 miles away, what is the relevant information to give to people quickly?

▲ Clarification of authority of organizations involved in the warning system. This is part of the reason the EAS was not activated on September 11, 2001. There was confusion as to who had the power to activate it—EAS officials, the president of the United States, the mayor of New York, or the governor of New York.

▲ Lack of clarity on whom to notify. If there is a hurricane heading toward the state, do you notify everyone or just those in the affected regions? You will have to determine what criteria to use.

▲ Physical ability to communicate. Is the communication equipment up-to-date and working?

▲ Conflicting information. During a disaster, information comes in quickly and a portion of it is usually inaccurate or conflicting with other information. You will need to choose an information source prior to disasters, if possible, and rely on it.

▲ Liabilities. What are the liabilities in terms of death, damage, and lawsuits if the warning is issued or not issued?

▲ Cost. What is the cost of protective action? Many organizations initiate emergency procedures when a "warning" is issued by the local emergency management agency. The cost of protective actions taken by local businesses, schools, agencies, and the public must be taken into consideration in issuing a warning.

▲ Feasibility. Is it possible to carry out an effective warning? There may be times when an effective warning is difficult to deliver because there is not any advanced indication that a disaster would occur. For example, if there is a chemical explosion at a warehouse and several people are killed instantly, there would not be a need for a warning.

▲ Timing. When do you issue a warning? For example, do you issue a warning when there is a threat of a tornado or do you wait for it to touch down?

8.3.3 Societal Issues

You have to consider the cost/benefit of issuing a warning on society as well. Below are the societal issues to consider.

▲ What are the costs and benefits of the warning system.
▲ Under what conditions should the warning system not be activated?

SELF-CHECK

- Issuing warnings in metropolitan areas requires coordination between neighboring jurisdictions. What would be some steps to ensure that warnings by jurisdictions do not confuse the local population?
- What are the societal issues to consider before issuing warnings?
- What are the technical issues to consider before issuing warnings?

8.4 Types of Warning Systems

Warning systems have been a part of our emergency management system for years. Initial efforts centered on radio broadcast warning systems. Today, warning systems include a variety of methods to warn the public.

Many communities have established ways of communicating with the public in the event of a disaster. Some of these systems are completely within the local emergency management agency. Others utilize commercial warning systems such as cable providers, radio stations, and companies that use Internet communications or a mass phone dialing capacity. Each system has the ability to quickly relay information to the public. Each system is different. For example, some allow you to identify and send a warning message to a specific part of the community in the case of a chemical incident. Each system has its pros and cons. Also keep in mind that the local media (radio, TV, and cable) all work closely with the emergency management community. You often see emergency warnings scrolling along the bottom of the screen on the TV. This is separate from the national emergency warning system currently in place.

8.4.1 Sirens

Many communities use sirens in a wide variety of disasters, including tornadoes, fires, and chemical accidents. Outdoor mechanical and electronic sirens are often used for tornadoes. Although the sirens can warn a large number of people at once, people must be close to the siren to hear it. Often, they must also be outside to hear the siren. Electronic sirens also have the capability of allowing voice warnings that are good for people who do not understand what a siren means. People must be close to hear electronic sirens as well and both types of sirens are not usually heard by people inside the building.

8.4.2 The Emergency Alert System (EAS)

Warnings from the NWS are often broadcast over the **Emergency Alert System (EAS).** EAS is a national initiative of over 13,000 radio, television, and cable systems that voluntarily organize and plan for warning of local communities. The EAS was established in 1994 by the Federal Communications Commission (FCC). The EAS replaced the EBS, or Emergency Broadcasting System. This system has many benefits that include the following:

▲ Any transmission means can be used to send and receive EAS alerts and tests (telephones, radios, pagers, etc.). Hospitals, chemical-processing operations, emergency responders, and medical personnel frequently have pagers that can be activated by their sponsoring organizations. In an emergency situation, the "hospital" or other sponsor can activate a pager. This is done with either a message or a call-back code or number alerting the person of an emergency. The person receiving the message then contacts the organization or takes other appropriate prearranged actions.

▲ EAS equipment can be programmed for very unique events and specific areas.

▲ These are Simple designations for EAS communications facilities.

▲ Automatic visual and audio messages can appear on broadcast stations and cable systems.

▲ The system can interface with computers.

▲ Time comparison of EAS messages to avoid duplicate or outdated messages.

▲ There is multiple monitoring of sources for EAS messages.

▲ Digital storage and retrieval of messages is possible.

▲ There are weekly tests at any time and monthly on-air tests for all EAS communications facilities in state or EAS local area.

▲ Incoming EAS messages are displayed on EAS equipment.

▲ Any FM or TV subcarriers can be used for transmitting EAS messages.

▲ There is interoperability with future NWS and FEMA warning systems.

▲ Equipment is automatically operated.

The EAS undergoes ongoing changes, but the system continues to face significant challenges in reaching the handicapped or impaired citizens or in providing detailed information on threats. The EAS also was not enacted on September 11, 2001, due to internal confusion as to who had the authority to send out the warnings (see Figure 8-4).

Due to these criticisms, a bill passed in Congress in 2005 that appropriates money to replace and or/upgrade the current EAS system. The legislative proposal specifies that technologies would be considered such as "telephone, wireless communications, and other existing communication networks" (White, 2004).

The Department of Homeland Security's (DHS) Federal Emergency Management Agency (FEMA) tested a digital EAS (DEAS) in the national capital region in 2004. This 6-month pilot was intended to demonstrate how Homeland Security can improve public alerts and warnings during times of national crisis through the use of local public television's digital television broadcasts. FEMA's Office of National Security Coordination coordinates the national-level (EAS). The pilot program is a joint venture among FEMA, DHS Information Analysis and Infrastructure Protection directorate, and the Association of Public Television Stations. Working with cell phone providers, television and radio broadcasters, hardware and software developers, and community leaders and emergency managers, Homeland Security used the pilot to identify best practices and to develop a foundation for deploying DEAS nationally. This system is intended to supplement and integrate with the existing national EAS. For more information, see www.fema.gov/news/newsrelease.fema?id=14924.

Figure 8-4

The Emergency Alert System (EAS) was not activated during the September 11, 2001, terrorist attacks.

Reverse 911

Reverse 911 is a call issued from one site that is transmitted by computer to homes and businesses. The message can be short or detailed. A phone notification system provides the following advantages in an emergency:

▲ Quick notification of an incident can be provided to a controlled geographic area.

▲ Limited notification of an incident can be provided to individuals affected—the activities of the larger population are not affected.

▲ The message can be customized for the event and even to specific neighborhoods.

▲ The technology is not complex and is easy to customize for a jurisdiction.

▲ Contractors are available to run this function. Not many jurisdictions would be capable of including this activity in their operations.

▲ The receipt of the message by a household can be verified.

A phone notification system also has the following disadvantages:

▲ Despite the large number of lines that a company may have, it does take time to make individual calls to those affected by an incident. Remember, once the call is made, the receiver must listen to the message. The message could last 30 seconds or more.

▲ The cost of the service can be significant. Many jurisdictions cannot afford this notification system without private organizations underwriting the cost of the service. Expect ongoing operational charges.

▲ The biggest limitation of this system is the accuracy of the phone records. In many jurisdictions, local phone companies do not make resident and business numbers available. The directory database is often out of date.

Intercoms, Teletype Writers, Telephone Devices, and Strobe Lights

These systems warn the deaf and people in large buildings. However, they have limited use and do not warn a large number of people.

Loud Speakers, Door-to-Door Notification, and Weather Radio

Police can drive through neighborhoods and use bullhorns and speakers to broadcast warnings. However, they have the same drawback as sirens in that they warn a limited number of people, and people inside may not hear the warnings.

Before Hurricanes Andrew and Katrina, local officials went door to door, urging people to evacuate. This is an effective way of issuing warnings as long as the people delivering the warnings are considered credible. The major drawback of this is that it requires an incredible amount of manpower. Door-to-door warnings are also very time-consuming. Few communities have the resources to spare, especially when they are preparing for a disaster.

The NWS broadcasts weather information and warnings to weather radios. However, most people do not have weather radios.

8.4.3 Barriers to Warnings

You must anticipate problems with warning systems. Develop a flexible system that can address the technical, organizational, and social issues that arise. Efforts must be taken to design a system that can respond effectively. Effectiveness is measured in terms of issuing warnings that are directed to the target population. A primary goal of any warning system is to alert the public of a potential disaster. But the public could perceive warning systems as inadequate. Mileti and Sorrensen (1990) note that warning systems encounter many barriers. The disadvantages of the warning systems we just discussed fall into one of these four categories:

▲ **Geographic barriers:** A warning system may not reach the entire community. Some neighborhoods are outside the range of sirens.

▲ **Language barriers:** In some cases, a warning is provided in written or spoken form and may not be understood by some residents. Many communities have a broad ethnic base. Some residents may not speak English.

▲ **Technical barriers:** Some warning systems are transmitted over radio, cable, or television. Members of the community may not have these communications systems.

▲ **Personal barriers:** Many communities use a telephone alert system to notify the public of an emergency. Unlisted phone numbers may not be included in the notification system group to be called.

8.4.4 Case Study: Evacuating the Area during a Nuclear Disaster

Let's examine what the procedure is for warning the public of a nuclear disaster. Two significant events—the Three Mile Island incident in 1979 and the terrorist attack on September 11, 2001—are partially responsible for a reevaluation of and improvements in the safeguards at our nation's nuclear facilities. The Nuclear Regulatory Commission (NRC), which oversees our nuclear facilities,

Figure 8-5

Warnings are a critical first step in the evacuation of areas
around nuclear power plants.

FOR EXAMPLE

9/11 Warnings

Prior to 9/11, there was no warning that the World Trade Center and the Pentagon would be attacked by terrorists who hijacked airplanes. The first Americans heard about the events was on the morning news when the events were already unfolding. Even if the EAS had been activated, it is unclear what protective actions New Yorkers could have taken. Congress, however, did evacuate after the Pentagon was struck, and there were reports that a plane was headed for the Capitol. The plane never reached the Capitol, as the the passengers fought the hijackers on board and the plane crashed in Shanksville, Pennsylvania.

shares emergency planning and preparedness for potential nuclear accidents or terrorist's attacks with FEMA (see Figure 8.5).

In the United States, there are 104 commercial nuclear power reactors at 65 sites in 31 states. Each site must have emergency plans in place. These plans are approved by FEMA and the NRC. These plans must provide adequate protective measures should there be a nuclear emergency. State and local officials are required to have emergency systems that can alert the public in approximately 15 minutes after learning that a situation requires public action.

There are four categories of nuclear power plant emergencies: notification of an unusual event, alert, site area emergency, and general emergency. In case of an unusual event or an alert, local officials would be notified, but not the general public. In these two cases, the problems can be resolved at the plant. In the case of a site area emergency or a general emergency, the public will be notified through the Alert and Notification System. Information will be available through radio and television. There are two emergency planning zones around each nuclear plant. The first planning zone extends about 10 miles in radius around a plant, and the second planning zone extends to a radius of about 50 miles. Residents within the first planning zone are regularly given emergency information materials. These publications include information on radiation, evacuation, and sheltering; arrangements for people with disabilities; and so on. Evacuation routes and shelters have been pre-planned, and the public will be asked to follow these routes and use designated shelters.

- What special populations are there in your community, and how should local authorities reach them in warnings?
- What are the advantages of using radio, television, and cable to provide local warning messages?
- Name and define two barriers to warnings.
- What are the benefits of an **Emergency Alert System (EAS)**?

8.5 Response

There are many common myths associated with emergency management. **Myths** are beliefs that are not supported by facts and do not accurately reflect the real world. These myths have influenced how managers plan for and respond to crisis events. The reality is, however, that myths are beliefs that are not supported by emergency management research. Mileti and Sorensen (1990) have examined the research and explain just how people will behave in a crisis or disaster. The myths are simply beliefs not supported by fact. The following principles provide a sound basis for the design of warning systems and their operational use:

▲ The public does not panic. They react to warnings rationally.

▲ The public rarely, if ever, gets too much emergency information in an official warning. The initial warning gets one's attention; more information is desired.

▲ Response to warnings is not diminished by what has come to be labeled the "cry wolf" syndrome. This is true as long as the public has been informed of the reasons for previous misses.

▲ People want information from a variety of sources.

▲ Most people do not respond with protective actions to warning messages as soon as they hear their first warning.

▲ Most people will not blindly follow instructions in a warning unless the basis for the instructions is given in the message. People also examine if the basis of the warning makes common sense.

▲ People do not remember the meanings of various siren signal patterns. However, they do try to find out the reason for the siren.

8.5.1 Case Study: Response to Hurricane Katrina

Emergency management officials in Louisiana, Alabama, and Mississippi used many different warning systems to warn residents about Hurricane Katrina. In

FOR EXAMPLE

Evacuations

Once evacuation orders are given, you must do everything you can to facilitate evacaution. Special populations that are not mobile will need help evacuating. Schools, nursing homes, and hospitals may have to be evacuated with school buses. Traffic jams are often a problem as well. During Hurricane Rita, all interstate lanes were open to outflowing traffic, and traffic trying to get into the city was rerouted.

Louisiana alone, the governor declared a state emergency on August 26, President George W. Bush declared Louisiana a disaster area on August 27, and Mayor Ray Nagin ordered a mandatory evacuation of New Orleans on August 28. Hurricane Katrina made landfall on August 29. Media reports discussed the damage that could occur. Evacuation orders were given by all three states, although at different times. Local officials and law enforcement went door to door in the most vulnerable areas asking people to leave. The EAS was used, and warnings were issued in different languages. Louisiana Governor Blanco noted in congressional testimony that 1.2 million people had evacuated from Louisiana without delay prior to landfall of Hurricane Katrina. For those who could not evacuate, they went to shelters. Despite the problems in the aftermath of Hurricane Katrina and the large death toll (1,400+), it was still one of the most successful evacuations in the nation's history.

SELF-CHECK

- List three **myths** of public response to warnings.
- What steps can you take to ensure that people take the correct action for a warning?

SUMMARY

Issuing warnings is one of the most critical job responsibilities for any emergency manager. In this chapter, you examined the warning process. You assessed the technical and organizational difficulties in issuing warnings. You compared and contrasted the different types of warning systems while examining the disadvantages and advantages of each. You then examined the myths behind the public response to warnings. By examining these myths, you discovered what actions you can take to ensure the public responds appropriately to all warnings.

KEY TERMS

Emergency Alert System (EAS)	EAS is a national initiative of over 13,000 radio, television, and cable systems that voluntarily organize and plan for warning of local communities.
Myths	Beliefs that are not supported by facts and do not accurately reflect the real world.
Warning system	A system of getting information about an impending emergency, communicating that information to those who need it, and facilitating good decisions and timely response by people in danger.

ASSESS YOUR UNDERSTANDING

Go to www.wiley.com/college/pine to evaluate your knowledge of warning systems. *Measure your learning by comparing pre-test and post-test results.*

Summary Questions

1. If a community hazard warning is issued early, people will have time to prepare for a disaster. True or False?

2. A warning system is composed of these three separate subsystems.

    (a) Detection, management, and response

    (b) Planning, mitigation, and recovery

    (c) Communication, assessment, and training

    (d) Analysis, leadership, and utilization

3. In the response phase of a warning system, individuals determine their own interpretation of the warning and what appropriate action is required. True or False?

4. The NOAA Weather Radio network is a commercial extreme atmospheric modeling enterprise. True or False?

5. The Emergency Management Weather Information Network (EMWIN) is a Web-based system to give information to the public relating to weather warnings, forecasts, and observations. True or False?

6. When issuing extreme weather warnings, an agency must:

    (a) coordinate with other organizations.

    (b) understand the roles and responsibilities of other organizations.

    (c) establish clear lines of authority.

    (d) All of the above

7. Warning systems do not require specialized technology for businesses and homes. True or False?

8. In developing processes for activating warning systems, you need to ensure that the correct information is not distorted or lost. True or false?

9. Only public agencies are allowed to take actions when a warning is issued in a community. True or False?

10. EAS only provides voice warning messaging. True or False?

11. A phone emergency warning notification system provides which of the following?

    (a) A quick notification of an incident to a specific geographic area

    (b) Contacts all industrial and commercial enterprises in a community

(c) A detailed warning message throughout a community regardless of the neighborhood

(d) Only utilizes public communication resources rather than commercial enterprises

12. Some barriers to effective warning systems include which of the following?

(a) Geographic and language barriers

(b) Emerging wireless systems

(c) Excessive preparation of the warning message

(d) Dependence on private telephone companies

(e) All of the above

13. Response myths in hazard warning include which of the following?

(a) The public panics in a hazard warning.

(b) The public gets too much information in a warning.

(c) Previous false alarms cause the public to dismiss warnings.

(d) All of the above

Review Questions

1. Why is issuing warnings important?

2. What is the role of the National Weather Service in weather warning?

3. Explain three barriers to effective community hazard warning systems.

4. Under what circumstances, if any, do people respond to warnings with panic?

5. How does a flood warning system work?

6. What is an example of a personal barrier to a warning? What is an example of a geographic barrier to a warning?

Applying This Chapter

1. Sirens located in a community may be activated to warn the local population of a variety of disasters. Discuss the type of disasters for which sirens would be suitable.

2. You have to warn a community that a hurricane is coming. You have a significant population of non-English speakers in your community. In addition, you have two deaf schools in your community. What steps do you take to warn these populations?

3. What steps do you take to ensure your communication system will work when you need it during a disaster?

4. You are the emergency manager for a community that is prone to flooding. What detection system do you implement and why?

5. You are the emergency manager for a city that is home to a nuclear power plant. Although there has never been a nuclear plant accident, you want to be prepared for one. How do you prepare for a warning and evacuation in the case of a nuclear power plant emergency?

6. Under what circumstances would you activate the Emergency Alert System (EAS)?

YOU TRY IT

Evacuating

You are the emergency manager for Miami, Florida, and have learned that a Category 4 hurricane is scheduled to make landfall in 3 days. Write a paper on how you warn the public. What instructions do you give?

Warning System

You are the emergency manager for a town that is in the path of tornadoes every year. You have been alerted that a tornado is heading for your community. What steps do you take before you issue a tornado warning?

Response

You are the emergency manager for New York City, and you were just told that terrorists will strike the subways tomorrow. You decide to warn the public. What type of public response do you expect?

9

OPERATIONAL PROBLEMS AND TECHNOLOGY
Making Technology Work for You

Starting Point

Go to www.wiley.com/college/pine to assess your knowledge of operational problems and technology.
Determine where to concentrate your effort.

What You'll Learn in This Chapter

▲ Barriers to implementing technology in emergency management agencies
▲ The role of the emergency manager in using technology
▲ The pitfalls of technology
▲ How to use technology to overcome organizational boundaries
▲ How to manage technology to ensure the technology contributes to the emergency management environment

After Studying This Chapter, You'll Be Able To

▲ Examine the reasons why emergency management agencies may be slow to implement technology
▲ Examine ways to adapt to change and help your organization adapt to change
▲ Compare and contrast the work qualities of humans and machines
▲ Analyze ways to use technology to overcome organizational boundaries
▲ Analyze the risks of heavy dependence on technology

Goals and Outcomes

▲ Design technology around your organization
▲ Assess the contingency approach and how to implement it
▲ Assess strategies to address common technology problems
▲ Select technology to support your organizational needs
▲ Assess the pitfalls of technology and how to overcome them to ensure technology meets your needs

INTRODUCTION

Technology allows us to do things we never before dreamed of. You can send volumes of information around the world within seconds. You can use satellites to take pictures of storms as they move through areas. You can communicate anywhere and anytime. And yet, technology is not the answer to all of our challenges. In fact, along with using technology comes a unique set of challenges. In this chapter, you will examine problems that you may encounter in using technology. Strategies to prevent and minimize the adverse impact of these problems will be presented. Recommendations for enhancing the use of technology will also be provided.

9.1 Examining Barriers in Implementing Technology in Emergency Management

It's difficult to imagine what our lives would be like without the information revolution we have experienced over the past 30 years. It's even more difficult to imagine the state of emergency management without the technological advances of the past three decades. For example, can you imagine working without e-mail? Can you imagine rushing to a disaster without a cell phone? Can you imagine trying to predict the path of a hurricane without access to the Web, the Weather Channel, or satellite images?

Technology is crucial. It provides an important way to link our internal system with our external partners. We have faster and more reliable access to others via phone and wireless Internet connectivity. The technology provides you with broad access to data. We also have the increased ability to collect data. This not only provides improved communication but also gives you additional flexibility. All organizations are heavily dependent on communications. The technology enables even small emergency management operations to function effectively.

You can also use highly specialized technology, such as hazard modeling, GIS, and remote sensing, that often requires expertise that takes years to develop. We supervise more specialists and become more interdependent with the expertise of others in our systems.

The ease of use of technology is critical. So much of the technology that is being used has come from highly technical research efforts. The technical development staff must package the technology in an easy-to-use manner. It will still, however, require training and support.

With technology, the data quality and availability is essential to any user. Documenting the source of the data and knowing its intended use should be understood by the emergency manager, especially where property and lives are at risk.

As amazing as technology is, it cannot solve all of our problems. In fact, technology brings us its own set of problems. Drabek (1991) conducted a study of how local government emergency management units use computer technology.

He found that emergency managers encountered many problems, including the following:

▲ Many technology systems require local data. Entering local data into systems requires time and resources.

▲ Technology was not often compatible. Communications systems are often unable to be linked.

▲ Users have high expectations. They expect technology to be easy to use and yet meet their needs.

▲ There is often a lack of money to invest in new technology or technology upgrades.

▲ As technology is brought into the emergency management system, the need for even more technology is identified. This is because emergency managers learn of the capabilities during the implementation process and want to do more than they had initially envisioned.

▲ Training an adequate technical staff to support the systems is a major barrier.

▲ Technical support staff do not always understand the needs of emergency management.

Gates (1996) also examined several issues associated with emerging technologies. These include the following:

▲ The need for adaptability in the use of technology and in networking

▲ The need for an enormous breadth of sources of data

▲ Usability of technology

▲ Data quality and availability

Despite the fact that these studies were completed over 15 and 10 years ago, respectively, they are still relevant today. In fact, further studies reinforce Drabek's work. Emergency managers use very little of the technology available today for the same reasons. Lindell and Perry completed a study in 2001 in which they took data from the Local Emergency Planning Chairs in Illinois, Indiana, and Michigan. This data indicated that only 59% of the LEPCs had used technology to calculate vulnerable zones around their community's hazmat facilities. Of those who had calculated them, only 36% used computer models such as CAMEO; only a small fraction of the LEPCs used computer-based methods to calculate vulnerable zones (Lindell et al. 2006). One could argue that this is in part because of the extensive training using models requires. However, emergency managers also fail to consistently perform simpler tasks such as posting hazard information to local Web sites (Lindell et al. 2006). Lindell's work further investigates the use of common computer applications such as word processing programs.

FOR EXAMPLE

Budgets and Technology

It can be especially difficult to receive approval for the necessary funds to buy the technology your organization needs. To combat this difficulty, first determine what types of technology your office needs and determine what the priorities are. You will have an easier time receiving approval for one or two technology solutions versus many pieces of equipment, software, or an expensive decision support system. If you do need a technology solution that is very expensive, build support before the proposal comes up for a vote and write a strong proposal as to why it is needed and how much money the solution could potentially save as well as the lives it could save.

Emergency managers most consistently and frequently use word-processing applications, e-mail, databases, and spreadsheets. Lindell refers to these applications as Category 1 applications. Category 2 applications include desktop publishing and statistical analysis. Infrequently used, more complex systems such as GIS, hazard modeling, and CAMEO are Category 3 applications. Lindell found that agencies do not appear to use Category 3 applications until they have used Category 1 and 2 applications extensively. Clearly, you can anticipate encountering problems and hesitation in applying technology.

SELF-CHECK

- Name two issues associated with emerging technologies.
- Name three problems associated with technology that emergency managers must overcome.

9.2 Creating Successful Emergency Management Organizations

As we have just learned, technology is not the total solution that many people imagine it is. The question remains as to how to build the most successful organization that can mitigate hazards, plan for hazards, and effectively respond to hazards. Is technology the complete answer? You cannot solve any problem with technology alone. To further illustrate this point, let us consider the failures of the local, state, and federal governments in Hurricane Katrina.

Hurricane Katrina was the most destructive hurricane in our history. Communities from Alabama to Louisiana had extensive damage to residential and business structures as well as highway and rail bridges. The levee breaches in New Orleans had unprecedented catastrophic impacts. After action reports by response agencies clarified many ways that emergency response efforts could be improved. In fact, these agencies acknowledged the use of technology to simulate a similar disaster. In 2004, federal, state, and local agencies used SLOSH, and other hurricane models to simulate a hurricane in a disaster exercise. The exercise, Hurricane Pam, had sustained winds of 120 mph. It produced up to 20 inches of rain in parts of southeast Louisiana. The storm surge topped levees in New Orleans. More than 1 million people had to evacuate the city in the exercise. The hurricane destroyed 500,000–600,000 buildings. If this scenario sounds familiar, it is because it is close to what happened a year later during the real Hurricane Katrina.

The Hurricane Pam exercise involved an extensive use of technology and planning. However, much more was needed to be prepared for Hurricane Katrina, which hit the Gulf of Mexico coastline in August 2005. Although many plans were developed following the exercise, it did not lead to the type of preparedness required by the devastating impacts from Hurricane Katrina. This is a perfect example of why the success of organizations is complex and depends on many factors. Effective emergency management relies on a combination of competent, hard-working professionals who can use the technology they need to achieve their goals. Public, private, and non-profit organizations are not like mechanical or natural biological systems; they are intentionally created by people. The fact that social organizations are created by human beings suggests that they can be established for many different objectives; further, they do not follow the same life-cycle pattern of birth, maturity, and death as do biological systems. Social systems are imperfect systems. The cement that holds them together is essentially psychological rather than biological or physical. They are anchored in the attitudes, perceptions, beliefs, motivations, habits, and expectations of human beings. The key is to appreciate and use technology to keep the system together.

Technology, through communication tools such as e-mail, computer video conferencing, or common phone conference calls, serves as a means of linking members of a system. By itself, the technology does not ensure that the system will work. It instead serves as a support mechanism to make it easier for members of the system to make contact. Because there are many ways that technology helps link emergency managers, it helps to make system more effective.

9.2.1 The Contingency Approach

Contingency theory is a management approach that suggests that there is no single way to deal with organizational problems and that the best solutions to problems must be responsive to changing environmental conditions. This theory suggests that success in an organization depends on many factors. Outcomes depend on a combination of factors, such as staff, technology, and financial resources. The approach suggests that there is no "one best way." There could be many acceptable solutions to organizational problems.

The designers of many technology systems often infer or openly state that there is a best way to solve a problem. The assumption that there is a one best-way approach does not recognize the adaptability of technology systems. It does not recognize that an effective solution could be achieved by alternate approaches. In fact, the best approach depends on many factors.

The use of GIS in local governments provides an excellent example of this "one-best" consideration. Mapping and GIS is quickly growing in use at the local level. Both Intergraph Corporation (GEOMEDIA) and ESRI (ArcGIS) have targeted local governments as priority users of GIS. Both systems provide a sound basis for serving the mapping needs of local jurisdictions. How to set up a mapping system depends on many local factors. No one approach fits all local factors. Developing a comprehensive mapping capability at the local level can be organized in many different ways. One way is to centralize the function in the chief executive's office. It could also be decentralized in many departments. These departments could be planning, public safety, utilities, public works, and emergency management. Since many local governments have a limited number of staff, designating one unit to serve the local government has proven to be one excellent approach. The best approach depends again on the goals and capabilities of the local government units and their willingness to assume a new role.

As an emergency manager, you know to expect the unexpected. You must be prepared to adapt in emergencies, crises, and disasters. Organizations must have **adaptive mechanisms,** processes and procedures that keep the system from changing too rapidly or slowly as required and allow the operation to adjust and not get out of balance. It also prevents the system from changing so slowly as to be ineffective in a response. For example, warning systems can be designed to provide immediate notification of an accidental hazmat release from a facility. An adaptive system can be created to provide backup of critical data. The data can be backed up to another city or to a critical Web site that can be activated when disaster strikes. An adaptive system is created to ensure that the operations center can run when disaster strikes. You need an adaptive system for when normal staffing patterns will not work because of snow, flooding, or sickness that keeps people at home.

9.2.2 Managing an Organization

The view of an organization as a system suggests a very special role for you. You must deal with uncertainties and ambiguities. You must be concerned with adapting the organization to new and changing requirements. Management is a process. The basic function of management is to align not only people, but also the institution itself, including technology, processes, and structure. It attempts to reduce uncertainty while at the same time searching for flexibility.

Organizations face a significant barrier in attempting to bring change to themselves. Reengineering occurs when we introduce new technologies and change the system (Champy, 1996). This barrier is management itself. New technologies require a new configuration and change. The introduction of new technologies provides an opportunity to reassess the emergency management process. You can also assess the role of technology. You must get close to the nature of change so that a full understanding of the implications of the change can be understood. You will need details to understand but you also really need breadth and perspective. You should examine the impact that the technology will have on the current system and how this change can be implemented effectively. These efforts are also known as **support mechanisms,** or efforts initiated by an organization to ensure that the operation functions efficiently and effectively.

Regardless of the organization or the system, there will be failures. Whether you are relying on a host of highly skilled professionals to respond effectively or whether you are using a hazard model, there will be failures. Many experts believe that failures of complex systems are inevitable. Failure happens regardless of the care of operations and the redundancy of safety mechanisms. One may thus assume that the system will fail; planning for alternative means of achieving goals is thus needed. Planning is the key.

FOR EXAMPLE

Adaptive Mechanisms and Staffing

In working with staff members, you have to remember that people are human and not machines. People can easily become ill, not be able to get to work, or have some emergency that prevents them from working their scheduled hours. Because of this, you must have alternative staffing plans, especially when disaster strikes. For the most crucial positions, you will want to cross-train other staff members so you have all the critical job responsibilities covered during a crisis. You will also want to ensure staff members are cross-trained on the software programs and other technology solutions you will need implemented during a crisis.

SELF-CHECK

- Define **contingency theory.**
- Give two examples of **adaptive mechanisms.**
- Give an example of technology that was used in preparation for Hurricane Katrina and what the outcome of using the technology was.

9.3 Using Technology to Overcome Organizational Boundaries

All organizations have their own "turf." They have boundaries, domains, or regions that define their activities. These boundaries separate communication and interaction between those on the inside and people on the outside. As we saw with Hurricane Katrina, there were many examples of ineffective use of technology for communications between organizations. Technology can be used to bridge these natural barriers. Technology can facilitate transactions necessary for organization functioning.

Technology offers you and others from different groups a way to work together despite jurisdictional boundaries. A regional shelter task force illustrates this concept. The regional shelter task force is composed of local emergency managers who represent different regions of the state. When disaster strikes, the task force is activated. Frequent communication and coordination is facilitated by phone conference calls, electronic mail, and even video conferences. The task

FOR EXAMPLE

Use of E-mail

E-mail is a great tool. GIS support staff at state and federal agencies across the United States used e-mail to communicate during Hurricane Katrina. The Operations Center in New Orleans was too busy, noisy, and crowded for all these staff to work effectively. Instead, staff worked from many locations, including the campus a few miles away, and sent maps or reports by e-mail to one another and especially to the State Operations Center. E-mail proved to be a fast means of communications. A record of each communication was maintained on computers in the Operations Center and the LSU campus. Fortunately, both the LSU campus and the Operations Center had electrical power and Internet connectivity.

force chair can use technology to communicate beyond his or her own organization. This keeps members up-to-date on current needs and polls members on input to problems. The task force uses e-mail as the primary means of communication. It allows all users quick access to information. E-mail is also easier to manage than frequent telephone calls. The key is that each use of technology is a normal part of operations and not something new brought out in a disaster. Problems with technology can be minimized by looking for ways to bring technology into our normal everyday operations.

SELF-CHECK

- What technology can help build teamwork in a community?
- How can e-mail break down barriers between agencies?

9.4 Pitfalls of Technology

Despite the fact that we can accomplish many goals with the use of technology, technology can cause us problems in emergency management. There are risks associated with any dependence on technology. Understanding how an organization is vulnerable to technology is just as important as what the technology can do for you. You should always design a backup system just in case the technology does not work.

9.4.1 Reliance on Technology

You can take advantage of mobile communication devices to stay in touch. You can access e-mail remotely. You can also access remote weather and hazard sensors to monitor a developing crisis. As you use the technologies, you will become even more dependent on accessing critical information. You are then more vulnerable when the connection to the remote source of information is terminated. A strategy for alternative access to critical data must be made prior to an emergency.

9.4.2 Obsolescence

Systems have a life cycle. A **system life cycle** is a time period in which the elements of a system—including software, hardware, or organizational conditions—change, requiring upgrades or operational changes. To help with obsolence within a system life cycle, Purchase new computers for critical needs and utilize older ones where they can be used effectively. Know that as one upgrades computers or software, unexpected problems can be encountered. Test and retest your upgraded systems to ensure that everything works as intended.

9.4.3 Information Overload

Increasing attention to technology may inadvertently result in information overload. As an illustration, we often use chemical databases to provide detailed information on hazardous substances in a chemical spill. Information from multiple sources may be confusing. The information may be far more detailed than is required.

9.4.4 Data Integration

Many organizations have been struggling to cope with increasing demands for timely and accurate data. In many cases, the data needed for timely decisions is distributed to multiple units. Maintaining integration between these units is critical in times of crisis. As we prepare for disasters and crisis, we will need to examine what data will be needed. We will also need to know how we can link our operations. The key is to recognize that we are increasing working in a shared and distributed environment. Documentation on the sources of data and data types will be critical. This will ensure that information is used for its intended purpose.

Data sharing and integration between local government units is always an issue. Cooperation between law enforcement and other public safety and social service agencies varies in each community. A critical task for you is to develop a cooperative spirit between these agencies to support emergency management activities.

9.4.5 Real-Time Response Data

You cannot make effective decisions without accurate information. Your information must be current and must reflect the precise situations that are occurring at that moment. Real-time response data enhances the basis for decision making. Technology allows you access to real-time response data.

Lack of access to updated weather data, traffic flow, or modeling applications could inhibit effective evacuation or sheltering decisions. However, if the computer fails, you will not be able to get this information. If you experience a loss of power, connectivity, or if the computer system fails, then you will not be able to use the computer to get access to the data. You must plan for alternative methods for obtaining information for these critical functions.

9.4.6 Security

Sensitive data exists on office computers. Limiting access to parts of the network may be required to ensure that the business operation is not compromised and remains secure. The application of technology does come with security risks.

FOR EXAMPLE

Real-Time Data

The USGS provides information on water levels in streams and rivers. Direct online access to this data is available through the Internet. You can use this data to determine road and bridge closings, warnings to the community, evacuation orders, and routing. Access to this data source is critical to communities that are subject to periodic flooding.

SELF-CHECK

- Define **system life cycle.**
- What steps can you take to enhance security of office computers?
- What is meant by data integration, and why is it important?

9.5 Managing the Technology

Organizational systems, including emergency management agencies, may be characterized as human- or mechanistic-centered operations. For an organization to operate well, it must take into account the strengths of both people and machines. Consider the following qualities for comparison (Alter 1996):

Category	Humans	Machines
Endurance	Get tired and bored	Never get tired and bored
Consistency	Often inconsistent	Never inconsistent
Speed	Slow	Fast
Memory	Forgetful	Retrieves complex data
Ability to perform programmed tasks	Yes, but may be bored	Can perform completely structured tasks
Understanding	See meaning in task	Cannot see meaning in tasks
Imagination	Invent ideas and associations	Unable to invent ideas
Ability to see the whole	Recognize the whole	Recognize the detail rather than the whole

Alter does not suggest that the choice is not whether to use human- or machine-centered system processes but how to design the technology to use the strengths of each. Alter suggests that steps may be taken to take advantage of the mechanistic systems that do not suppress human-centered systems. These steps are as follow:

▲ Make sure the technology system must be user-friendly.

▲ Recognize that technology can have a positive and negative impact on worker health and safety, including video display terminals, keyboard design—ergonomics).

▲ Make use of the automation that fits human needs.

▲ Preserve and enhance social relationships with technology.

▲ The technology needs human skill and knowledge, thus training is critical to have effective implementation.

▲ Involve staff in planning for changes in the business process to ensure understanding and commitment.

▲ Remember that privacy may be an issue with employees, clients, or the public.

▲ Monitor information access and data input processes.

Technology makes a positive contribution to emergency management. For example, cell phones give us individual mobile connectivity that has only recently been available by the use of radios. GPS units allow us to see precisely where we are at any given time. This capability is extended to the use of cell phones (Adler 1996). You need to assess the outcomes of technology on an ongoing basis. Look at tangible and intangible benefits of different systems. There may be a tendency to understate the cost of technology and information.

▲ **Evaluate the technology with an eye on your goals and priorities.** The question is not to select either distance education or computer assisted training; we might use both to upgrade our skills. The key is to identify your goals and priorities. We will need to gain knowledge, skills, and abilities in different ways than in the past. New developments in technology-based education using the Internet, CDs, or other distance learning applications may be used in addition to traditional workshops and conferences. Distance education will complement what emergency managers are taking advantage of in the current system.

▲ **Recognize that technology will have a life cycle—it will need to be replaced.** The use of new technology will initially have high start-up costs. These are lowered over time. Data storage devices are costing less today than in the past. At the same time, the capacity of these devices continues to grow. Individual computers or phone systems need to be upgraded every few years as our systems become more powerful and integrated; maps, phones, and databases are becoming seamless and mobile.

▲ **Design technology to be maintainable.** All parts of the technology will change. Build into any application the notion that programs will need to be adapted, computer hardware upgraded, new devices added, and storage and imaging displays added. The data and the programs will change as users point out needed developments. Changing the technology in any form will require that the components be maintained.

▲ **Use off-the-shelf programs.** You may want to evaluate using integrated emergency management software with third-party software. The third-party software is usually designed to address a single function, such as weather forecasts, emergency alert, or specific database maintenance. Usually the integrated emergency management software does have a higher cost. The cost, however, may be balanced with greater assurances of upgrades, maintenance, training, and user acceptance. As tasks increasingly become computer aided, there is a greater need for linking the programs and access to the information throughout the system. In the end, the software could be more cost-effective. It could allow you to link to other agencies. However, dependence on information technology is not absolute. Firefighters can continue to put out fires without computerized maps. Managers can write reports with pen and paper. But continued improvements in the quality, efficiency, accessibility, and dependability of information using technology can enhance our capacity to manage in emergencies. Technology may be driven from a user-center system. This makes the interface between man and machine easier and more useful. For example, there could be speech, touch screen, or visualization applications.

▲ **Develop user-centered systems.** Technology must be created for the user. Ease of use and application to the operations staff are of critical importance. They must be kept in the forefront of the system and application design. Input by a variety of users must be included early on in the system design. As a result, a broader interdisciplinary team may need to test the system to ensure its successful application. This facilitates a broader understanding of the system and encourages collaboration. In addition, training staff in the use of the system is fundamental to ensure successful response. Technology will work best when it is packaged in a format that can be understood by the novice as well as the experienced user.

▲ **Support and control the technology.** Many users of technology express their frustration in confronting problems with hardware or programs. Technology works best when adequate technical support is available to users. In addition, the support can be used as a means of ensuring that the technology system is being installed and used as designed.

▲ **Pay attention to network security and control.** Our dependence on technology raises security concerns. Our infrastructure must build tighter controls and safeguards. Wired and wireless networks provide greater linkages within and between organizational units, but they also make us vulnerable to security breaches.

Before you can install and use the technology you need, you must first have the funds to pay for it. It can be a challenge to receive the necessary funding for the tools you need. You will continue to face financial constraints. Public agencies rarely receive the funding they request. To receive funding for new technology, you must prove that the technology will be cost-effective. This is especially true when the technology is used in non-emergency operations. Public agencies will be shaped by technology, politics, economics, demographics, and environmental change. Governments will encourage efficiency in their operations. They will have spending restraints. Agencies will continue to seek out partnerships with the private and non-profit sectors to maximize the use of all resources (including technology). You will be a catalyst to bring government agencies closer to other public entities, nonprofits, and the private sector. Technology helps facilitate this connectedness, openness, and accessibility in an ever-changing environment (Stanley and Waugh 1999).

FOR EXAMPLE

Security and Management Controls

Many emergency 911 operations provide an excellent illustration of how to introduce security and management controls. Through technology, 911 operations use caller identification as a management control; This allows the operators to determine callers are who they claim to be. Emergency operators computerized mapping systems. They have up-to-date street and road addresses so as to verify the caller's address. They have photographs of the local community for use in geographic information systems. And they have easy-to-use communication systems that provide quick access to response agencies. Their rapid introduction and adaptation to new technologies using security and management controls together demonstrate that technology systems can be effective. Emergency management can embrace similar new tools to enhance their operations.

SELF-CHECK

- Name three ways humans differ from machines.
- Under what circumstances would you want to use off-the-shelf programs and why?
- What is meant by a user-centered system?

SUMMARY

While technology offers you many tools, you must choose and implement technologies that work for you. In this chapter, you examined reasons why emergency managers can be slow in implementing technology. You also examined ways to overcome reluctance to use technology. You assessed the pitfalls of technology and how to avoid them. You examined how technology can be used to overcome organizational boundaries. You also assessed ways to evaluate technology with your office's goals and priorities in mind.

KEY TERMS

Adaptive mechanisms	Processes and procedures in an organization that keep the system from changing too rapidly or slowly, and allow the operation to adjust and not get out of balance.
Contingency theory	A management approach that suggests that there is no one best way to deal with organizational problems and that solutions must be responsive to changing environmental conditions.
Support mechanisms	Efforts initiated by an organization to ensure that the operation functions efficiently and effectively.
System life cycle	A time period in which elements of a system—including software, hardware, or organizational conditions—change, requiring upgrades or operational changes.

ASSESS YOUR UNDERSTANDING

Go to www.wiley.com/college/pine to evaluate your knowledge of operational problems and technology.
Measure your learning by comparing pre-test and post-test results.

Summary Questions

1. Local data should not be loaded into systems because it requires too much time and allocation of resources. True or False?
2. Technology is designed in such a manner as to ensure that the parts of a system are always compatible. True or False?
3. Training and adequate technical staff are essential elements of effective use of technology. True or False?
4. Contingency theory suggests that there are no solutions to most complex problems. True or False?
5. An adaptive mechanism keeps a system from changing so rapidly that the parts get out of balance. True or False?
6. Systems are self-organizing and thus will never go out of date. True or False?
7. New developments in information technology prevent information overload. True or False?
8. Effective technology systems have which of the following requirements?
   (a) Must be user-friendly
   (b) Assume that technology will only have a positive impact on workers
   (c) Allow for breaks to preserve social relationships
   (d) All of the above
9. Technology may initially have high start-up costs but may be lower over time. True or False?
10. Technology helps facilitate openness and accessibility in a changing environment. True or False?

Review Questions

1. Name two applications of technology in emergency management.
2. List two pitfalls associated with technology and how to overcome them.
3. Name two things you can do to manage technology so it is effective for an emergency management agency.

4. Why do many emergency managers fail to use technology to their benefit?

5. What tasks are people better at versus computers? What tasks are computers better suited for?

6. When using technology, is there one approach that is the best for all jurisdictions?

Applying This Chapter

1. You are the director of the state emergency management agency. Some of the local emergency management agencies in your state do not have Web sites for the public or use statistical analysis programs and other necessary technologies. What steps do you take to encourage the use of technology among the local emergency managers?

2. You are the local emergency manager for a town that is prone to hurricanes. You know that a hurricane could take out your information system. What preparations do you take to ensure you still have access to the data you will need?

3. You are the local emergency manager for New York City, and you get large volumes of information on a daily basis about possible hazards, including terrorism. With what agencies do you want to share this information, and why? What technology can you use to share the information?

4. You are the local emergency manager and your staff is reluctant to use new technology. What factors do you consider when you develop a user-centered solution?

5. What steps can you take to ensure that technology does not suppress the natural capabilities and skills your staff brings to their positions?

YOU TRY IT

Using Technology

You are a local emergency manager with a staff of 10 people. They are all reluctant to use any software applications beyond word-processing programs. You want to train three of them to use databases and GIS. What are the first steps you should take?

Staffing Needs

During an emergency, critical staff will need a break. What steps can you take to ensure that you could con-tinue critical parts of your operations 24 hours a day, for 2 days or longer?

Technology Needs

You are a local emergency manager with a staff of 10 people. In the past, your office has been underfunded, but through a grant you now have money to purchase technology tools. Besides a few computers with basic programs and printers, you do not have any technology. How do you determine what your office needs?

10

TRENDS IN TECHNOLOGY
New Tools for the Challenges of Emergency Management

Starting Point

Go to www.wiley.com/college/pine to assess your knowledge of trends in technology.
Determine where to concentrate your effort.

What You'll Learn in This Chapter

▲ Types of information exchange
▲ Benefits of mapping technology
▲ Sources of emergency management information on the Web
▲ Ways to manage the technology in an effective manner that benefits all participants

After Studying This Chapter; You'll Be Able To

▲ Appraise the usefulness of emergency management technologies by researching them on the Web
▲ Apply remote technologies to emergency response
▲ Examine how information exchange can be used to acquire new knowledge and skills
▲ Manage new technology in an effective way, ensuring that technology supports personnel effectively

Goals and Outcomes

▲ Support your career and increase your knowledge of emergency management through information exchange
▲ Assess new Internet resources for information on hazards
▲ Evaluate how to use mapping and modeling technologies in a disaster
▲ Predict the limits of technology in responding to and managing disasters

INTRODUCTION

Technology applications are constantly changing. New developments, including communications, information access, training, and modeling, will help you respond more effectively. With the new tools, you will be able to save more lives. Software innovations will continue. You will use new technologies never before considered possible. In this chapter, you will examine ways you can further your knowledge of emergency management through information exchange. You will also examine how training can be completed through the Web. You will then move on to remote technology and how modeling, mapping, and decision-support systems can support your emergency management efforts. Finally, you will look at ways to manage the technology so it enhances your workflow rather than becoming a burden.

10.1 Using Technology for Information Exchange

In discussing how to meet national needs for the exchange of information in the coming decade, the focus is shifting from "networks" to "information infrastructure." This means that the emergency management system will depend on networks. It will also involve more than networks. An information infrastructure makes use of communications networks that support other services and access to information. Therefore, you will continue to see innovations. These could be in communicating using wireless technology or running complex models over networks. This will enable to move beyond the simple transfer of data. You can use mapping, modeling, or communicating technology. This will help you solve problems easily and quickly. You will see new applications on the Internet that take advantage of these developments to provide information, research, and education. The Web provides us with an extensive choice of information services. Simple search capabilities allow the user to find a list of resources relating to any topic. The Internet is also providing innovative examples of information exchange.

10.1.1 Emergency Preparedness Information Exchange (EPIX)

EPIX allows the user to exchange ideas and information on disasters. The site identifies new technologies that are a part of the communications network. The site was developed by the Centre for Policy Research on Science and Technology. This is located at Simon Fraser University, Vancouver, Canada. See the EPIX site for a description of this innovative service (http://hoshi.cic.sfu.ca/epix).

FEMA has also facilitated information exchange or a clearinghouse after disasters for both hurricanes and earthquakes (for hurricanes, see www.katrina.lsu.edu; for earthquakes, see http://maximus.ce.washington.edu/~nisqually/). FEMA wants to facilitate easy access to data, contacts, and resources. This will aid in response, recovery, mitigation, and even in research.

10.1.2 Television and Internet Information

Newspapers, television organizations, and cable providers give users information. These media allow users to obtain current information instantaneously. Users can monitor extreme weather, emergency incidents, or other regional incidents. Today, many Internet providers give real-time information on developments in a disaster. Many of us look to www.weather.com for current information on local or regional weather conditions. Even local media provide current news stories or updates on disasters worldwide.

10.1.3 Digital Libraries and Publications

The digital environment of the Web is an excellent means of making information available. A **digital library** is a Web-based storage system that enables you to search for books, articles, studies, and videos, similar to the services provided by a conventional library. Borbinha (1996) contends that these digital libraries can go well beyond just the preservation and dissemination of knowledge. Digital libraries are active partners with the potential to stimulate, support, and register the process of creation of that knowledge. Users of the library can view the data/knowledge from different perspectives. Users can raise complex questions that can lead to answers.

The digital library is an "assemblage of digital computing, storage, and communications machinery together with the content and software needed to reproduce, emulate and extend the services provided by conventional libraries based on paper and other material means of collecting, cataloging, finding, and disseminating information. A full service digital library must accomplish all essential services of the traditional libraries and also exploit the well-known advantages of digital storage, searching and communications" (Gladney et al. 1994).

Borbinha (1996) suggests that technology can convert our memory and knowledge to a digital format and store it at an affordable cost. The resulting digital format may be made available to everyone through the Internet, CDs, or by other electronic means. Borbinha wrote, "Computers were first introduced in libraries to help in the management of catalogues. . . . Finally, the technology brought digital publication. It became easy to write a text, to be stored in a server, and to have it accessible worldwide".

Libraries are also index databases. This allows users the opportunity to find specific information for their use. In addition, the digital library may include photos, maps, or other graphics in a compressed digital format.

The Consortium for International Earth Science Information Network

The Consortium for International Earth Science Information Network provides an innovative gateway to massive amounts of data stored in locations around the world. Visit the Web site at http://sedac.ciesin.org/index.html.

Natural Hazards Center at the University of Colorado

Universities are one of the largest sources of information. Several universities have emergency management programs. They have hazard resources available via the Web. The University of Colorado has a Natural Hazards Center. The staff produces a printed newsletter, the *Natural Hazards Observer,* as well as numerous papers, bibliographies, and special publications. The following is a more detailed description of their offerings.

Natural Hazards Observer: The bimonthly *Observer* carries current information on disaster issues. Articles are on various topics, including research, policy developments, and new programs. Notices of upcoming conferences are included as well. There are over 14,000 subscribers in the United States and abroad. The *Observer* is free and can be accessed at www.colorado.edu/hazards/o/nov04/nov04c.html.

Publications: Applying research findings is one of the main goals of the center. The staff works toward this goal by editing and publishing many types of books, reports, and bibliographies. These materials are designed to provide information to a wide range of readers. They produce works that appeal to everyone from government officials to emergency managers in private industry. Because they are trying to appeal to this wide audience, the books are edited and produced in nontechnical language. A complete list of all center publications is on their Web site www.colorado.edu/hazards.

The Disaster Research **electronic newsletter and network:** The center also produces and distributes a moderated e-mail newsletter called *Disaster Research.* Disaster Research comes out approximately twice a month. The e-mail includes some of the news items that appear in the *Observer* as well as other articles. It is distributed worldwide through the Internet to over 3,000 subscribers. The information is also reposted on numerous bulletin boards, gopher servers, Internet home pages, and other networks. All past issues are archived and are available on the Web. You can subscribe by filling in your name and e-mail address at www.colorado.edu/hazards/dr/drsub.html.

Annual workshop: To bring together researchers and practitioners, the center has a workshop each summer in Colorado. This brings these groups together to share hazard-related problems as well as ideas for their solutions. The workshop is unique. It involves participants from a wide range of disciplines and provides people an opportunity to learn new perspectives and determine how their work impacts others. Session summaries from past hazards workshops are available on the Web site.

Research program: The center also conducts both an in-house research program and a grant program enabling a quick response study of disasters. With funds from the National Science Foundation, the center funds social scientists traveling to the scene of a disaster immediately after the disaster's impact. This allows the scientists and the center to gather information that might otherwise be lost. The center, for example, provided 25 grants in the aftermath of Hurricane Katrina. Their findings were subsequently published by the center in brief Quick Response Reports. The latest reports are available on the Web site.

Library research services: The heart of the center's work is the library that it shares with the University of Colorado. The library includes over 14,000 books, articles, reports, journals, and other documents. These focus on the social, economic, and behavioral aspects of natural disasters. The holdings are cataloged in a computerized, bibliographic database called Haz-Lit.

FEMA

The Emergency Management Institute within FEMA has established an online library. This enables you to search for books, articles, studies, and videos at the Learning Resource Center. This collection may be searched at www.lrc.fema.gov.

MCB University Press

Emergency management journals, newsletters, and bulletins are going online. MCB University Press manages over 400 journals. These journals include *Environmental Management and Health* and *Disaster Prevention and Management*. Users subscribe to a journal and have access to the journal articles in a digital format.

The Center of Excellence in Disaster Management

The Center of Excellence in Disaster Management has created a large digital library. The library includes disaster-related journals. You can review these journals at http://website.tamc.amedd.army.mil.

Natural Hazards Research Center

The Natural Hazards Research Center is associated with Macquarie University in North Ryde, NS, Australia. It is a great resource for natural hazards publications.

FOR EXAMPLE

Louisiana State University GIS Information Clearinghouse

The LSU GIS Information Clearinghouse was established in the aftermath of Hurricanes Katrina and Rita. It was initiated through the collaborative efforts of LSU and FEMA. The clearinghouse has geospatial data for Hurricanes Katrina, Rita, and Wilma. It also contains hundreds of pre- and post-hurricane raster images. While some of this information is password protected, other information is publicly accessible. For more information see www.katrina.lsu.edu

The center publishes the *Natural Hazards Quarterly* (NHQ). The center can be reached at www.es.mq.edu.au/nhrc. The publications from the center are an excellent resource and reflect a growing number of organizations making publications available by the Internet. Their focus is on natural hazards research and applications in the Australia-Pacific Asia region.

10.1.4 Distance Learning

It can be argued that the most significant form of information exchange is **distance learning.** Distance learning is an extended learning effort that includes everything from self-paced individual learning to forums or chat rooms that bring together students and instructors. Students and instructors use the Web to allow more timely access to learning and a digital classroom environment. Several groups have initiated innovative extended learning efforts that bring together informed experts. The future may include a new form of classroom that uses the Internet to allow more timely access to learning.

Introductions to topics associated with disasters are available on the Internet. The ease of access to education without leaving home is invaluable to individuals interested in learning and keeping up on the latest news. Tutorials are available from FEMA at the National Emergency Training Center, the National Weather Service, the United States Geological Survey (USGS), universities, and many not-for-profit groups.

Today, many conferences are available on the Internet in real time. Regardless of where you are, you can log on. You can view the presentation and discussion. Or you can tune in later and view a digital recording. Technology, also exists that allows you to communicate directly with the speakers. For example, a national conference on rebuilding New Orleans after Hurricane Katrina was hosted in November 2005. It linked over 50 sites and hundreds of viewers by using Webcast technology. You can see the Webcast conference at www.acorn.org. On this Web site, you can go to the archives and watch the conference in its entirety.

Although we frequently associate distance learning with obtaining educational degrees, distance learning can also be used for training. Through the Internet, you can take part in a training session with professionals from different states and from the federal government. You can use the Internet for training. This cuts down on travel expenses. Or you may need to train people quickly in a crisis. For example, the E Team staff trained emergency managers on how to use their software remotely over the Internet in the aftermath of the terrorist attacks on September 11, 2001.

FEMA has recognized the need for making training more available to public, private, and nonprofit agencies. More classes are going online and are available at a distance from the Emergency Management Institute in Emmitsburg, Maryland. Some of the classes are available on an independent study basis. See http://training.fema.gov/EMIWeb/IS/ for more information.

SELF-CHECK

- Define **digital libraries.**
- Define **distance learning.**
- What Internet sources of information are most useful to you in keeping up with technology?
- What are the advantages to using a Webcast to keep up and learn via the Internet and Web for training efforts?

10.2 Using Remote Technology: Modeling, Mapping, and Decision Support Systems at a Distance

With the help of the Internet, you can also work remotely. You can now use hazard modeling, mapping, and decision support systems on individual computers. Rather than install and run separate programs on a user's computer, you can now go to **centralized Web-based systems.** A centralized Web-based system is a Web-based program that runs hazard models, GIS, and decision support systems on a centralized system rather than on a single-user computer. You can use a centralized Web-based system to understand the depth of the water in a geographic area, find addresses and transportation routes, and determine the dangers associated with a hazardous substance. Access to many of these tools is open to anyone. The tools are easy to use. In the future, you may be able to utilize each of the following types of technology from our wireless phones or other small-computer technologies. It seems impossible now, but consider the types of modeling, mapping, and decision support systems that you use over the Internet. In the near future, you should be able to obtain information for decision support from the field, the classroom, or in your cars or planes. What seems impossible today may be here sooner than you think.

10.2.1 Wildfire and Earthquake Situational Maps: Using a National and International Approach

Public agencies use Web-based mapping approaches to share information on recent and historic hazard events. You can understand current hazard events through static maps as illustrated by the following examples. Some of the maps show the location of current disasters. Others show maps explaining the potential for hazard events to occur (such as wildfires or earthquakes).

The National Interagency Fire Center provides up-to-date information on current wildfires. Figure 10-1 shows an example of a current fire location in a

map format. The use of national mapping programs provides critical information. See www.nifc.gov/firemaps.html for a list of the types of map products that
are available for fire hazards. For additional information on fire maps, see
http://activefiremaps.fs.fed.us/.

Many federal agencies and universities have applied Web-based mapping
technology to show current conditions of hazardous events similar to the large
wildfire map in Figure 10-1.

▲ **Large Wildfire Events** (http://activefiremaps.fs.fed.us/lg_fire2.php#). The
USGS monitors earthquake events as shown at http://earthquake.usgs.gov/
recenteqs/. You can monitor current hazard events or examine past events
that apply to current situations.

Figure 10-1

Map of current fire locations for June 22, 2006.

10.2.2 Applying Technology in Hurricane Katrina: A Case Example

In 2005, Hurricane Katrina damaged the coastlines of Louisiana, Mississippi, and Alabama. Entire communities were destroyed. Some lost nearly all of their buildings and homes. In New Orleans, Louisiana, the levees that separated Lake Ponchartrain from the city were breached and 80% of New Orleans was flooded. Hurricane Katrina was the costliest disaster in terms of dollars in United States history. It was the second deadliest natural disaster in terms of loss of life. Because of the losses and the wide area in which the disaster hit, the response to the hurricane was enormously challenging. Fortunately, recent technology helped overcome some of the challenges in several different ways.

Responders made extensive use of technology by utilizing up-to-date cell and satellite communications. Responders and emergency managers were able to transfer geospatial data at high speeds over the Internet, cell, and satellite systems. Portable handheld computers were used to record damage to local infrastructure and accurately map direct observations on responders. High-speed hazard models were run on supercomputers. The computers sent their outputs over the Internet to decision makers in both the public and private sectors. Instant messaging provided another way for people to communicate. Even the challenges with donations were made easier by technology. IT systems were used to track donations of food, other goods, and services.

Figure 10-2

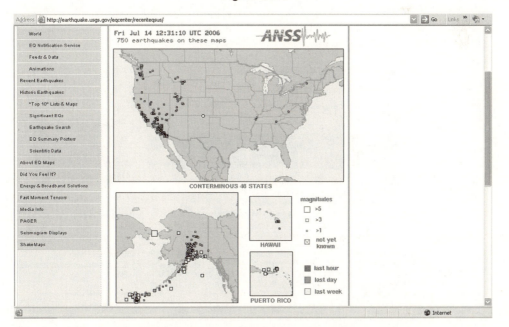

Map of recent earthquake activity as of July 14, 2006
(http://earthquake.usgs.gov/recenteqs/).

One of the biggest challenges was in rescuing people who were stranded either inside their homes or on the roofs of their homes. Simple solutions often proved to be the best answers. A request by the Louisiana State Police for local street maps of New Orleans was made to the GIS unit in the State Emergency Operations Center. The initial response was to prepare a large map of New Orleans and an associated street index. Unfortunately, this would take time to prepare and print. A call to a commercial mapping company resulted in a digital street map of New Orleans. It could be printed on any size paper, either in color or black and white. The map was formatted on multiple pages. It was suitable for printing on several pages that would be easy to read. Within just a few minutes, the state police had street maps for officers who would be part of the bus evacuation process.

Keeping it simple allowed the technology to be used quickly and in a cost-effective manner. Many requests for landing coordinates for rescue helicopters were made. These requests were fulfilled by staff using the address finder utility provided by Google Earth (www.earth.google.com). Agency staff with initial assistance by GIS staff quickly became capable users of this Web-based technology. Google Earth

Figure 10-3

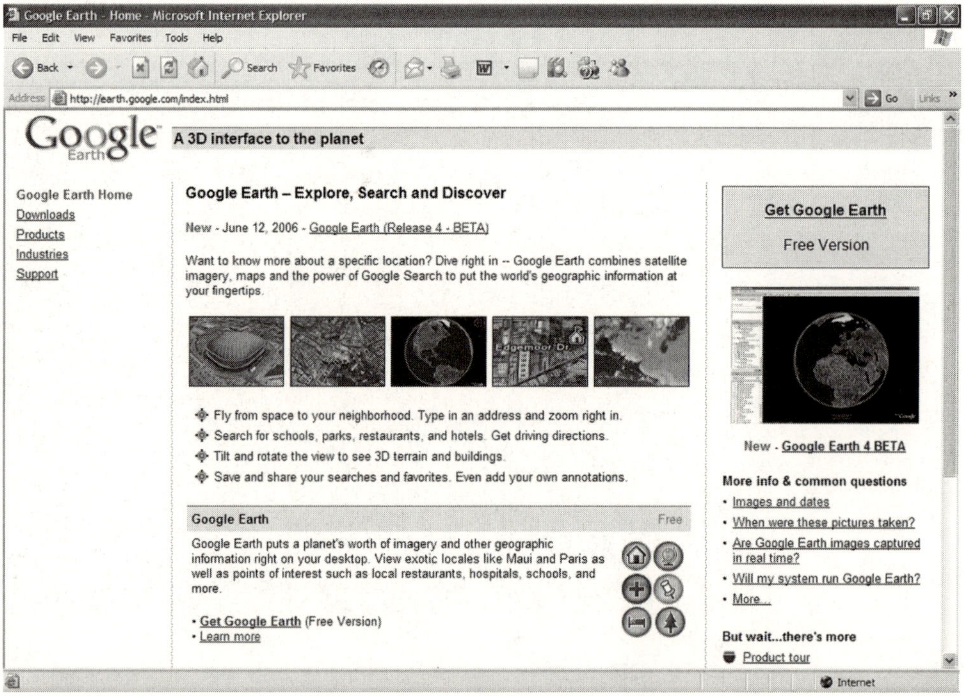

The Homepage for Google Earth.

staff were made aware of the extensive use of their technology (see Figure 10-3). They were excited with the application of their mapping tools. They responded by providing access to licenses for emergency operations personnel in the use of their Web-mapping software and high-resolution images of New Orleans.

This free and easy-to-use mapping software provided critical information to responders during both Hurricanes Katrina and Rita. With limited training, staff operating in the Louisiana Department of Homeland Security and the Emergency Response Center were able to use the tools in Google Earth. They were able to find critical mapping information to pass along to rescuers in the early days of Hurricane Katrina. Easy-to-use technology that was available over the Internet met their mapping information needs.

But Google Earth provided more than just maps. In collaboration with federal agencies such as NOAA and National Geospatial Agency (NGA), preliminary storm damage assessment were provided to the public and to the emergency management community. Figure 10-4 represents a snapshot of the damage as of September 5, 2005.

Figure 10-4

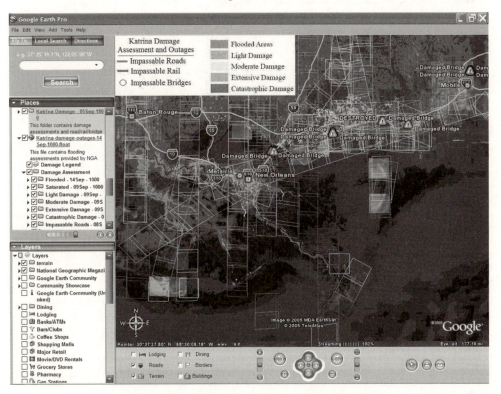

The damage inflicted by Hurricane Katrina.

Other companies saw the need for spatial information following Hurricane Katrina. Google Earth was a highly sophisticated mapping program with many capabilities. Other companies saw a simple solution for individuals who wanted to know the depth of flood water at their homes. For example, C & C Technologies Inc. is a privately owned surveying and mapping company. It operates worldwide. They designed a simple Web-based mapping program that provides limited information on the depth of flooding. This cutting-edge technology and inspiring workplace created an innovative map for New Orleans following Katrina. The open-access as demonstrated in Figure 10-5, map allows users to find an address and determine the level of water from the flooding. The user can insert an address in the mapping utility. Users are then given the highest water level from the flood. Comprehensive background information is provided on how the flooding estimates were determined. . This tool provided invaluable information for both citizens and public officials interested in flooding throughout the city of New Orleans. In the future, we will likely see similar applications that are based on sound science and provide critical information to the public in a timely manner. For more information see http://mapper.cctechnol.com/floodmap.php.

These examples remind us that the key is to be aware of our goals and select technology tools and applications that make the best fit. The technology is a means to accomplishing an end. These tools help us to prepare, mitigate, respond, and recover in an efficient and effective manner.

Figure 10-5

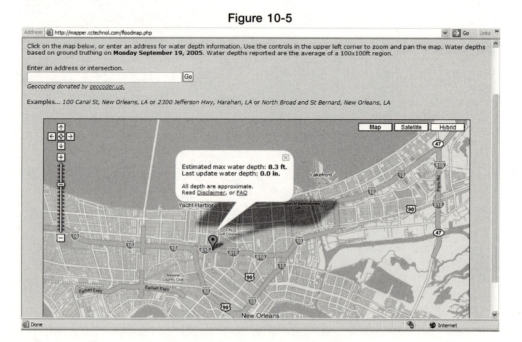

C & C map from Hurricane Katrina.

SELF-CHECK

- Define centralized Web-based system.

- What is the advantage of using a Web map rather than having a GIS on a computer?

- Give two examples of how mapping technology was important in Hurricane Katrina.

- What is Google Earth and in what situations would you use it?

10.3 Managing the Technology

Technology in emergencies has brought many tools that enhance response, recovery, mitigation, and preparedness. You have seen that with the introduction of many of the technology tools. However, when you evaluate whether you should use technology, you have to recognize the limits of technology. The following are some things to keep in mind:

▲ **Person-centered technology:** Person-centered technology refers to a technology system that is designed to fit and adjust to the needs and uses of the individual user. To acheive this, monitor for operator errors or difficulties in using the technology. You will also need to ensure that the application is used to support operations in a productive way.

▲ **Scale of application:** Keep it simple. Too often users fail to recognize that the technology is overkill when a simpler option is available.

▲ **Recognize that the software has limitations and bugs:** Monitor for any problems and efforts and solicit feedback from users as to any difficulties they are experiencing.

▲ **Data errors:** Assessing the quality of the data in an application is critical to ensure that objectives are being met. You want to avoid surprises that undermine the operations.

▲ **Dependence on community infrastructure:** Emergency management does not operate in a vacuum but in an interdependent manner with the community. Anticipate what your strategies will be for loss of power or the loss of the use of your facilities.

▲ **Security:** Today's atmosphere on homeland security suggests that we constantly determine how our operations may be vulnerable to security breaches. Dependence on collaboration with many local, regional, state, and national resources opens you up to potential security problems. Monitoring network and site security on an on-going basis is a must.

▲ **Inadequate system performance:** Users expect to high-performance computers, software, networks, and systems support. Test new technology to ensure that acquisitions enhance your operations. This is critical and avoids costly mistakes.

▲ **Liability for system failures:** The issue is not a legal one. It centers on ensuring that systems perform at the highest degree. Your goal is to prevent the loss of lives and property. Systems failures that could be prevented work against this goal.

Technology has a life cycle. Once it is developed, it evolves over time, gaining operational capabilities; it is reduced in size and is more compatible with other technology. Today very small computers can do mapping, modeling, Internet communication. They can be highly mobile, durable, and compatible with more powerful computer systems. Today, you can collect data on damaged buildings, bridges, and other structures as a part of damage assessments. You can record the precise location as well as store images of the damaged site. Digital cameras are linked to GPS systems and small computers. You will continue to see new technology that allows us to collect data on current conditions. You will be able to store the data, map the precise location of the area, and record digital images of the event. All of this will be in smaller packages, with seamless linkages. It will also be easier to operate.

FOR EXAMPLE

Issuing Debit Cards

The Louisiana Department of Social Services (DSS) issued debit cards to over 350,000 Louisiana residents who needed public assistance following Hurricanes Katrina and Rita. The food stamp funds were issued monthly. This was to help those who were forced from their homes. They were issued to those who qualified for the support under this program. The DSS staff could monitor expenditures as card users shopped not only in Louisiana stores but anywhere in the United States. This program could track expenditures by city, county, zip code. It could follow transactions to determine if the cards were used fraudulently. The monitoring program has reduced incidents of fraud in the food stamp program. It allowed the agency to direct other social services to geographic areas where evacuees were settled. New technology is being used not only in small portable computers but also in large agency programs that can have unexpected utility as with DSS. A large agency program intended to serve those in need was used by creative staff to also help establish where evacuees were living and shopping.

For example, new handheld wireless technology is being introduced by communication companies. A device that is purchased today will soon be obsolete. Other devices will have new capabilities, faster connections, and new services. Prices for the devices are high but appear to drop as new services are added. Take a look at the latest personal communication wireless devices offered in your community. See what new services and capabilities are offered that could be used by emergency services organizations in the public, private, and nonprofit sectors.

SELF-CHECK

- Define person-centered technology.
- What steps can you take to ensure that your office and staff can operate successfully in a disaster?
- What is meant by scale of application?

SUMMARY

New technology tools that can help you do your job more effectively are constantly being developed. You have learned through this chapter that information exchange is now possible, and you discovered the many benefits of information exchange. You can even work with others who live halfway across the world. New technologies such as modeling and mapping also help you be more effective in managing and responding to disasters. As you use the new technology tools, you will want to make sure you can manage the technology. You will want to use only the tools that will be beneficial to you in your goal of saving lives and protecting property.

KEY TERMS

Centralized Web-based systems	A Web-based program that runs hazard models, GIS, and decision support systems on a centralized based system rather than on a single-user computer.
Digital library	A Web-based storage system that enables users to search for books, articles, studies, and videos similar to the services provided by a conventional library.

Distance learning

Extended learning efforts, including self-paced individual learning to forums or chat rooms that bring together students and instructors who use the Web to allow more timely access to learning and to a digital classroom environment.

Person-centered technology

A technology system that is designed to fit and adjust to the needs and uses of the individual user.

ASSESS YOUR UNDERSTANDING

Go to www.wiley.com/college/pine to evaluate your knowledge of trends in technology.

Measure your learning by comparing pre-test and post-test results.

Summary Questions

1. An information clearinghouse is used to facilitate the exchange of information. True or False?

2. Information exchange includes:

   (a) remote training

   (b) distance learning

   (c) digital library

   (d) all of the above

3. A digital library emulates the services provided by conventional libraries but in a digital environment. True or False?

4. Distance electronic learning replaces the traditional classroom learning environment. True or False?

5. The development of remote technology Web applications replaces individual computer modeling, mapping, and decision support systems. True or False?

6. Many federal agencies and universities have applied Web-based mapping technology to show current conditions of hazard events. True or False?

7. The Google Earth mapping application replaces the need for individual-based GIS applications. True or False?

8. A Web-based program that runs hazard models is a:

   (a) GIS.

   (b) digital library.

   (c) centralized Web-based system.

   (d) Google Earth.

Review Questions

1. What Web communications technology could be used to keep you up-to-date on technology?

2. How can Web-mapping programs help you in responding to disasters?

3. What are some limits of technology?

4. What are some qualities of technology that you would need to consider when evaluating the technology?

Applying This Chapter

1. You are the emergency manager for New Orleans, which was just devastated by Hurricane Katrina. You have a database that contains sensitive information in it. How do you protect it against security breaches?

2. You are the emergency manager for a town that was just flooded. You are working with the coast guard, which is trying to rescue people. The coast guard members are not familiar with the town. What technology can you use to make their job easier?

3. You are the newly appointed director of FEMA. After a poor performance during hurricane season, you decide to invest in technology for training. What do you invest in and why? How do you deliver training to people scattered across the United States?

4. You are the local emergency manager for a town that is prone to flooding, and you and your staff are trying to determine the best ways to mitigate future flooding. What Web resources do you consult and why? What Web resources would you want your staff to have constant access to and why?

Information Exchange

You are the emergency manager for a town in California that sits on a seismic fault line. Name three sources you could consult for information on earthquakes and emergency management response to past earthquakes.

Training

You are the director of a county emergency management agency. When and why would you train people remotely using the Internet as the communication medium?

Internet

Consider the field of emergency management before and after the availability of the Internet. Name three ways the Internet has changed emergency management. Include the advantages and disadvantages of the use of the Internet in the field of emergency management.

BIBLIOGRAPHY

Adventure GPS. 2006. Buyer's guide to GPS receiver features. http://www.gps4fun.com/how-to-use.html.

Alter, S. 1996. *Information systems: A management perspective.* Menlo Park, CA: Benjamin/Cummings.

Anderson, P. S. 1995. The biggest mutual aid system on Earth: The Internet in emergency management. *NCCEM Bulletin* (Summer): 7–9.

Antenucci, J. C., K. Brown, P. Croswell, and M. Kevany. 1991. *Geographic information systems: A guide to the technology.* New York: Van Nostrand Reinhold.

Aronoff, S. 1991. *Geographic information systems: A management perspective.* Ottawa: WDL.

Bates, R. J., Jr. 1992. *Disaster recovery planning: Networks, telecommunications, and data communications.* New York: McGraw-Hill.

Baum, H. R., K. McGrattan, and R. G. Rehm. 1997. *Three dimensional simulations of fire plume dynamics.* Gaithersburg, MD: National Institute of Standards and Technology.

Baumann, P. Flood analysis: 1993 analysis. In Applications in remote sensing, vol. 4 of the Remote Sensing Core Curriculum. http://umbc7.umbc.edu/ ~tbenja1/baumann/baumann.html.

Beroggi, G. E. G., L. Waisel, and W. A. Wallace. 1994. The role of virtual reality technology in emergency management. In *International Emergency Management and Engineering Conference: Bridging the gap between theory and practice,* ed. J. D. Sullivan and S. Tufekci. Dallas: International Emergency Management and Engineering Society.

Berry, J. K. 1995. Raster is faster, but vector is corrector. *GIS World* 8 (6): 35.

Bidgoli, H. 1989. *Decision support systems: Principles and practice.* San Francisco: West.

Birkin, M., G. Clarke, M. Clarke, and A. Wilson. 1996. *Intelligent GIS: Location decisions and strategic planning.* New York: Wiley.

Borba, G. 1995. The Internet and disaster response. *Australian Journal of Emergency Management* 10 (4): 42–43.

Borbinha, J. L. B., and J. C. M. Delgado. 1996. Networked digital libraries. *Microcomputers for Information Management: Global Internetworking for Libraries* 13 (3–4): 195–216.

Brown, J. S. 1991. Reinventing the corporation. *Harvard Business Review* (Jan.–Feb.): 108.

Bryson, J. 1997. *Managing information services: An integrated approach.* Brookfield, VT: Gower.

Burkhart, F. N. 1991. *Media, emergency warnings, and citizen response.* Boulder, CO: Westview.

Bush, V. 1945. As we may think. *Atlantic Monthly,* July. http://www2.theatlantic.com/atlantic/atlweb/flashblks/computer/bushf.htm.

Butler, D. 1995. Information systems and knowledge transfer: Prospects for better understanding, opportunities for increased hazard mitigation. Unpublished paper, Natural Hazard Research and Application Information Center, University of Colorado at Boulder.

Cain, B. 1998. The historic flood of 1997 at Louisiana State Penitentiary. *ASPEP Journal,* 15–32.

CAMEO: A Case Study. Materials drawn from CAMEO and the following Web site from EPA: http://www.nsc.org/ehc/cameo.htm.

Campbell, J. B. 1996. *Introduction to remote sensing.* 2nd ed. New York: Guilford Press.

Carlson, G. R., and B. Patel. 1997. *A new era dawns for geospatial imagery. GIS World* 10 (3): 36–40.

Carrara, A., and F. Guzzetti, ed. 1995. *Geographic information systems in assessing natural hazards.* Hingham, MA: Kluwer Academic.

Champy, J. 1995. *Reengineering management.* New York: Harper Business.

Coile, R. C. 1997. The role of amateur radio in providing emergency electronic communication for disaster management. *Disaster Prevention and Management* 6 (3): 176–185.

Computer Science Telecommunications Board. 1994. *Realizing the information future: The Internet and beyond.* Washington, DC: National Academy Press.

Computer Science and Telecommunications Board. 1996. Application needs for computing and communications. In *Computing and communications in the extreme: Research for crisis management and other applications.* Washington, DC: National Academy Press.

Computer Science and Telecommunications Board. 1996. *The unpredictable certainty: Information infrastructure through 2000.* Washington, DC: National Academy Press.

Cooperative Institute for Research in the Atmosphere. Introduction to GOES I-M. http://www.cira.colostate.edu/ramm/tutorial/g8mo-dpg1.htm.

Dana, P. H. The geographer's craft project. University of Texas Department of Geography. http://www.utexas.edu/depts/grg/gcraft/notes/gps/gps.html.

Davenport, T. H. 1993. *Process improvement: Reengineering work through information technology.* Boston: Harvard Business School Press.

Drager, K. H., G. G. Lovas, J. Wiklund, and H. Soma. 1993. Objectives of modeling evacuation from buildings during accidents: Some path-model scenarios. *Journal of Contingencies and Crisis Management* 1 (4): 207–214.

Drury, S. A. 1990. *A guide to remote sensing.* New York: Oxford Science Publications.

Ecember, J., N. Randall, and W. Tatters. 1995. *Discover the World Wide Web.* Indianapolis: Sams.net Publishing.

eLib. 1996. eLib project details. http://ukoln.ac.uk/elib/projects.html.

Elsevier Science. TULIP final report. http://www.elsevier.nl/locate/tulip.

Environmental Systems Research Institute. 1992. *Understanding GIS.* Redlands, CA: Environmental Systems Research Institute.

ESRI. 2005. Red Cross utilizes GIS for Hurricane Katrina and Hurricane Rita efforts. http://www.gisuser.com/index2.php?option=content&task=view&id=7077&pop=1&page=0.

Federal Emergency Management Agency. 1996. *Emergency alert system: A program guide for state and local jurisdictions.* Parts I–III. Washington, D.C: Federal Emergency Management Agency.

Federal Emergency Management Agency. 1997. *Hydrologic hazards: Multi hazard identification and risk assessment.* Washington, D.C: Federal Emergency Management Agency.

Federal Emergency Management Agency. 2003. *HAZUS-MH riverine flood model technical manual.* Washington, D.C: Federal Emergency Management Agency.

Fischer, H. W., III. 1998. The role of the new information technologies in emergency mitigation, planning response and recovery. *Disaster Prevention and Management* 7 (1): 28–37.

Forbes. 1993. When machines screw up. June 7, 110–111.

Fortune. 1993. Information technology special report. Autumn.

Fortune. 1993. Welcome to the revolution. December 13, 66–78.

Gates, B. 1996. *The road ahead.* New York: Penguin.

Gividen, J. R., and K. Mantyla. 1997. *Distance learning: A step-by-step guide for trainers.* Alexandria, VA: American Society for Training and Development.

Golombek, M. P. 1998. The Mars Pathfinder mission. *Scientific American* 279 (1): 40.

Goodchild, M. F., B. O. Parks, and L. T. Steyaert. 1993. *Environmental modeling with GIS.* New York: Oxford University Press.

Greenway, A. R. 1998. *Risk management planning handbook: A comprehensive guide to hazard assessment, accidental release prevention, and consequence analysis.* Rockville, MD: Government Institutes, Inc.

Grinberg, A. 1995. *Computer/telecom integration.* New York: McGraw-Hill.

Grinberg, A. 1997. *Seamless networks.* New York: McGraw-Hill.

Haimes, Y. Y., R. Krzysztofowicz, J. H. Lambert, D. Li, and V. Tulsiani. 1996. *Risk-based evaluation of flood warning and preparedness systems.* Vols. 1 and 2. Springfield, VA: Water Resources Support Center National Technical Information Service.

Herring, T. A. 1996. The global positioning system. *Scientific American* (February): 44–50.

Jarman, A. M. G. 1993. Smart spatial information systems: Extending geographic information systems in the space age. *Journal of Contingencies and Crisis Management.* 1 (4): 229–240.

Johnson, G. O. 1992. GIS applications in emergency management. *URISA Journal* 4 (Spring): 66-72.

Kara-Zaitri, C. 1996. Disaster prevention and limitation: State of the art tools and technologies. *Disaster Prevention and Management* 5 (1): 30–39.

Keller, A. K., E. L. Coles, and R. Heal. 1996. Experiences gained from the first Internet Disaster Conference. *Disaster Prevention and Management:* 5 (5): 31–33.

Kiester, E., Jr. 1997. Water, water, everywhere. *Smithsonian* 28 (3): 34–45.

Kirkwood, A. S. 1994. Why do we worry when scientists say there is no risk? *Disaster Prevention and Management* 3 (2): 15–22.

Korte, G. B. 1992. *A practitioner's guide: The GIS book.* Santa Fe, NM: On Word Press.

Lilley, D. G. 1996. Fire modeling. *National Fire and Arson Report* 14 (4): 10–17.

Logsdon, T. 1992. *The Navstar global positioning system.* New York: Van Nostrand Reinhold.

Mann, B. W. 1997. Emergency alert. *Emergency Preparedness Digest,* April–June.

Markus, M. L., and M. Keil. 1994. If we build it, they will come: Designing information systems that people want to use. *Sloan Management Review* (Summer): 11–25.

Martin, E. W., D. DeHayes, J. Hoffer, and W. Perkins. 1991. *Managing information technology: What managers need to know.* New York: Macmillan.

McCoy, L. C. Satellites and fiber optics: Communications for the twenty-first century. National Institute for Urban Search and Rescue. See http://niusr.org/archives/tincan.html.

McCoy, L. C., J. R. Harrald, D. McManis, and J. O. Tuttle. Crisis management as a function of information exchange. National Institute for Urban Search and Rescue. http://niusr.org/programs.html.

Menard, R. J., and J. L. Knieff. 2002. GPS at Ground Zero: Tracking the World Trade Center recovery. GPS World. http://www.gpsworld.com/gpsworld/article/articleDetail.jsp?id=30686&searchString=Ground%20Zero.

Mileti, D. S., and J. H. Sorensen. 1990. Building and evaluating a warning system. Ch. 3 in *Communication of emergency public warnings: A social science perspective and state of the art assessment.* Oak Ridge, TN: Oak Ridge National Laboratory/FEMA.

Mileti, D. S., and J. H. Sorensen. 1990. Organizational aspects of warning systems. Ch. 4 in *Communication of emergency public warnings: A social science perspective and state of the art assessment.* Oak Ridge, TN: Oak Ridge National Laboratory/FEMA.

National Academy of Public Administration. 1993. *Coping with catastrophe: Building an emergency management system to meet people's needs in natural and manmade disasters.* Washington, DC: National Academy of Public Administration.

National Climatic Data Center. n.d. *About NOAA's satellites.* Asheville, NC: National Climatic Data Center.

National Institute for Occupational Health and Safety. 1994. *NIOSH pocket guide to chemical hazards.* Washington, DC: United States Government Printing Office.

National Weather Service. 1997. *Automated local flood warning systems handbook.* Silver Spring, MD: National Oceanic and Atmospheric Administration.

National Weather Service. 1997. *The Fort Collins flash flood of July 28, 1997: Service assessment initial report.* Silver Spring, MD: National Weather Service.

Nellist, J. G. 1996. *Understanding telecommunications and lightwave systems: An entry level guide.* 2nd ed. New York: Institute of Electrical and Electronics Engineers.

Newcott, W. R. 1998. Return to Mars. *National Geographic* 194 (2): 2–29.

Newkirk, R. T. 1993. Extending geographic information systems for risk analysis and management. *Journal of Contingencies and Crisis Management* (1) 4: 203–206.

O'Brien, J. A. 1993. *Management information systems: A managerial end user perspective.* 2nd ed. Homewood, IL: Irwin.

O'Connor, J. E., and J. E. Costa. 2003. *Large floods in the United States: Where they happen and why.* Reston, VA: United States Department of the Interior.

Oyen, R. 1996. 911: The system behind the phone number. In *Information systems: A management perspective,* ed. S. Alter, 690–692. Menlo Park, CA: Benjamin/Cummings.

Pan American Health Organization. 1996. The Internet: Tending to the basics. *Disasters: Preparedness and Mitigation in the Americas* 65: 1, 7.

Parker, D., M. Fordham, S. Tunstall, and A. M. Ketteridge. 1995. Flood warning systems under stress in the United Kingdom. *Disaster Prevention and Management* 4 (3): 32–42.

Pecar, J. A., R. J. O'Connor, and D. A. Garbin. 1993. *The McGraw-Hill telecommunications factbook.* New York: McGraw-Hill.

Pfeiffer, J. 1994. *Competitive advantage through people: Unleashing the power of the work force.* Boston: Harvard Business School Press.

Pine, J. C. 1997. Hazards analysis—Extremely hazardous substances: Sterlington, Louisiana. Technical report, Institute for Environmental Studies, Louisiana State University.

Rapoza, J. 2005. FEMA's IE-only form: Just what Katrina victims don't need. *eWeek,* September 9.

Rogers, G. O. and J. H. Sorensen. 1988. Diffusion of emergency warnings. *The Environmental Professional* 10: 281–294.

Rogers, G. O., and J. H. Sorensen. 1991. Diffusion of emergency warning: Comparing empirical and simulation results. In *Risk analysis,* ed. C. Zervos. New York: Plenum.

Rubin, C. B. 1998. What hazards and disasters are likely in the twenty-first century—or sooner? Natural Hazards Working Paper 99, Natural Hazards Research and Applications Information Center, University of Colorado at Boulder.

Sanley, E. M., Sr., and W. L. Waugh, Jr. 1999. Emergency managers for the new millennium. In *Handbook of crisis and emergency management,* ed. A. Farazman. New York: Marcel Dekker.

Simard, A. J. 1996. The Canadian wildfire fire information system. In *The Disaster 96 first Internet conference.* London: MCB University Press.

Simard, A. J. 1996. A global emergency management information network initiative: GEMINI. In *The Disaster 96 first Internet conference.* London: MCB University Press.

Srinivas, E. 1996. Applications in hazard assessment and management. Vol. 6 of *Explorations in geographic information systems technology.* Geneva: United Nations Institute for Training and Research.

Srinivas, E., and J. X. Kasperson. 1996. Disaster communication via the information superhighway: Data and observations on the 1995 hurricane season. *International Journal of Mass Emergencies and Disasters* 14 (3): 321–342.

State University of New York at Buffalo and GIS Resource Group. 1997. *Helping local government create a GIS.* Vols. 1,2, and 3. Buffalo: State University of New York at Buffalo and GIS Resource Group.

Sullivan, J. D., J. L. Wybo, and L. Buisson, ed. 1995. *Proceedings of the International Emergency Management and Engineering Conference.* Dallas: International Emergency Management and Engineering Society.

Thomas, E. 2005. How Bush blew it. *Newsweek,* September 19.

Tobin, R. 1997. *Emergency planning on the Internet.* Rockville, MD: Government Institutes, Inc.

Tomaszewski, B. 2005. Erie County emergency response and planning application performs plume modeling. http://dssresources.com/cases/eriecounty/index.html.

Tzemos, S., and R. A. Burnett. 1995. Use of GIS in the Federal Emergency Management Information System (FEMIS). Paper presented at the Fifteenth ESRI User Conference, Redlands, CA. Available online at http://www.esri.com/base/common/userconf/proc95/to350/p345.html.

United States Census Bureau. 2001. *Home computers and Internet use in the United States: August 2000.* Washington, DC: United States Census Bureau.

United States Environmental Protection Agency. Integrated Risk Information System. http://www.epa.gov/ngispgm3/iris/index.html.

United States Environmental Protection Agency, Federal Emergency Management Agency, and United States Department of Transportation. 1987. *Technical guidance for hazards analysis: Emergency planning for extremely hazardous substances.* Washington, DC: United States Environmental Protection Agency, Federal Emergency Management Agency, and United States Department of Transportation.

United States Environmental Protection Agency and the National Oceanic and Atmospheric Administration. 1996. *ALOHA users manual.* Washington, DC: U. S. Environmental Protection Agency and the National Oceanic and Atmospheric Administration. Also available online at http://www.nsc.org/ehc/cam/aloha.html.

United States Flood Insurance Administration. 1996. *Users guide to the Q3 digital flood insurance rate maps.* Washington, DC: United States Flood Insurance Administration.

United States Geological Survey EROS Data Center. 1995. *Historical Landsat data comparisons: Illustrations of the earth's changing surface.* Washington, DC: United States Geological Survey.

University of Buffalo Department of Geography. GIS development guides. http://www.geog.buffalo.edu/ncgia/sara.

Vermeiren, J. C., and C. C. Watson, Jr. 1994. New technology for improved storm risk assessment in the Caribbean. *Disaster Management* 6 (4): 191–196.

Volume 2: Survey of Available Data, Evaluating Hardware and Software, Database Planning and Design, Database Construction and Pilot Studies and Benchmark Tests.

Volume 3: Acquisition of GIS Hardware and Software, GIS System Integration, GIS Application Development, GIS Use and Maintenance.

Wahl, K. L., W. O. Thomas, Jr., and R. M. Hirsch. 1995. *Stream-gauging program of the U.S. Geological Survey.* United States Geological Survey Circular 1123. Reston, VA: United States Geological Survey. Available at http://water.usgs.gov/public/realtime.html.

Walker, G. R. 1997. Current developments in catastrophe modeling. In *Financial risk management for natural catastrophes,* ed. N. R. Britton and J. Oliver. Brisbane: Aon Group Australia Limited.

Walter, L. S. 1997. *Remote sensing satellites for disaster reduction.* Greenbelt, MD: Earth Sciences Directorate, Goddard Space Flight Center.

White, L. 2004. Emergency communications: The Emergency Alert System (EAS) and all-hazard warnings. *CRS Report for Congress.*

Williams, R. S., J. Heckman, and J. Schneeberger. 1991. *Environmental consequences of the Persian Gulf War 1990–1991: Remote sensing datasets of Kuwait and environs.* Washington, DC: National Geographic Society Committee for Research and Exploration.

Wood, M. 1996. *Disaster communications.* South Daytona, FL: APCO Institute.

GLOSSARY

Adaptive mechanisms   Processes and procedures in an organization that keep the system from changing too rapidly or slowly as required and that allow the operation to adjust and not get out of balance.

Aerial locations of hazardous atmospheres (ALOHA)   A chemical dispersion model developed by EPA and NOAA as a guide for emergency responders to track a chemical-release plume and determine its potential impact on nearby populations.

Analog transmission services   A continuous wave or signal (such as the human voice) for which conventional telephone lines are designed.

ARPANET   The first packet switching network.

Base station   Final destination for the information from the sensors. Information is accepted, processed, displayed, and forwarded to the appropriate computers and personnel.

Centralized Web-based systems   A Web-based program that runs hazard models, GIS, and decision-support systems on a centralized based system rather than on a single-user computer.

Closed system   A system that is not open to any inputs and does not interact with its environment.

Coaxial cable   A copper data transmission wire that has an outer insulator and electrically grounded shielding.

Communication network   A set of lined devices that transfer information between users.

Contingency theory   A management approach suggests that there is no one best way to deal with organizational problems and that solutions must be responsive to changing environmental conditions.

Data   A fact or thing that is known.

Digital library   A Web-based storage system that enables you to search for books, articles, studies, and videos, similar to the services provided by a conventional library.

Direct sensors   Gages and instruments that are in direct contact with a phenomena that provide information.

Distance learning   Extended learning efforts, including self-paced individual learning to forums or chat rooms that bring together students and instructors who use the Web to allow more timely access to learning and to a digital classroom environment.

Distributed network   A collection of interconnected related network systems that facilitate information sharing.

Emergency Alert System (EAS)   EAS is a national initiative of over 13,000 radio, television, and cable systems that voluntarily organize and plan for the warning of local communities.

Event-reporting sensors   Programmed with prerecorded measurements that trigger the transmission of warning signals.

Federal Emergency Management Information System (FEMIS)   An automated decision support system that makes it possible to preplan for emergencies and to coordinate operations and make decisions during an emergency.

Focusing event   A national disaster resulting in losses that receives extensive media coverage.

Forum   An online chat hosted by an organization that allows you to ask questions.

Geocoding   A graphic representation, usually in the form of a point on a map, of information in a database that includes street addresses or other location information.

Geographic information system (GIS)   A computer-based information system that provides a means for the capture, storage, manipulation, analysis, and display of geographical reference information for solving complex problems.

Geostational operational environmental satellite (GOES)   An airborne remote sensing system that revolves in a fixed spot off Earth's surface and collects continuous observations relating to cloud cover, atmospheric temperature, and moisture in the air.

Global positioning system (GPS)   A system to identify and record a geospatial reference point on Earth's surface using a set of satellites orbiting Earth.

Hazard   An event or physical condition that has the potential to create loss (economic, social, or environmental).

Hazard modeling   A simulation of a real system or replication of a potential hazard event.

HAZUS-MH model   Suite of hazard models was developed by FEMA to describe the nature of hazardous conditions for earthquakes, wind, coastal, and flooding hazards and their economic and social impacts.

Immediately dangerous to life or health (IDLH) level   The IDLH is an exposure limit to hazardous chemicals and established to provide guidance to industry and emergency response personnel.

Information   Data that is processed or used in some form of analysis.

Internet   A digital transmission technology that allows users to search, sort, convert, and transfer information over a network.

Landsat   A remote sensing satellite program developed by NASA.

Latitude   Measurement used to describe the north–south position of a point as measured usually in degrees or decimal degrees above or below the equator.

Line   A map object that is defined by a set of sequential coordinates that represents the shape of a geographic feature.

Local area network (LAN)   A collection of users within an enterprise (business or public agency) that facilitates information sharing.

Longitude   Measurement used to describe the east–west position of a point.

Management information system   A set of digital databases that may be sorted, merged, retrieved, displayed, and used to make decisions or calculations.

Metadata   Data about data. Includes information on where the data was obtained, when, how it was formatted or altered, geospacial references if available, purpose of the data, and ownership.

Mitigate   To take actions and enact strategies that reduce vulnerability to hazards.

Myths   Beliefs that are not supported by facts and that do not accurately reflect the real world.

National Emergency Management Information System (NEMIS) An information system that was designed to automate and support vital emergency response and recovery operations by the federal government.

Network   A collection of parts that provide information to users.

Open system   A group of interacting parts that interacts on an ongoing basis with its environment to achieve a specific end.

Person-centered technology   A technology system that is designed to fit and adjust to the needs and uses of the individual user.

Point   An object on a map in a GIS that represents information for a specific location.

Polar orbiting satellites   An airborne remote sensing system that collects continuous observations such as data transmitted from Earth; high-resolution photos of Earth; images such as cloud cover, smoke, haze, or storm path on a specific orbit over the poles.

Polygon   An area vector data feature in a GIS that defines a perimeter by a series of enclosing segments.

Radar images   Data collected by remote sensing collecting observations at any time, regardless of weather or sunlight conditions. Data reveals environmental conditions such as flooded areas, oil spills in the water, or wetlands mapping.

Raster data   A graphic representation of a geographic area from an optical or electronic device in the form of an aerial photograph, scanned picture, land classification, or ground contour image. The image is represented by rows and columns of cells that may have data values.

Remote automated weather stations (RAWS)   A network of weather stations run by the U.S. Forest Service and Bureau of Land Management and monitored by the National Interagency Fire Center.

Remote sensors   Instruments or gages that can detect phenomena that are not in direct contact with it.

Saffir-Simpson Hurricane Scale   Scale that was developed as a general guide for use by public safety officials during emergencies to communicate and describe the nature and intensity of hurricanes.

Sea, Lake, and Overland Surges from Hurricanes (SLOSH)   A model used by the National Weather Service to calculate potential surge heights from hurricanes.

Single-frequency repeater   Increases the transmission range of event-reporting sensors by regenerating, amplifying, and transmitting to a base station.

Stability class   A classification system used in dispersion modeling to describe wind speed, atmosphere turbulence, and solar radiation.

Support mechanism   Efforts initiated by an organization to ensure that the operation functions efficiently and effectively.

Synergy   The notion that the whole is greater than the sum of its parts.

System   A group of interacting parts that function on a regular basis to achieve a specific end.

System life cycle   A time period in which elements of a system—including software, hardware, or organizational conditions—change, requiring upgrades or operational changes.

Technology   The application of scientific methods or objects to achieve a practical purpose.

Vector data   Coordinate-based data in a GIS that represents features on a map in the form of points, lines, or polygons.

Warning system   A system of getting information about an impending emergency, communicating that information to those who need it, and facilitating good decisions and timely response by people in danger.

Weather station   A sensor that collects information on the temperature, precipitation, wind direction and movement, barometric pressure and humidity by way of direct contact with the phenomena.

Web   A distributed information system that can be constructed on a local or wide area basis or an unlimited basis as with the World Wide Web.

Webcasting   Streaming audio and video through the Web.

Wide area network (WAN)   A collection of selected users that may span a large geographical region and include multiple enterprises or agencies.

Window of opportunity   A chance to compare the local area to areas that have garnered media coverage due to disasters. This chance allows emergency management officials to argue that the "same thing could happen here" in an effort to attain greater resources and funds for emergency management.

Wireless network   A communication network that connects users by radio or wireless means.

Wireline network   A series of network elements and the hard-wire lines interconnecting them.

FIGURE CREDITS

Figure 1-2:   Jay D. Edwards, Louisiana State University, Baton Rouge.

Figure 2-1:   www.fema.gov

Figure 2-2:   www.floridadisaster.org

Figure 2-3:   www.floridadisaster.org

Figure 3-4:   Photo by Don Jacks/FEMA, FEMA Web site, Image Number 5744

Figure 3-5:   Permission Pending, Cisco Press.

Figure 4-1:   New York City Office of Emergency Management, www.ci.nyc.ny.us/oem/pdf/gis_brooklynlanguages.pdf

Figure 4-2:   Prepared by John C. Pine

Figure 4-3:   Prepared by John C. Pine

Figure 4-4:   Prepared by John C. Pine

Figure 4-5:   Prepared by John C. Pine

Figure 4-6:   www.usgs.gov

Figure 4-7:   www.usgs.gov

Figure 4-8:   The Center for Public Health Impacts of Hurricanes at Louisiana State University

Figure 4-9:   www.usgs.gov

Figure 4-10:   www.usgs.gov

Figure 4-11:   www.fema.gov

Figure 4-12:   Prepared by John C. Pine

Figure 5-1:   www.noaa.gov

Figure 5-2:   www.nasa.gov

Figure 5-3:   www.nasa.gov

Figure 5-4:   www.nasa.gov

Figure: 5-5:   www.nasa.gov

Figure 5-7:   Louisiana State University, Coastal Studies Institute

Figure 5-8:   www.usgs.gov

Figure 5-9:   www.usgs.gov

Figure 5-10:   ww.usgs.gov

Figure 5-11:   www.noaa.gov

Figure 5-12:   http://digitalglobe.com/images/Katrina

Figure 6-1:   www.usgs.gov

Figure 6-2:   www.epa.gov/enviro/index

Figure 7-1:   www.nws.noaa.gov/mdl/marine/hugo.htm

Figure 7-3:   Prepared by John C. Pine

Figure 7-4:   http://www.fema.gov/hazus

Figure 8-4:   Photo by Andrea Booher/FEMA; FEMA Web site, Image Number 4124

Figure 8-5:   Credit: PhotoDisc, Inc./Getty Images; Image Number 38309

Figure 10-1:   http://activefiremaps.fs.fed.us

Figure 10-2:   http://earthquake.usgs.gov

Figure 10-3:   www.earth.google.com

Figure 10-4:   www.earth.google.com

Figure 10-5:   http://mapper.cctechnol.com

INDEX